The House of Wisdom

JIM AL-KHALILI

The House of Wisdom

*How Arabic Science Saved Ancient
Knowledge and Gave Us the Renaissance*

THE PENGUIN PRESS

NEW YORK

2011

THE PENGUIN PRESS
Published by the Penguin Group
Penguin Group (USA) Inc., 375 Hudson Street, New York, New York 10014, U.S.A. •
Penguin Group (Canada), 90 Eglinton Avenue East, Suite 700, Toronto, Ontario, Canada M4P 2Y3
(a division of Pearson Penguin Canada Inc.) • Penguin Books Ltd, 80 Strand, London WC2R 0RL, England •
Penguin Ireland, 25 St. Stephen's Green, Dublin 2, Ireland (a division of Penguin Books Ltd) • Penguin Books
Australia Ltd, 250 Camberwell Road, Camberwell, Victoria 3124, Australia (a division of Pearson
Australia Group Pty Ltd) • Penguin Books India Pvt Ltd, 11 Community Centre, Panchsheel Park,
New Delhi–110 017, India • Penguin Group (NZ), 67 Apollo Drive, Rosedale, North Shore 0632,
New Zealand (a division of Pearson New Zealand Ltd) • Penguin Books (South Africa) (Pty) Ltd,
24 Sturdee Avenue, Rosebank, Johannesburg 2196, South Africa

Penguin Books Ltd, Registered Offices:
80 Strand, London WC2R 0RL, England

First American edition
Published in 2011 by The Penguin Press,
a member of Penguin Group (USA) Inc.

Illustration credits appear on pages xi-xii.

Library of Congress Cataloging-in-Publication Data
al-Khalili, Jim.
The house of wisdom : how Arabic science saved ancient knowledge and gave us the Renaissance / Jim al-Khalili.
p.   cm.
Includes bibliographical references and index.
ISBN 978-1-59420-279-7 (hardback)
1. Science—Arab countries—History.   2. Science—Philosophy—History.   3. Science, Medieval.   4. Science—
Methodology—History.   5. Arab countries—Intellectual life—History.   6. Science, Renaissance.   I. Title.
Q127.A5A4   2011
509.17'67—dc22   2010053136

Printed in the United States of America
1 3 5 7 9 10 8 6 4 2

To Julie

He who finds a new path is a pathfinder, even if the trail has to be found again by others; and he who walks far ahead of his contemporaries is a leader, even though centuries pass before he is recognized as such.
Nathaniel Schmidt, *Ibn Khaldūn*

Contents

CONTENTS

List of Figures

List of Plates

1. Abbasid Caliph Harūn al-Rashīd and King Charlemagne, oil painting by Julius Koeckert (1827–1918). (Maximilianeum Foundation, Munich)

2. Hārūn al-Rashīd and the barber in a Turkish bath, fifteenth-century oil painting. (British Library, London, UK/ © British Library Board. All Rights Reserved/The Bridgeman Art Library)

3. The ruins of the eighth-century Abbāsid Palace of Ukhaidhir, south of Baghdad. (alimdi.net/photographersdirect.com)

4. The spiral cone minaret of the Sāmarra mosque. (Thomas J. Abercrombie/Getty Images)

5. The ruins of the tenth-century palace-city complex Medinat al-Zahrā', outside Córdoba. (Medjai)

6. Description of the eye in Hunayn ibn Ishāq's *Ten Treaties on the Eye*. (The Art Archive/Kharbine-Tapabor/Boistesselin)

7. Brass astrolabe from Saragossa (*c.* 1079–80). (Germanisches Nationalmuseum, Nuremberg (Nuernberg), Germany/The Bridgeman Art Library)

8. A trickster in eleventh-century Baghdad; thirteenth-century painting. (Institute of Oriental Studies, St Petersburg, Russia/ The Bridgeman Art Library)

9. Page from the *Canon of Medicine* by Ibn Sīna. (Wellcome Library, London)

10. Medieval Muslim surgical instruments, from *Kitab al-Tasrīf*.

Preface

Sargon, king of Akkad, overseer of Ishtar, king of Kish, anointed priest of Anu, king of the country; he defeated Uruk and tore down its walls. Lugalzaggisi, king of Uruk, he captured in this battle, and brought him in a dog collar to the gate of Enlil.

Ancient text

An hour's drive south of Baghdad lies the town of Hindīyya. This was where I spent my last few happy teenage years in Iraq before leaving for good in 1979. The town takes its name from the Hindīyya Barrage, which was built across the Euphrates in 1913 by the soon to be departing Ottomans. I have an abiding and powerful memory of this bridge. On cool autumn days I would skip afternoon school with my three best friends, Adel, Khalid and Zahr il-Dīn, and walk across the Barrage to the riverside tourist resort on the opposite bank. We would buy a six-pack of *Farīda* beer and sit down by the water discussing football, philosophy, movies and girls.

Those happy days contrast dramatically with a second powerful image that is seared into my memory and which took place during the first Gulf War of 1991. I remember watching a CNN news report showing footage of a gun battle in Hindīyya in which a lone and terrified woman was trapped in crossfire while walking across the Barrage. For most viewers this would have been just another scene depicting the horrors of war in a far-off land. But for me, instantly recognizing the setting, it suddenly brought home the reality of the plight of the country I had left behind twelve years earlier. I had walked past the spot where this helpless woman now stood frozen in terror dozens of times.

But that was a world away. As I write, I have yet to return to Iraq. I say 'as I write' for I have not ruled out a brief visit at some point in the future when, coward that I am, I deem it safe enough.

The year I left Iraq was a momentous one in the Islamic world. In 1979 Anwar Saddat of Egypt and Israel's Menachem Begin signed a peace treaty in Washington, the first Islamic republic was created in Iran after the deposed shah fled to Cairo, the holy city of Mecca witnessed a gun battle to put down a fundamentalist insurrection following the killing of hundreds of pilgrims, the Soviet Union invaded Afghanistan and the Iranian hostage crisis began in the US embassy in Tehran. During all this turmoil, Saddam Hussein had taken over the presidency of Iraq from Field Marshal Muhammad Hassan al-Bakr, thus making life a great deal grimmer for the vast majority of the population there. My family and I arrived in Margaret Thatcher's Britain at the end of July – exactly two weeks after Saddam had come to power. We had escaped just in time, as it turned out, for within months he had declared war on Iran. Had we not left that summer, my brother and I would undoubtedly have been conscripted to fight in that pointless and terrible conflict and I doubt that I would have lived to tell the tale. Having a British mother and a Shi'a Muslim father of Persian descent who had flirted with the Iraqi Communist movement in the 1950s marked my brother and me as 'undesirables', and certainly expendable frontline fodder.

And life in Iraq seems to have gone downhill ever since. Things have changed there dramatically since my childhood in the 1960s and 1970s when life for a kid from a middle-class background was comfortable and relatively easy. My father, a British educated electrical engineer, had served as an officer in the Iraqi air force. His various postings around the country meant that we were used to moving house regularly. But in the early 1970s, the ruling Ba'ath party decreed that any Iraqis with British wives were suddenly no longer to be trusted in the armed services. So, having reached the rank of major, he now had to find work as a civilian for the first time in his adult life. He soon landed a job as the head of engineering at Ma'mal al-Harīr, a chemical firm in Hindīyya that produced artificial rayon fibres.

We lived in Baghdad for a few years before eventually moving to Hindīyya to spare my father the daily commute. This was fine with me. I made friends quickly, set up my new football team: the Rayon Dynamos (I still have the tatty number 9 shirt I wore) and, together with my brother, would tune in to the BBC World Service to catch the English football scores on 'Sports Report' on Saturdays. Actually, the World Service was pretty much a constant background in our house. When possible, I would make regular visits to the British Council's library in Baghdad for my supply of English books. And I grew up knowing that living under a dictatorship was bearable, as long as you kept your head down and never criticized the government or the Ba'ath Party, even in private.

A fun day out for my family and me was to visit the Hanging Gardens of Babylon, an hour's drive south-east of Hindīyya. The ruins of this mythical place held no great mystique as I had often trudged around the site on school trips. But despite the less than impressive ruins and my indifference born of familiarity, the excitement of a day away from class never lost its appeal, and the site still radiated a powerful aura that whispered of past glories too ancient for me to comprehend. Once, while on a family picnic there when I was in my early teens, we came across two chunks of clay brick, each the size of a fist and each clearly marked with ancient cuneiform writing on one surface. It is still a source of a long-running and good-natured family dispute as to whether it was my brother, my mother or I who actually picked up these bricks. In any event, my mother hid them in the bottom of our food hamper and we smuggled them back home.

This probably sounds like an outrageous case of archaeological theft. Surely we should have handed over such national treasures to the local authorities or, probably more sensibly, to the Iraqi Museum in Baghdad. But we kept them. In our defence, similar cuneiform-etched Babylonian bricks were strewn among the rubble all around us. And in comparison with the later damage wrought on the ruins of ancient Babylon – first by Saddam Hussein's astonishingly vulgar rebuilding of the Ishtār Gate in the 1980s, and more recently by the US forces in 2003 who levelled a whole section of one of the world's most precious archaeological sites to create a landing area for helicopters and a parking lot for heavy military vehicles – our theft seems pretty tame.

It was only recently that I asked an acquaintance, Irvine Finkle, the Curator of Ancient Mesopotamia at the British Museum, to take a look at the two bricks. He confirmed that they date back to the seventh century BCE and the reign of King Nebuchadnezzar II, when the Hanging Gardens were built. Apparently, the symbols are fragments of a common inscription that reads: 'Nebuchadnezzar, King of Babylon, who provides for Esagila and Ezida [the temples of two Babylonian gods Marduk and Nabu], the eldest son of Nabopolassar'.

The seventh century BCE may sound quite ancient to Europeans, and even more so to Americans, but by Iraqi archaeological standards the period of Nebuchadnezzar's reign is practically the Middle Ages. It is sometimes hard to imagine that the heritage of those struggling to lead a semblance of normal life in today's Iraq stretches back over seven thousand years, to the birth of some of the very first civilizations on earth. Archaeologists have dated the remains of the Ubaid culture in southern Iraq to the middle of the sixth millennium BCE; and the succeeding Uruk civilization, which saw the invention of the wheel, as well as such vital technical advances as the fusion of metals, the potter's wheel, the seal, the brick mould and the temple plan, to around 4100 BCE. And it was in Uruk that an invention – possibly even more important than the wheel – was made. For it was here that writing first appeared.

The rest, as they say, is history.

The first powerful ancestor of today's indigenous Arab people of Iraq was Sargon, Semite king of the Akkadians, who conquered the Sumerians in the twenty-fourth century BCE. Very little is known about Sargon, but it is believed that he founded a new capital, Akkad, not far from today's Baghdad. Within a short time his empire extended from the Mediterranean in the west to Persia in the east and he would take the title 'King of the Four Parts of the World'.

The Akkadians were followed by the dynasty of Ur. It is estimated that the city of Ur in southern Iraq had grown (by around 2000 BCE) to become the largest in the world, with a population of more than sixty thousand. It is from this city that Abraham, patriarch of the three great monotheistic religions of Judaism, Christianity and Islam, is supposed to have originated.

The first Babylonian dynasty began not long after this, during which we encounter the greatest of all the ancient kings of Iraq, Hammurabi, who reigned for more than forty years (1792–1750 BCE). It is during his rule that we find the world's first schools as well as the earliest written legal code. Of all the great rulers who followed Hammurabi, and there were many, none would come close to his achievements for a thousand years, until the Assyrian king, Ashurbanipal, founder of the great library of Nineveh near the modern city of Mosul in the north of the country.

The decline of Iraq's self-rule began several hundred years before the birth of Christ and marked the beginning of more than two millennia of almost uninterrupted outside occupation; by the Persians, Greeks, Mongols, Turks and, briefly – between 1917 and 1921 – the British, after which the modern state of Iraq was born. The great Abbāsid Empire, which lasted from 750 to 1258 CE, should certainly not be regarded as an occupying power. For long periods, however, its caliphs were mere puppets of foreign dynasties, notably the Persian Buyids and the Turkish Seljuks in the tenth and eleventh centuries.

The earliest Persian rule over the land known as Mesopotamia (from the Greek 'Land Between Two Rivers' – the Tigris and Euphrates – which largely corresponds to what is modern Iraq) ended with defeat at the hands of Alexander the Great in 333 BCE. The death of Alexander signalled the division of his great empire among his generals: Egypt for Ptolemy, who ruled from Alexandria, and Asia for Seleucus, who built his new capital, Antioch, in north-west Syria, a city that would later play a vital role in the transfer of scientific knowledge from the Greeks to the Arabs.

By the time of the arrival of Islam in the early seventh century CE, what we now call the Middle East was divided between the Persian and Byzantine empires. But with the spread of this new religion from Arabia, a powerful empire emerged, and with it a flourishing civilization and a glorious golden age.

Given how far back it stretches in time, the history of the region – and even of Iraq itself – is too big a canvas for me to paint. Instead, what I hope to do in this book is take on the nonetheless ambitious task of sharing with you a remarkable story; one of an age in which great geniuses pushed the frontiers of knowledge forward to such an extent that their work shaped civilizations to this day.

I have for some time had the strong desire to bring this story to a wider audience. That I do so now lies in my belief that it has never been more timely, nor more resonant, to explore the extent to which Western cultural and scientific thought is indebted to the work, a thousand years ago, of Arab and Persian, Muslim, Christian and Jewish thinkers and scientists. Popular accounts of the history of science typically show a timeline in which no major scientific advances seem to have taken place during the period between the ancient Greeks and the European Renaissance. In between, so we are told, Western Europe and, by extrapolation, the rest of the world, languished in the Dark Ages for a thousand years.

In fact, for a period stretching over seven hundred years, the international language of science was Arabic. For this was the language of the Qur'an, the holy book of Islam, and thus the official language of the vast Islamic Empire that, by the early eighth century CE, stretched from India to Spain.

I must also stress at the outset that my task is not to cover the whole of the history of science around the globe. I am well aware of the richness and variety of scientific achievements in other parts of the world, particularly in China and India, and there have been many books written – and no doubt many more yet to be written – about these two glorious civilizations. But that is not my story.

I have been helped tremendously in my task of exploring the subject through the making of a recent BBC television series, *Science and Islam*. But unlike in the series, I have had the luxury in this book of exploring in more depth both the science and its associated social, political and historical influences and implications. Of course, the extensive travelling I undertook around the Islamic world in the making of the series was useful in two ways. First, and probably most importantly, it brought the subject alive for me in a way that the many books and scholarly articles I have buried myself in could not do. Secondly, it provided me with an opportunity to meet and discuss ideas with many scholars and historians from a wide range of backgrounds. I hope this book does them justice too.

Naturally, there will be those who might suspect that, having grown up in Iraq, I see the Muslim world through rose-tinted glasses, a biased partisan on a mission to demonstrate what a wonderful and enlightened religion Islam is. However, as an atheist my interest in Islam is cultural rather than spiritual. So if Islam as a belief system, unencumbered by the misconceptions and misinterpretations of many of today's Muslims and non-Muslims alike, comes out of my account in a positive light, then so be it.

There is no doubt that, to the ear of many non-Muslims around the world today, the term 'Islam' too comfortably evokes a negative stereotype that contrasts with our Western secular, rational, tolerant and enlightened society. This lazy view can make it difficult to acknowledge that a thousand years ago the roles were reversed. Think of the Crusades: which side back then was the more enlightened, the civilized, the 'good guys'? Even those in the West who have a vague awareness of the contribution of the Muslim world to science tend to think of it as no more than a reheating of Greek science and philosophy with the odd bit of originality subtly added, like Eastern spice, to enhance the flavour. A grateful Europe then eagerly reclaimed its heritage once it awoke from its slumber during the Renaissance of the fourteenth and fifteenth centuries.

I shall address many questions that have long intrigued scholars of the history of science. How much science, for instance, did the Arabs actually know? How important were the contributions of Persian culture, Greek philosophy and Indian mathematics? How and why did scientific scholarship flourish under the patronage of certain rulers? And, possibly most interestingly, why and when did this golden era come to an end?

As a practising scientist and a humanist, I believe that what is referred to as the 'scientific method', and the knowledge that humanity has gained from rational science, gives us far more than just 'one way of viewing the world'. Progress, through reason and rationality, is by definition a good thing; knowledge and enlightenment are always better than ignorance. Growing up in Iraq, I learnt at school about such great thinkers as Ibn Sīna (Avicenna), al-Kindi and Ibn al-Haytham (Alhazen), not as remote figures in history but as my intellectual ancestors. Many in the West will have heard, for instance, of the Persian scholar Ibn Sīna. But there are very many other great names that have been largely forgotten. Even in Iraq, I encountered these characters not in science classes but in history lessons. For the teaching of science in the Muslim world today follows the Western narrative. While it is not surprising that European children are taught that Copernicus, Galileo and Kepler were the fathers of astronomy, that nothing of note came before them, it is rather more disappointing that children in the Muslim world are taught the same thing. Might they not sit up and take notice if they were told that most of the stars we see in the night sky have Arabic names? For instance, the names of five of the seven main stars that make up the constellation Ursa Major (or 'Great Bear') – also known as the Big Dipper or the Plough – are Arabic in origin: Dubhe, Megrez, Alioth, Mizar and Alkaid.

The scientists who feature in this book truly were pathfinders, both literally and metaphorically. The title of the book is taken from a quotation about the fourteenth-century scholar Ibn khaldūn, but is in fact applicable to all those whose stories and achievements I touch upon. For they all broke new ground in advancing mankind's knowledge, yet most have been forgotten.

The transmission of science, especially that of mathematics and astronomy (referred to by historians as the 'exact' sciences), is one of the most powerful tools for establishing relationships between different civilizations. Other areas of human thought – such as religion and philosophy – are transferred more slowly and will only gradually diffuse into, and influence, a particular culture. But the exact sciences require the direct use of treatises and other written work and so can tell us a great deal about the circumstances of the time. And while my motives for trying to piece together a complete picture of Arabic science are no different from those of a historian, I should stress that my primary interest is in the origin and development of the science itself. For this reason, it does not really concern me whether the science in question was developed by Greeks, Christians, Muslims or Jews. And while I devote a chapter to examining how the Islamic Empire inherited the science of the Greeks and other civilizations, I nevertheless wish in this book to explore the ideas themselves, in the fields of natural science, medicine, philosophy and mathematics, which emerged and matured during medieval Islam.

For a theoretical physicist more familiar with the inner workings of the atomic nucleus, this has been an exhilarating and refreshing journey. I am particularly pleased therefore to have turned over many stones that others before have either ignored or had not seen fit to describe to a wider audience.

This book has been three years in the writing, throughout which time I have been on a relentlessly steep, yet hugely enjoyable, learning curve. I have been helped enormously in my research and education by many people; some are experts on the subject of Arabic science, others have provided insightful comments and helpful advice. Each one of them has added to this book and helped me turn it into something I am immensely proud of. First and foremost, I thank my wife Julie for her constant encouragement and companionship. I also owe a huge debt of gratitude to my agent Patrick Walsh, and commissioning editor at Penguin Press, Will Goodlad, both of whom have shared my enthusiasm for the subject and helped me mould my initial clunky, diffident and tentative draft into a more assured final product that I hope is both accurate and readable. I would also like to thank Afifi al-Akiti, Ali al-Azzawi, Nader al-Bizri, Salim al-Hassani, Faris Al-Khalili, Salima Amer, Amund Bjørnøs, Derek Bolton, Paul Braterman, Anna Croft, Misbah Deen, Okasha El Daly, Kathryn Harkup, Ehsan Masood, Peter Pormann, George Saliba, Mohammed Sanduk, Simon Schaffer, Andrea Sella, Paul Sen, Karim Shah, Adel Sharif, Ian Stewart, Rim Turkmani, Tim Usborne and Bernardo Wolf. I am hugely grateful to them all.

A Note on Names, Pronunciations, Spellings and Dates

It is common for English speakers to mispronounce Arabic names – not because some of the guttural-sounding letters have no English counterpart, but because the wrong syllables are often stressed. For instance, the Iraqi city of Kerballa was often mispronounced by news reporters during the Iraq invasion in 2003 as Ker*ba*lla or Kerbe*llah* rather than the correct *Ker*balla. To transcribe Arabic words in English correctly, diacritical symbols should be added above or below letters to give them the correct pronunciation. However, I have not been overly pedantic or rigorous on this front, and have instead aimed at a 'halfway house' convention that closely approximates to the correct vowel sounds without worrying too much about the more awkward consonants. Therefore, you will find many names with a macron over a vowel to extend its sound. For instance, the Persian scholar *Ibn Sīna* is phonetically pronounced *ibin seena*. Without the macron over the 'i', *Sina* would more likely be pronounced by a native English speaker as *sinner*, which would be wrong. For Arabic words familiar in English I dispense with all diacritical marks. Thus, I do not bother to write Baghdād, Islām, Qur'ān or Irāq (provided the 'a' in Iraq is understood to sound like it does in 'car' rather than 'cat'). Even for less familiar words, if I can get away without a diacritic then I will. Thus, the Arabic for 'book', *kitab*, should be written as *kitāb*, but since it is natural for a native English speaker to pronounce it correctly anyway, with a short 'i' and longer 'a' (ki*tab*) then the bar is deemed unnecessary.

In scholarly works, historians often insist on a comprehensive transcription of Arabic words into English with additional diacritics, such as dots underneath consonants. But I feel no obligation to follow this convention closely. Let me give you an example of what I mean: a famous text by the eleventh-century scholar Ibn al-Haytham, translated as 'The Book of Optics', is traditionally transcribed as *Kitab al-Manazir*. But the 'z' should really be written with a dot underneath it, ẓ, denoting the Arabic letter ظ. The correct way to pronounce this letter is like the hard 'th' in 'the' (and not soft as in 'think'), but with the tongue protruding further outside the mouth, which is more rounded. So, for me, a more faithful and closer pronunciation would be to spell the word as 'al-Manathir'. The only reason to use a 'z' is if the word were pronounced in the colloquial style of certain Arab countries today, such as Egypt. So, my decision not to use any diacritical marks with consonants means I sometimes stray from the conventional scholarly transliteration and focus on a more natural transcription that is closer to the correct classical Arabic.

In some cases, I have deferred to tradition. Thus, the word 'ibn' ('son of') is really pronounced *ibin* but it is usual not to include the second 'i' in the spelling; in any case it is difficult not to include a vowel sound between the 'b' and the 'n'. Likewise, the name *al-Khwārizmi* – a mathematician we shall meet later – is always spelt this way, but the more accurate Arabic, and Persian, pronunciation is to include a vowel (an 'a' or an 'o') after the 'Kh'.

In a break with popular Western tradition on this subject, I believe there is no excuse not to refer to people by their correct Arabic or Persian names rather than the Latin derivation that has been passed on to us. Thus, I refer to Ibn Sīna and Ibn Rushd rather than the better known, in the West, Avicenna and Averroës. Finally, most Persian scholars have Arabized names with the definite article 'al' placed in front of the name. Thus al-Bīrūni and al-Tūsi would simply be Bīrūni and Tūsi in Persian. I have, however, stuck with the more familiar (usually Arabic) version of their names and hope that Iranian readers are not too offended. Thus, while I keep the more familiar Persian name of the mathematician Omar Khayyām, another Persian, Khwarizmi, is better known by the Arabized al-Khwārizmi.

Many of the characters we shall encounter have impressively long names that involve not only their forenames and family names but, sandwiched in between, the names of their fathers and grandfathers. They may also pick up a *laqab* (nickname) or *nisba*, based on an attribute of their personality, profession or origin, such as describing someone from Baghdad as 'al-Baghdadi'. They can even be known by the name of their eldest son. Thus the word *Abū* (pronounced *aboo*) means 'father of'. If a man does not have children then his first name is often associated with a prominent character in Arabic or Islamic history who would have had a son. Among many Shi'ite Muslims, the name *Ali* is always associated with that of Imam Ali and his son, Hussein. Thus, when a man is referred to as Abū Hussein, he may either have an eldest son named Hussein or may simply be an Ali with no sons.

For example, the mathematician al-Khwārizmi has the full name Abū Abdullah Muhammad ibn Mūsa al-Khwārizmi, which means his first name is Muhammad but his son is Abdullah and his father's name is Mūsa (Moses). Sometimes he is referred to as Muhammad ibn Mūsa, but is far better known as al-Khwārizmi, named after his birthplace Khwārizm (modern Khiva in Central Asia).

The common language used universally across the Arab world is referred to as classical Arabic. This is the Arabic of the Qur'an, and the Arabic of the educated classes. However, Arabic dialects differ widely from one country to the next and certain letters are pronounced differently. Thus a 'j' in Iraq is pronounced the same as in English, whereas in Syria it would be pronounced as in the French *bonjour* and in Egypt as a 'g' sound. But more than just accents differentiate Arabic dialects. Often words are completely different. For instance, in Iraq, the word for 'yes' is *ee*; in Egypt, it is *aywa*, but in classical Arabic, it is *na'am*. I mention this because classical Arabic, being the language of the Qur'an, has not changed at all in fourteen centuries, making the writings of the early Islamic scholars as accessible today as they were then.

On the issue of dates, there are several standard conventions, and I have chosen the one most commonly used by contemporary historians. Apart from the early chapters, when I cover the sciences of antiquity and have to use the 'BCE' notation (Before the Common Era, or Before the Christian Era), years not so identified should be taken to denote the Common Era (or Christian Era), CE. For brevity, I have chosen not to include Muslim *Hijri* dates – the calendar that began in 622 CE.

A Note on the Term 'Arabic Science'

Throughout the book, I use the term 'Arabic science' in its broadest sense. I do not mean by this only the science practised by people of Arab blood, and therefore carefully refrain from referring to it as 'Arab science'. That would necessarily constrain the discussion to the inhabitants of Arabia (modern Saudi Arabia and southern Syria and Mesopotamia) many of whom, outside the cities, were in any case simple Bedouin desert tribes. What I mean by 'Arabic science' is that carried out by those who were politically under the rule of the Abbāsids, whose official language was Arabic, or who felt obliged to write their scientific texts in Arabic, the lingua franca of science in the medieval world. A large part of the scientific body of work was initially (in the ninth and tenth centuries) carried out in today's Iraq, in the cities of Basra, Kūfa and, most importantly, Baghdad.

Many of the scientific figures we shall encounter along our journey, such as al-Bīrūni and Ibn Sīna, were Persians, and were often even anti-Arab in their sentiments. But what matters in this context is that most of their scientific work was written in Arabic, not Persian. Nor indeed do we find that all the scientific work was carried out by Muslims, despite the undeniable fact that this explosion in scientific creativity would not have been possible without the spread of Islam, as I shall explain later on. Many important contributions were made by Christians and Jews, particularly in the early days of the Abbāsid era when the main body of translation from Greek texts was being carried out. But even they shared with their Muslim rulers a common culture that encompassed their customs, thinking, education and language.

Thus, when I speak of 'Arabic' scientists I do not mean the word in the sense that they had to have been born and educated in today's

Arab and Arabic-speaking countries and would have regarded themselves as Arabs, rather that it was the Arabic language that united
them. I therefore include the great Persian scientists as part of this
broad definition.

A nice example to emphasize this point is that of the Alexandrian
astronomer Ptolemy, author of the *Almagest* (*c.* 150 CE), one of the
most important astronomical texts ever written. Those who would
question whether the work of Persians such as al-Bīrūni and Ibn Sīna
is rightly part of Arabic science cannot then class the work of an Egyptian such as Ptolemy as part of Greek science. However, it is
acknowledged universally that Ptolemy's work was no less a part of
the science of the Greeks than that of Euclid, Archimedes or Aristotle.

Naturally, you might ask whether it is not more appropriate to
define this as Islamic, rather than Arabic, science. There are three
reasons why I have not done so. The first is one that I have alluded to
already: not all the important scientific advances were carried out by
Muslims. Before the spread of Islam in the seventh century, much of
the Middle East was Christian. Its two main sects were the Nestorians
(chiefly in the cities of Hīra in southern Iraq and Edessa and Antioch
in northern Syria) and the Monophysites (who were spread throughout Syria, Anatolia and Egypt). In addition, large parts of the region
before Islam also practised the ancient Mazdean and Zoroastrian religions, even Buddhism. Consequently, during the golden age of Arabic
science many of the leading figures were not Muslims. The greatest of
all the translators of Baghdad, Hunayn ibn Ishāq, was a Nestorian
who never converted to Islam. Other Christian scientists of ninth-
century Baghdad include the astronomer Yahya ibn abi Mansūr and
the physicians Jibrīl ibn Bakhtyashū and Ibn Massāwayh. Likewise,
many Jewish philosophers and scientists, such as the translator Sahl
al-Tabari, the medic Ishāq ibn Amrān and the astronomer Mashā'allah,
all made valuable contributions to the intellectual culture of Baghdad.
Nor can we ignore the many contributions of the Andalusian Jewish
scholars between the eighth and eleventh centuries, or even later, such
as the great medieval Jewish philosopher and physician Maimonides,
who was born in Córdoba but spent much of his life in Egypt.

The second reason is that Islam is today practised by more than a
billion people across the world. The subject of this book does not

extend to include the scientific heritage of those Muslim countries such as Pakistan or Malaysia, which would have also been influenced by Indian and Chinese science. I am defining my subject matter more narrowly.

Of course we cannot hope to understand the context of Arabic science if we do not explore the extent to which the religion of Islam influenced scientific and philosophical thinking. Arabic science throughout its golden age was inextricably linked to religion; indeed it was driven by the need of the early scholars to interpret the Qur'an. Furthermore, politics in Baghdad during the early Abbāsid rule was dominated by a movement of Islamic rationalists, known as the Mu'tazilites, who sought to combine faith and reason. This led to a spirit of tolerance in which scientific enquiry was encouraged.

Many have argued that the scientific creativity of the Islamic world was short-lived because it came into conflict with religious teaching within Islamic society, culminating in the work of the Muslim theologian al-Ghazāli (the equivalent in terms of importance in Islamic teaching as Thomas Aquinas was to Christianity). However, many of the sciences, such as mathematics, medicine and astronomy, continued to flourish long after al-Ghazāli.

The third reason why I resist the temptation to refer to my subject matter as Islamic science is because of an unfortunate anti-scientific attitude among some Muslims today (although this is of course not restricted to Muslims). It is sad to think that a minority of contemporary Islamic scholars do not seem to be endowed with the enquiring minds of their forefathers. For the early scholars of Baghdad, there would have been no conflict between religion and science. The early thinkers were quite clear about their mission: the Qur'an required them to study *alsamawāt wal'arth* (the skies and the earth) to find proof of their faith. The Prophet himself had besought his disciples to seek knowledge 'from the cradle to the grave', no matter how far that search took them, for 'he who travels in search of knowledge, travels along Allah's path to paradise'. Of course, this knowledge (*'ilm*) referred primarily to theology, but in its early years Islam never made a clear-cut distinction between religious and non-religious scholarly pursuits.

The seemingly comfortable compatibility between science and religion during the Abbāsid Empire contrasts starkly with the tensions between rational science and many different faiths around the world today. None of our modern-day angst existed in early Baghdad. One can of course argue that the science of the time was itself not so far removed from superstition – a mix of metaphysics and folklore. So it could be more easily absorbed into theological ideas. But what we shall also see is that, in contrast to many of the Greek philosophers' abstract notions, the Arabic scientists were grounded in something very close to the modern scientific method in their reliance on hard empirical evidence, experimentation and testability of their theories. Many of them, for instance, dismissed astrology and alchemy as not being part of real science and being quite distinct from astronomy and chemistry.

It is clear that there is a broad continuum of attitudes held by today's Muslim population towards science; all are no doubt sincerely held. Those who see the importance of science and who are able to disentangle it from religion would claim that 'the Qur'an tells us how to go to heaven, not how the heavens go'. Many devout Muslim scientists feel it is their religious duty to try to understand the universe from an empirical, rationalist scientific standpoint. Then, armed with this new-found knowledge, they can return to the words of the Qur'an in the hope of gaining a deeper and more profound understanding than they had before their scientific enlightenment. I have no problem here since their faith does not influence how they conduct their science. Only when the process is reversed do alarm bells start to ring: when one hears the argument that it is not necessary to try to understand the world around us from a scientific perspective since all we ever need to know is already written in the Qur'an anyway.

Ultimately, there can be no such thing as *Islamic* science or *Muslim* science. Science cannot be characterized by the religion of those who engage in it, as the Nazis in 1930s Germany attempted to do when disparaging Albert Einstein's great achievements as 'Jewish science'. The term 'Islamic science' may likewise be used by those with similar racist notions who wish to downplay its importance. Just as there is no 'Jewish science', or 'Christian science', there cannot be 'Islamic science'. There is just *science*.

The one misgiving I have about my chosen term of 'Arabic science' (aside from its likely unpopularity among the population of today's Iran, Uzbekistan or Turkmenistan, all proud homes of great scholars of the golden age) is that even choosing to name a scientific age by the language of its communication is problematic. After all, we do not refer to the scientific achievements of the European Renaissance as those of 'Latin science'. Even stranger would be to refer to modern-day science as 'English science'. But I nevertheless feel that 'Arabic' rather than 'Islamic' science is somehow more honest and less problematic. And I really do need to call it something to distinguish it from Greek or Indian or European Renaissance science, the meaning of all of which is quite clear; and to keep referring to it as 'the science practised by the scholars of the golden age of Islam' is, I am sure you agree, a bit of a mouthful.

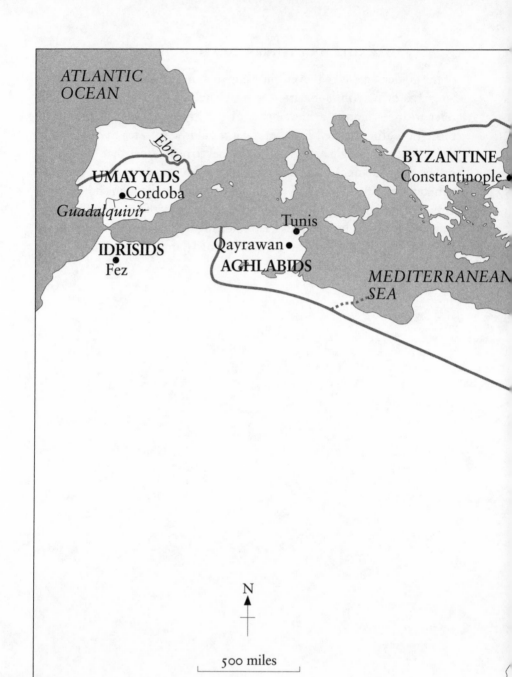

**MAP 1: THE ABBASID CALIPHATE
AT THE BEGINNING OF THE NINTH CENTURY**

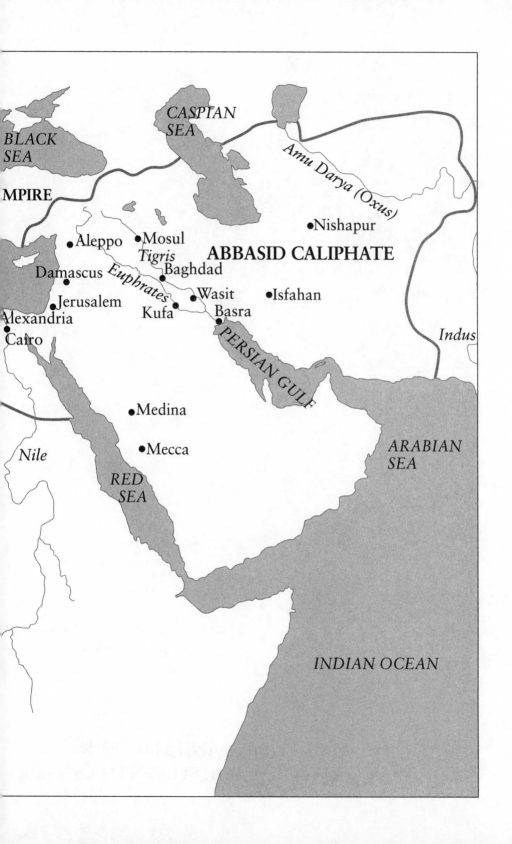

ATLANTIC
OCEAN

BYZANTINE

Constantinople

Toledo

Ebo

Guadalquivir

Valencia

Cordoba

Seville

Granada

ZIRIDS

ALMORAVIDS

Tunis

Bijaya

Qayrawan

Fez

Tlemcen

Mahdiyya

Marrakesh

*MEDITERRANEAN
SEA*

HAMMADIDS

FATIMIDS

N

500 miles

**MAP 2: THE MIDDLE EAST AND MAGHRIB,
TOWARDS THE END OF THE ELEVENTH CENTURY**

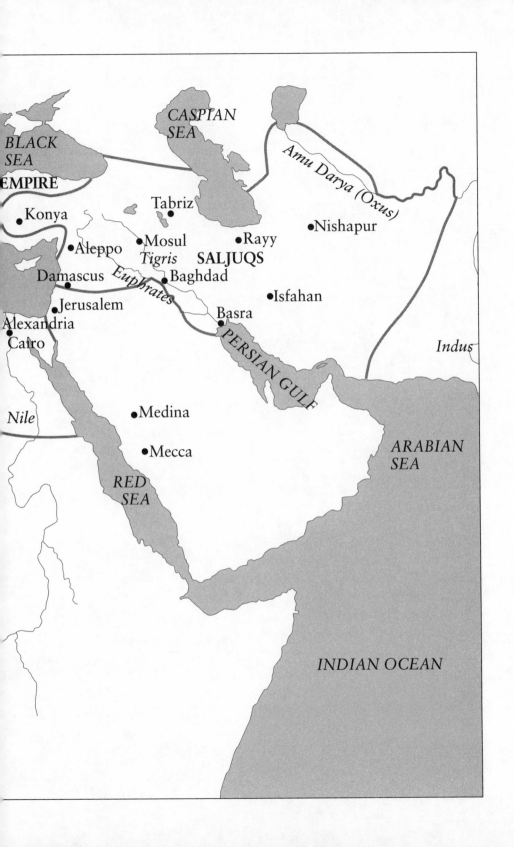

The House of Wisdom

I

A Dream of Aristotle

One night the Caliph Harūn al-Rashīd summoned his vizier Ja'far and said to him, 'I wish to go into the city to find out what is happening and to question the people about the conduct of my administrators, so that I may dismiss those of whom they complain and promote those they praise.'

From 'The Tale of the Three Apples',
The Thousand and One Nights

The Bab al-Sharji district in the centre of Baghdad derives its name, which means East Gate, from the medieval fortifications of the city. It was part of the walls probably built around the first half of the tenth century. During the brief British stay at the end of the First World War, its gatehouse was used as a garrison church (and in fact referred to by the British as the South Gate, since the only other surviving gate, called *Bab al-Mu'atham*, was to its north). Nothing of those medieval walls, or the East Gate, remains today; I remember Bab al-Sharji as a hot, smelly, noisy, bustling and congested square, with its food stalls and second-hand record shops scattered around the busy bus depot and taxi ranks, but its name is a reminder of the expansion and transformation of this proud city over the years since its foundation in 762 CE as the new seat of power of the mighty Abbāsid Empire. For Baghdad has grown and shrunk and grown again, with the centre of government shifting over the centuries from one side of the Tigris river to the other as successive rulers chose the most suitable spot to build their elaborate palaces. If we probe into the history of the city we see that whatever suffering its present-day inhabitants have had to

3

endure, they are in very good company. For no other city on earth has had to put up with the levels of death and destruction that Baghdad has endured over the centuries. And yet, as the capital of one of the world's great empires, this had been the richest, biggest, proudest, most supercilious city on the planet for half a millennium.

Exactly twelve hundred years after its foundation, I was born in a Baghdad hospital in Karradat Mariam, a Shi'a district with a large Christian community, just a stone's throw away from today's Green Zone on the opposite bank of the river. That hospital is a few miles south of the spot where one of Baghdad's most famous rulers was born in 786 CE. His name was Abū Ja'far Abdullah al-Ma'mūn. Half Arab, half Persian, this enigmatic and fascinating caliph is central to my story, for he was destined to become the greatest patron of science in the cavalcade of Islamic rulers, and the person responsible for initiating the world's most impressive period of scholarship and learning since ancient Greece.

In order to understand how and why this golden age took place, we shall need to dig deeper into the motives and psyche of early Muslim society and its rulers and carefully examine those factors (both internal and external) that helped shape and influence the period. But before we begin our journey in earnest, allow me to introduce you to this remarkable ruler.

Al-Ma'mūn was not the only caliph to support scholarship and science, but he was certainly the most cultured, passionate and enthusiastic. He created an environment that encouraged original thinking and free debate like no other Islamic ruler before or since. He was in fact the son of an even more famous caliph – in the West at any rate – called Harūn al-Rashīd (763–809), which translates as 'Aaron the Righteous', who pops up frequently as a character in the tales of *The Thousand and One Nights* (see Plate 2). Al-Rashīd oversaw the Abbāsid Empire's expansion as far north as Constantinople and maintained diplomatic ties with China and the European Emperor Charlemagne, with whom he frequently exchanged delegations. They recognized each other as the most powerful men of their respective cultures, and diplomatic ties between the two rulers helped encourage strong trade relations. Charlemagne sent 'Frisian' cloths to Baghdad to correct a 'balance-of-payments' problem caused by Western tastes for Abbāsid silks, rock crystal and other luxury objects. In return, al-Rashīd sent many gifts to Charlemagne, including an elephant and an elaborate brass water clock, both of which must have amazed the European emperor. There are many stories of al-Rashīd's wealth, and his collection of gems was particularly legendary.[1] He is said to have bought a famous pearl called *al-Yatima* ('The Orphan Pearl') for 70,000 gold dinars. Charlemagne is also believed to have given him what is thought to have been the world's largest emerald.

Al-Rashīd took a personal interest in many campaigns against the neighbouring Byzantine Empire, leading military expeditions against them throughout his reign. In 797 the defeated Empress Irene agreed to pay a large sum of money to al-Rashīd as the terms of her surrender. When her successor, Emperor Nicephorus I, withheld the payment, al-Rashīd declared war again, and Arab forces defeated the Byzantine emperor in a battle in Phrygia in Asia Minor (Turkey) in 805. The following year, he invaded Asia Minor again, this time with more than 135,000 men. Nicephorus was humiliated into agreeing to pay a yearly tribute of 30,000 nomismata (Byzantine gold coins).[2]

There is a further account of a sum of 50,000 dirhams[3] sent by Nicephorus as a ransom to al-Rashīd for a female slave captured during the incursion of 806. It seems that the woman was betrothed to Nicephorus' son and that the emperor's offering to Baghdad was part of a larger exchange that involved brocade garments, falcons, hunting dogs and horses.

Back in Baghdad, however, al-Rashīd was a poor administrator, who owed his success to the running of the affairs of state by a powerful Persian family known as the Barmakis (referred to in the West as the Barmakids). The Islamic Empire was at its most powerful under al-Rashīd's reign and many historians and poets have, over the centuries, referred to this period as the pinnacle of Baghdad's golden age. However, this view was to a large extent based on nostalgia towards a bygone era before the cracks in the empire began to appear, which they soon did. It is remarkable that for a city which would remain as the most important in the world for five hundred years, the decline in its glory would begin, as we shall soon see, just fifty years after its foundation. Certainly al-Rashīd has been the beneficiary of almost universal sentimental glorification ever since.

5

Al-Ma'mūn (786–833) was born the same year that his father became caliph. His mother was a Persian slave concubine named Marajil who had arrived in Baghdad originally as a prisoner of war. She was the daughter of Ustath Sis, a Persian rebel leader defeated by the Abbāsids in Khurasan in what is today western Iran. Marajil worked in the kitchens of al-Rashīd's palace. Historians have unkindly recorded that, as a forfeit for beating him in a game of chess, al-Rashīd's Arab wife Zubayda insisted that he sleep with the ugliest and dirtiest slave in the kitchen. After much pleading he agreed and had sexual intercourse with Marajil, and she bore him his first son, Abdullah, to whom he gave the title al-Ma'mūn ('The Trustworthy'). Marajil died soon after childbirth and al-Ma'mūn was placed in the care of the Barmaki family.

On assuming the caliphate, Harūn al-Rashīd had moved across the river from his father's palace on the east side to the magnificent Qasr al-Khuld ('Palace of Eternity') that had been built by his grandfather and founder of Baghdad, the Caliph al-Mansūr. Within six months of the birth of al-Ma'mūn, Zubayda herself bore the caliph a second son, al-Amīn (787–813). The two boys were destined to grow up in very different worlds. Like al-Rashīd, Zubayda was of pure and noble Arab blood – she was a granddaughter of al-Mansūr and thus al-Rashīd's cousin – and their son, al-Amīn, was the natural successor to the caliphate over his older half-brother, the son of a Persian slave girl. Unsurprisingly, al-Ma'mūn was never close to his stepmother but was certainly loved by his father, for there are many accounts of him as a young boy playing with the caliph in the beautiful gardens of the palace and on the banks of the Tigris.

As a young man, al-Ma'mūn memorized the Qur'an, studied the history of early Islam, recited poetry and mastered the newly maturing discipline of Arabic grammar. He also studied arithmetic and its applications in the calculation of taxes and inheritance. Most importantly, he was a brilliant student of philosophy and theology, or more specifically what is referred to in Arabic as *kalām*, which is a form of dialectic debate and argument. The early Muslim theologians found that the techniques of *kalām* enabled them to hold their own in theological arguments with the Christian and Jewish scholars who lived alongside them, and who had had a head start of several centuries to hone their debating skills by studying the writings of philosophers such as Socrates, Plato and Aristotle – historical figures from ancient Greece whose names would certainly have been known to the young Ma'mūn. It is even quite likely that some of their work had already been translated into Arabic. Al-Ma'mūn's interest in *kalām* was to later play a big part in his lifelong obsession with science.

By the beginning of the ninth century, the teenage prince would have known a Baghdad at the very height of its glory: a vast and beautiful city characterized by the domes and archways of its famously intricate Abbāsid architecture. Although just four decades old, Baghdad was already the largest city in the world, with some estimates putting its population at more than a million.[4] Certainly far larger in area than Rome, Athens or Alexandria had been at their grandest, Baghdad boasted dozens of sumptuous palaces, occupied by the members of the caliph's family, his generals and viziers.

Given its turbulent history, almost nothing survives of early Abbāsid Baghdad today. It is worth remembering that, unlike for other, far older, cities such as Rome and Athens, there are no stone quarries in Iraq (although significant limestone and marble deposits could once be found in the north and the west of the country). All the buildings in Baghdad, including the palaces, were constructed mainly from sun-dried mud bricks, making them susceptible to the regular destruction of invading armies, fires and floods. But we can get a sense of the scale of these palaces from one of the very few surviving Abbāsid buildings of that early period.[5] Known as the Palace of Ukhaidhir, its ruins stand about 120 miles south of Baghdad (see Plate 3). I vividly remember school trips there, during which my friends and I would race each other, completely unsupervised, around its precarious 65-foot high perimeter walls. It had originally been built as a private retreat by a wealthy member of the caliph's family in the second half of the eighth century.

Most of Baghdad's palaces could be found along either bank of the Tigris, and not all were for residential purposes. The grand vizier (derived from the Arabic word *wazīr*, meaning 'minister'), Ja'far al-Barmaki, another familiar character in *One Thousand and One Nights*, built a pleasure palace known as *al-Ja'fariyya* ('the Palace of Ja'far') in an undeveloped, secluded part of east Baghdad. It would later become the residence of al-Ma'mūn himself and the centre of a district containing a whole complex of palaces and luxury homes known as *Dar al-Khilāfa* ('Home of the Monarchy'). Ja'far had been appointed as the young al-Ma'mūn's personal tutor and he is credited with instilling in the future caliph a love for learning and scholarship.

The palaces, along with many of the important administrative buildings, were tall, multi-storey structures. Many were crowned with elaborate weathervanes depicting warriors on horseback, symbolizing the caliphs' might. One account, for instance, tells how members of a captured rebel group attempting to escape from the caliph's throne room – having realized that they would not be able to defeat his bodyguards – jumped from a window and fell nine floors to their death in the courtyard below.

Within the houses of the wealthy, marble was widely used for pillars, tiled floors and the flights of steps leading down to courtyards or the riverbanks. The plastered walls of the houses would have been draped with ornate tapestries, their floors paved with ceramic or marble tiles, with beautiful rugs that would be spread out during the winter months, then taken up during the heat of the summer. Families would have sat on embroidered cushions laid out on the floor. The rooms on the ground floor would often have had one side open onto a central courtyard, sometimes containing a small fountain. The kitchen would often have been below ground level but ventilated in its ceiling through a metal grid in the floor of the courtyard. In order to beat the summer heat, families would have slept up on the flat roof at night and in the cool basement (*sirdab*) for their afternoon siestas.

In contrast, life for the poorer residents of Baghdad was in overcrowded multi-storey buildings, with floors separated by beams of palm-tree trunks, which were far more solid than the clay and sun-dried bricks that made up the walls and held the buildings together. In one account, a ninth-century Baghdadi landlord complains – as have all landlords before and since – about his tenants who

> constantly risk burning the building down by cooking on the roof, reducing the value of the property by clogging the drains, yanking on the doors and breaking the locks and hinges, and pounding their laundry on the floor instead of on the stone provided for that purpose.

Their children dig holes in the courtyard, driving sticks into the walls and break the wooden shelves. And when they move out, they steal everything they can carry, including the ladders and water jars.[6]

On the whole, this was a well-managed city, for the broad avenues and boulevards were kept clean and swept, and complex canals were used to ensure that water was carried in from the Tigris for the city's inhabitants. The air would have been alive with the strong scent of local and imported spices and perfumes and, along the banks of the river, with the unmistakable smell of the local delicacy, a grilled freshwater carp known as *shabbout* that is still popular to this day.

Among my own most pleasant childhood memories of modern Baghdad are the sultry summer evenings out with my family on Abū Nou'was Street. Named after one of Baghdad's most famous poets and a contemporary of al-Ma'mūn, this tree-lined avenue along the east bank of the Tigris, with its parks and cafés, has always been a favourite meeting place. More than a thousand years earlier, Baghdadi families would no doubt have enjoyed similar riverside walks.

But the Baghdad of my youth and the Baghdad of al-Ma'mūn's youth have another, sadder, parallel. For in each case, the city was destined to suffer the ravages of a war that would banish its peaceful beauty, leaving much of its infrastructure destroyed and its glory in tatters. In both cases, the years of war and hardship would end in the same way: with the removal of the incumbent ruler from power. In 1980 Saddam Hussein's Iraq declared war on Iran following many years of border disputes. The senseless eight-year-long conflict that followed would claim the lives of a million young men from both sides. And worse was to follow within just a few years when, in 1991, US fighter planes bombed Baghdad heavily in response to Saddam's invasion of Kuwait. But they would wait a further decade – long enough for him to rebuild his powerbase and continue his acts of genocide while the population suffered the indignity of crippling international sanctions – before returning to finish the job in 2003.

Twelve hundred years earlier, older, wiser and more ruthless than the innocent young student of Ja'far, al-Ma'mūn would himself be personally responsible for the destruction that befell his city.

When it became necessary for al-Rashīd to choose an heir, he is said to have deliberated long and hard before deciding finally in favour of the younger and far less able but pure Arab-blooded al-Amīn. In 802, on the occasion of a pilgrimage to Mecca with his two teenage sons, the caliph formally announced their respective rights of succession following his death: al-Amīn as successor to the caliphate in Baghdad, with al-Ma'mūn sovereign over the eastern provinces of the empire, in Khurasan, with his seat in the city of Merv (now in Turkmenistan). His sons' oaths of allegiance to stick to his wishes (what is called the Mecca Protocol) were recorded in documents that were rolled up, placed in boxes and stored within the Ka'ba.[7] As a further part of the full succession agreement, al-Rashīd's third and youngest son, al-Mu'tasim (794–842), was to become governor of Asia Minor and oversee the protection of the empire's borders against the Byzantines.

Al-Rashīd knew very well that the half-Persian al-Ma'mūn would make the better ruler: more intelligent, more determined and with sounder judgement. But he was pressured by those around him, particularly his wife Zubayda, to name the shallower and more frivolous al-Amīn. Once he had made up his mind, the extent of al-Rashīd's determination to ensure his wishes were carried through is clear. He cut off the influential Persian Barmaki family from power and even went as far as having his loyal vizier Ja'far, who was of course very close to al-Ma'mūn, executed.[8]

But it seems that al-Rashīd's gift of Khurasan to his eldest son was more than a consolation prize. The province was highly symbolic, for this was where the Abbāsid revolution had started in the middle of the eighth century and from where it had spread to seize power from the first Islamic dynasty, the Umayyads. Moreover, al-Ma'mūn seems to have been given absolute power in Khurasan, providing him with an opportunity to rise up against his brother. Did their father predict this would happen? Did al-Rashīd carefully engineer things so that it would look as though he had favoured al-Amīn just to keep his wife and the Abbāsid family happy, while at the same time leaving the door open for al-Ma'mūn to snatch power if he so desired? No one can be sure, and al-Rashīd's motives remain subject to conjecture. It has been speculated that he already harboured serious doubts about al-Amīn during the famous 802 pilgrimage.

In 805 a rebellion broke out in Khurasan. The people of the province had risen up against the governor in protest against the extortionately high taxation. Matters slowly worsened until, in 808, al-Rashīd was obliged to personally ride east with his son al-Ma'mūn at the head of an army to quash the rebellion. Although still only in his early forties, al-Rashīd became ill from the exertions of the long trek across mountains and deserts and died on the way. His death changed the whole complexion of the campaign, for al-Ma'mūn now automatically assumed the governorship of this volatile part of the empire. However, most of his father's army deserted him to return to their families in Baghdad. This setback proved to be a minor one for the 23-year-old al-Ma'mūn, who, after successfully putting down the rebellion, immediately set about establishing his powerbase. He was helped in this by his close adviser and confidant al-Fāthl ibn Sahl, a Persian who had replaced Ja'far the Barmaki as vizier. Slashing the high taxes in the province proved to be a hugely popular early policy. In addition, al-Fāthl advised him in no uncertain terms to improve his public image. Al-Ma'mūn was renowned for his love of good wine and the company of beautiful slave women, but he would need to come across as a far more pious Muslim if he wished to lay claim to the caliphate in Baghdad from the newly installed al-Amīn. All the while, he slowly and methodically put together his new army, recruited from across Central Asia.

Back in the capital, the new caliph began flexing his muscles and trying to assert his authority in the East. He challenged his brother's role as governor of Khurasan by demanding that tax revenues be sent back to Baghdad, recalling those in the original army who had remained loyal to al-Ma'mūn and even naming his own son as his direct successor, ahead of his brother.

Armed conflict between the two men was quickly becoming inevitable. Al-Ma'mūn was fortunate to be served by the loyal and highly able Persian General Tāhir, who claimed an early victory over al-Amīn's army on the outskirts of present-day Tehran, giving al-Ma'mūn control over much of Persia. Al-Amīn, suddenly growing concerned, appealed in vain first to his brother to see sense and to respect the wishes of their father, and then to his subjects in order to recruit new troops, mainly from among the Arabs of Syria. But al-Ma'mūn's army kept advancing westwards, finally arriving at the outer walls of Baghdad in April 812. And so the great siege of Baghdad began. By this time most of the empire outside the immediate environs of Baghdad itself had already declared its allegiance to al-Ma'mūn.

For more than a year the beleaguered caliph held his ground against the armies of his half-brother and pretender to the throne, who continued to reside in Merv. Al-Amīn initially found an unexpected source of popular support among the city's trapped population, who fought with crude homemade weapons against the well-armed and well-trained Khurasani soldiers. Tāhir seemed initially unable to break down Baghdad's defences and could not understand what was driving this newly emerged resistance from within. Al-Amīn, who had been living in the Qasr al-Khuld by the river, retreated within the fortified walls of the old Round City built by his great-grandfather, al-Mansūr, the founder of Baghdad. While Tāhir's forces used catapults to pound the walls and buildings as they advanced through the vast metropolis, al-Amīn's men set whole neighbourhoods on fire to slow down the enemy advance. By the time Tāhir had reached the Round City walls, much of Baghdad was in ruins.

The ninth-century Baghdadi poet Abū Tammam wrote: 'the death announcer has risen to mourn Baghdad', comparing the city to 'an old woman whose youth has deserted her, and whose beauty has vanished'.[9] Given Baghdad's long and bloody history since that time it sounds strange to hear of it being referred to as an 'old woman' just half a century after it was founded.

After more than a year of siege, the stalemate was finally broken in the autumn of 813 when Tāhir persuaded the merchants of Baghdad to destroy the pontoon bridges across the Tigris that had served as critical communication routes between the resisting forces. The ensuing chaos offered the assembled eastern army the opportunity to attack. Anticipating eventual defeat, al-Amīn listened to the advice of his closest advisers who convinced him that he stood a chance of a future counterstrike against his brother if he escaped from the north and made his way to Syria or Egypt where he could organize a new powerbase. Tāhir, however, apparently having caught wind of the plan, sent a message to the troops loyal to al-Amīn, threatening to retaliate by destroying not only their property inside Baghdad but their estates in the country as well if they did not dissuade al-Amīn from this decision. Al-Amīn was soon 'convinced' by his advisers of the benefit of surrender instead – a decision that would prove fatal for him.

Although the civil war had originated with al-Rashīd's ill-advised decision over the succession – for al-Amīn was never cut out for great leadership – it also revealed the first cracks within the Abbāsid Empire. It was a question not merely of a personal rivalry between the two brothers, but of a conflict between different politico-religious trends that had become apparent during the preceding reign; al-Amīn had emphasized traditionalism and Arab culture, while al-Ma'mūn, who was open to new philosophical movements and outside influences, had courted the support of Persian intellectuals and was a strong supporter of the rationalist movement known as Mu'tazilism, a doctrine of open questioning and enquiry that opposed the literal interpretation of the Qur'an.

The medieval historian al-Mas'ūdi recounts how al-Amīn's mother, Zubayda, had predicted ill fortune for her son: in each of three separate dreams, a different woman appeared to her and described her son's future rule as despotic, corrupt, weak, unjust and extravagantly wasteful. On each occasion Zubayda awoke in great horror. On a final visit, all three women appeared together to make their harshest prediction yet by not only graphically describing al-Amīn's violent death (despite his surrender to Tāhir) but defending it as a fitting and glorious outcome.

But we should not get too carried away with this depiction of al-Ma'mūn as the worthier of the two brothers. A cursory review of the literature of the civil war might at first strike one as overwhelmingly supportive of al-Ma'mūn – not so surprising, given that the sources were written after his victory and needed to be seen as being on the right side. However, despite his weakness al-Amīn had been a relatively popular caliph during his four years in power. More importantly, while this was not the first case of regicide in Islamic history it was nevertheless the first violent end to befall an Abbāsid caliph. It thus left an indelible mark on the collective consciousness of Islamic society. Al-Mas'ūdi's story of Zubayda's dreams, therefore, seems a harsh reflection on al-Amīn and has more to do with the historian's hagio-graphic support for al-Ma'mūn.

There does, however, seem to be some doubt over al-Ma'mūn's part in his brother's death. Several historians recount how Tāhir sent a message to al-Ma'mūn from Baghdad asking what he was to do with al-Amīn if and when he was finally captured. Al-Ma'mūn is said to have sent back to the general a shirt with no opening in it for the head. Tāhir interpreted this as al-Ma'mūn's wish to have his half-brother beheaded and as soon as he captured the caliph he carried out his master's wishes.

Some accounts describe how al-Ma'mūn had his brother's head displayed on a pole in the central courtyard of his palace in Merv after it had been carried back by his victorious troops on a two-week, 1,000-mile journey from Baghdad; and that he distributed sums of money among his military commanders, ordering whoever felt he had earned this reward in his service to come to the courtyard to curse the gruesome trophy. However, other Arab historians have argued that the execution of al-Amīn was a decision taken in the field by Tāhir himself and that al-Ma'mūn was horrified and grieved when he dis-covered what had happened. They claim that he wept openly when al-Amīn's head was presented to him and that he cursed Tāhir for carrying out a deed he had not ordered.

Al-Ma'mūn remained in Merv for a further five years, a period in which he did not endear himself to many of his subjects across the vast empire. This was partly due to his attempts to heal the divisions between the two main sects of Islam: Sunnism and Shi'ism.[10] His sym-pathies towards the latter were such that he adopted its green flag instead of the black flag of the Abbāsid dynasty. It was also partly due to his sympathies, like his father's, towards Mu'tazilism, a school of thought not shared by all Muslims. He certainly surrounded himself with Mu'tazilite sympathizers, among them his influential adviser, al-Fāthl. He even went so far as to declare that his successor would not be a member of his own family, but Ali al-Ridha, a descendant of the Prophet's cousin and son-in-law, Ali, the spiritual leader of Shi'ism.

This last decision was extremely unpopular among the Sunnis in Iraq and, in Baghdad, his uncle Ibrahim decided to lay claim to the caliphate. This seems to have been the final straw, and al-Ma'mūn had a change of heart and headed for Baghdad to put down this insurrection personally. Mysteriously, his two closest allies, the Persian vizier al-Fāthl and Ali al-Ridha, both met with their death in suspicious circumstances on the long journey west. Ali al-Ridha is regarded by the Shi'a as the martyred eighth Imam, or saint, and his shrine in the city of Mashhad in north-east Iran is still of great religious importance.

Al-Ma'mūn arrived in Baghdad in 819, with the destructive siege six years earlier now a distant memory and the city mostly rebuilt and back to its former glory. One Baghdadi historian recounted how, as a young child, he was lifted up by his father over the heads of the crowds lining the streets of the capital to watch the caliph as he rode past, and remembered being told never to forget this momentous day.

Upon his arrival in the city, al-Ma'mūn abandoned his policy of reconciliation between Sunnis and Shi'a and quickly reinstated the traditional black Abbāsid flag. But his sympathies towards the Mu'tazilite movement only grew stronger. He subscribed wholeheartedly to their rationalist world-view that borrowed from the works of the Greek philosophers, as well as to their notions of indeterminism and free will, a philosophical standpoint that is, surprisingly, broadly in line with thinking in modern science, based on current theories in theoretical physics.

Under al-Ma'mūn's patronage, and the spirit of openness and inclusiveness towards other religions and cultures that he fostered, many scholars from all over the empire gravitated towards Baghdad, drawn by a vibrant sense of optimism and freedom of expression that epitomized the mood of this golden age. The fusion of Greek rationalism and Islamic Mu'tazilism led to a humanist movement the like of which would not be seen again until fifteenth-century Italy. This attitude is best expressed by one famous Baghdadi scholar, al-Jāhith (c. 776–c. 869), who wrote in his famous *Book of Animals*:

> Our share of wisdom would have been much reduced, and our means
> of acquiring knowledge weakened, had the ancients [the Greeks] not
> preserved for us their wonderful wisdom, and their various ways of life,
> in writings which have revealed what was hidden from us and opened

what was closed to us, thereby allowing us to add their plenty to the little we have, and to attain what we could not reach without them.

Interestingly, this spirit of tolerance and inclusiveness towards other faiths did not apply to those holding different ideologies within Islam itself. Late in his life, al-Ma'mūn instigated an uncompromising inquisition (*mihna*) against the Islamic conservatives and traditionalists of his day who would not subscribe to the Mu'tazilite ethos.

As for al-Ma'mūn himself, his interest in science is known to have started when as a young boy he was imbued with a love of scholarship and learning by his tutor Ja'far. He would certainly have been aware of the great legacy of the ancient Greeks and their passion, even obsession, with trying to understand the world around them. However, one particular episode in his life is said to have affected him so dramatically that it would change his life for ever. Not long before returning to Baghdad, he had a vivid dream. The Arab historian from whom we obtain almost the entirety of our information on this wonderful yet probably (and sadly) apocryphal story is Ibn al-Nadīm, the tenth-century author of the *Fihrist* (*Index*), a biographical account of the scholars of Baghdad as well as a catalogue of all books written in the Arabic language. In it he writes:

> Al-Ma'mūn dreamed that he saw a man of reddish-white complexion and high forehead, bushy eyebrows, bald head, dark blue eyes and handsome features, sitting on a chair. Al-Ma'mūn said, 'I saw in my dream that I was standing before him, filled with awe. I asked, "Who are you?" He replied: "I am Aristotle". I was delighted to be with him and asked, "O philosopher, may I ask you some questions?" He replied, "Ask". I said: "What is the good?" He replied: "Whatever is good according to intellect." I asked: "Then what?" He replied: "Whatever is good in the opinion of the masses". I asked: "Then what?" And he replied: "Then there is no more 'then'."'[11]

Whether or not this story is true, there is no doubting that al-Ma'mūn devoted the rest of his life to following the advice granted him by this vision, and sought everywhere to satisfy his craving for knowledge – whatever he deemed 'good according to intellect'. Although we shall see that the Abbāsids' thirst for ancient texts from Greece, Persia and

India, and for having them translated into Arabic, began before al-Ma'mūn, it was he who turned this into a personal obsession. And it was during his reign that we see the first true geniuses of Arabic science.

Yet in order to understand this sudden flourishing of scholarship, we must look back in time to see how Islam rose out of the Arabian desert two hundred years earlier. Why did this golden age of science take place during the reign of the Abbāsids of Baghdad, when nothing of any real intellectual consequence had taken place in that part of the world since the decline of the Library of Alexandria hundreds of years before the arrival of Islam?

2

The Rise of Islam

The ink of the scholar is more sacred than the blood of the martyr.

The Prophet Muhammad

With the weakening of the Roman Empire at the beginning of the fifth century, Western Europe slipped rapidly into what is now known as the Dark Ages, from which it would not emerge for a thousand years. By the time of the fall of Rome itself, the centre of imperial power in Europe had long since moved eastwards to Constantinople, the capital of the Byzantine Empire. Its rule covered Anatolia, Greece, southern Italy, Sicily, Syria, Egypt and the North African coast, with an eastern border that ran roughly north–south between modern-day Iraq and Syria. The official language of the Byzantines was Greek, but they did not reach anywhere near the great intellectual heights of scholarship and learning achieved by the Greeks of Athens and Alexandria. And although there were Jewish settlements scattered throughout the empire, as well as many pagans, the official and dominant religion of the Byzantines was Christianity.

To its east, four centuries of Persian Sasanid rule produced an empire stretching from Iraq and Iran through to Central Asia. The Sasanids had come to power in the year 224 CE, under the leadership of Ardashīr I, when they defeated the Parthians. Their capital, Ctesiphon, lay on the banks of the Tigris river just a few miles south-east of present-day Baghdad. All that remains of this great city is the ruins of the imperial palace. With its famously huge archway, it is still a favourite tourist destination for Iraqis.

The middle of the sixth century marked the start of nearly a hundred years of long and costly wars between the Sasanians and Byzantines over the lands of Iraq and Syria, with their mutual border in constant flux as they each advanced and retreated in a continuous and bloody dance. By the early seventh century these two once power-ful empires were exhausted and had only themselves to blame for their humiliating defeats at the hands of the powerful and highly organized Muslim armies that rode north out of Arabia after the Prophet Muhammad's death in 632. First, the Byzantines were pushed out of Syria and Asia Minor, then the Sasanians were defeated and crushed.

Before the arrival of Islam, the only other sovereign power in the region lay in the far south-western corner of the Arabian peninsula, in Yemen, where several small kingdoms had ruled for more than two millennia before Islam, and whose power and wealth had come from their geographical location and exclusive trade access to both south-ern Asia and eastern Africa.

The rest of Arabia was inhabited mostly by nomadic Arab tribes. Long before the birth of Muhammad, however, these peoples were already beginning to develop a sense of cultural identity. Despite their wide range of different dialects, a common Arabic language had begun to develop, mainly through the reciting of poetry. The *qasīda*, or ode, was an important feature of the cultural life of Arabia, often telling of lost love or a tribal victory. These poems, which would be recited at festivals, feasts, in market towns or palace courts, came to be known collectively as *diwan al-Arab*, or 'the register of the Arabs', and became a way of preserving a maturing sense of Arab identity and communal history.[1] Most of them were not written down but memorized. How-ever, some were preserved in the ancient Aramaic script. The Arabic script that was to be later used in the Qur'an still had some way to go before it would reach the level of maturity it has today, and its rules and grammatical nuances would take centuries to be established by scholars keen to remove any ambiguities of meaning from the Qur'an.

But not all Arabs belonged to nomadic tribes. Two great cities in western Arabia had been trading centres for hundreds of years before the arrival of Islam. Their names were Macoraba and Yathrib and they were destined to become the two holiest cities in Islam: Mecca and Medina.[2]

The city of Mecca lies in an arid and barren valley surrounded by imposing mountains. Its life force was the well of Zamzam, which provided the city's water. For a century or so before Islam there had been a massive migration of population from southern to western Arabia (the region known as the Hijaz) and further north to Syria and Palestine. With its prime location along this trade route between Yemen in the south and the Mediterranean in the north, Mecca had grown rich and powerful, not only as a trade centre but as a financial one too.

More importantly, its role as a holy centre for the many pagan religions of the Arabians dating back to antiquity made it a safe haven for those wishing to escape the widespread violence that regularly broke out among the tribes in the region. Mecca housed many shrines and sanctuaries for the worship of several hundred different gods. A century before the birth of Islam one of the most powerful tribes in Arabia, the Quraysh, began to spread its influence in Mecca, both politically and commercially. And it was from one of the less influential clans within this tribe that a 40-year-old illiterate merchant named Muhammad announced in the year 610 that the angel Gabriel had appeared before him to reveal the word of God while he was meditating alone in a cave in Mount Hirā overlooking the city.

According to Islamic history, Muhammad was initially distressed at seeing the vision of an angel. When he came down from the mountain he was consoled by his wife Khadija and taken to speak to her Christian cousin, Waraqah ibn Nawfal, who immediately informed Muhammad that he had been chosen as a new prophet, for God had also sent the angel Gabriel down to Moses two thousand years earlier, and it was Gabriel who had told Mary that she would give birth to Jesus. Muhammad declared his mission, and his very first convert was Khadija herself, followed by members of his family and his close companions. Within a few years, during which he continued to receive revelations, Muhammad began preaching publicly, but he was soon met with open hostility from many of the inhabitants of Mecca. Despite this opposition and the slow start, his teachings marked the beginnings of the new religion of Islam that would soon grow rapidly and spread into one of the world's greatest spiritual, political and cultural forces.

The Arabic word for God, *Allāh*, comes etymologically from a contraction of the word *al-Ilāh*, meaning 'The God' and can be traced back to early Semitic writing. The definite article is included here to make the point that in Islam, in common with the other monotheistic religions of Christianity and Judaism, there is but one divine Creator. The message being spread by the Prophet Muhammad did not therefore go down too well with the pagan Arabs of Arabia, who worshipped a multitude of gods. For instance, of the three most powerful goddesses, al-Lāt, Manāt and al-'Uzzā, the first of these was supposedly the daughter of another god, al-Lāh, the Lord God of Mecca. All these gods had sanctuaries in or near Mecca, including within the Ka'ba itself, which is of course now the most powerful and holy symbol of Islam and the destination of millions of Muslims for the *Hajj*. Indeed, pre-Islamic pagans would make pious visits to Mecca from all over Arabia, and even walk around the Ka'ba, giving offerings to their gods. Once his mission became clear, Muhammad would order all such shrines and sanctuaries destroyed, but the Ka'ba itself remains to this day, situated within the largest mosque in the world, al-Masjid al-Harām.

Arabic-speaking Christians and Jews also use the same word *Allāh* to mean God in their religions. Islam is of course a much younger religion, but at its heart it has much in common with Judaism and Christianity. This is not surprising given that all three originated in the same part of the world, and among the same race of people, who all claim to be the descendants of Abraham. Muhammad himself had of course interacted with many Christians and Jews while accompanying his uncle on regular trade trips to Syria.

In the early years, as support for Muhammad and his message grew – particularly within his close family, but also among many of the young men of Mecca, as well as traders, craftsmen and slaves – the leaders of the Quraysh turned against him. His call to them to abandon their polytheism and rituals was seen as an intolerable attack on their whole way of life. Circumstances changed when, in 619, Muhammad was devastated by the death of his wife and confidante, Khadija, followed shortly afterwards by the death of his uncle and lifelong guardian, Abū Tālib. Now he no longer had the support of these two powerful figures in his life, the Quraysh leaders stepped up their harassment of Muhammad and even took the decision to have him killed. And so, after twelve years of persecution, he decided to leave Mecca with his followers for the city of Yathrib, 200 miles north, from which he had received an invitation to act as an arbiter in another bitter tribal conflict.

The journey he took in 622 CE is called the *Hijra* ('Migration') and marks the beginning of the Islamic, or *Hijri*, calendar. Yathrib gradually became known as *Medinat al-Nabi* ('The City of the Prophet') or just Medina for short. There had been a number of conflicts between the two Arab tribes in Yathrib, Banū Aus and Banū Khazraj. The large Jewish community in the city was also split in its allegiance to one or other of the two sides. Unlike the Meccans, the exposure to monotheistic Judaism, with its prophets and holy book, had made the Arabs of Yathrib far more receptive to Muhammad's message and teaching and they welcomed him, with relief, as someone people would listen to and who could bring peace and stability to their city.

Eventually, armed conflict broke out between the two cities of Mecca and Medina. Fighting continued for several years, culminating with the Meccans' failed siege of Medina and the famous battle of the Ditch (*ma'rakat al-Khandaq*). A ten-thousand-strong Arab and Jewish army (the latter an exiled tribe from Medina) had advanced on Medina in 627, but instead of the traditional military tactic of marching out to meet them in open combat, the much smaller Muslim army within Medina chose a different solution. One of the Prophet's closest generals, Salmān the Persian, proposed the digging of a deep trench around the weaker northern side of the city, a feat achieved in just six days. It proved successful and, combined with the strong fortifications around the other sides of Medina, it halted the advance of the Meccan army, who, after a two-week-long ineffective siege, eventually gave up and dispersed.

The Meccans finally realized that they would not be able to break the resolve of the growing Muslim army or halt the continuing spread of the message of the Prophet. In any case, the years of conflict were having a devastating effect on trade. Finally, the peace treaty of

Hudaybiyya between the Quraysh of Mecca and the followers of Muhammad was signed in 628. Two years later Mecca itself surrendered to the army of the Prophet, who entered the city unopposed.

Throughout this time, Muhammad had continued to receive revelations, which he passed on to his followers. They, in turn, memorized them or wrote them down. After his death, they were collected in a series of 114 chapters, or *suras*, in a book known universally as the Qur'an (meaning 'recitation'). Most scholars agree that the final version of the Qur'an was not agreed upon until the time of the third caliph, Uthmān, who ruled between 644 and 656. The word 'caliph' (*khalīfa* in Arabic) literally means 'successor' to the Prophet.

By the time of the Prophet's death in 632, Islam, which translates as 'submission [to the will of God]', had spread throughout the Arabian peninsula. But all was not well in this embryonic nation, for strong divisions surfaced within the Prophet's own family over the issue of succession. Uncertainties were quickly dismissed, however, when Abū Bakr, the Prophet's father-in-law, took on the mantle of the first of four caliphs known as *al-Rashidūn* ('The Rightly Guided Ones'). He quickly crushed several revolts that had broken out across Arabia and was successful in stabilizing the rapidly expanding Islamic Empire. In doing this he was fortunate to be served by one of the greatest military commanders the world has ever seen: Khālid ibn al-Walīd, who had already masterminded many of the victories of the new Muslim army. Under his command, one city after another, deep into Byzantine territory to the north of Arabia, fell to the Muslims, with Damascus itself coming under their control in 634. Abū Bakr died after just two years and was succeeded by the second of the Rashidūn caliphs, Umar ibn al-Khattāb (634–44), under whom the empire expanded its frontiers through ever more ambitious military campaigns into Syria, Egypt, Iraq and Persia.

In 637 Khālid's army inflicted a famous and devastating defeat on the much larger Byzantine forces in the battle of Yarmūk east of the Sea of Galilee on the frontier between the modern Syria, Israel and Jordan. The Emperor Heraclius had assembled an army comprising Christian Arabs from the Levant along with Armenians, Slavs, Franks and Georgians. But they were no match for Khālid's tactical genius. Heraclius himself was forced to flee from northern Syria back to his capital Constantinople as the Islamic armies overran the cities of Jerusalem, Aleppo and Antioch. At the same time that the Byzantines were in retreat, the conquering Muslim armies were turning their attention to the east and the Persian Empire. It would take them almost two decades, but they finally brought Sasanian rule to an end in 651, although it would be many generations before the majority of Persians converted to Islam.

The third caliph, Uthmān (644–56), was a softer touch than Umar. While more compassionate and generous, he was also weak as a leader and easily influenced by a corrupt and power-hungry clan called the Umayyads. This weakness would lead to unrest across the empire culminating in his assassination at the hands of rebels from Egypt. He was succeeded by the fourth and last of the Rashidūn caliphs, Ali ibn abi Tālib (656–61). Ali was the Prophet's son-in-law and is to this day revered by millions of Muslims worldwide as the first of the imams of Shi'ism. He moved his capital from Medina to the Muslim garrison city of Kūfa in Iraq, which now had a far more important strategic location at the heart of the new empire. But a separate powerbase was already beginning to build up in Jerusalem, where Uthmān's governor of Syria, Mu'awiya, from the Umayyad clan, was gaining in power and influence.

A fanatical group called the *Khowārij* blamed Ali for not dealing once and for all with Mu'awiya. They even accused him of being an enemy of Islam, and assassinated him in 661, bringing to an end the reign of the Rashidūn caliphs. In the ensuing unrest, Mu'awiya won control of the caliphate and shifted the capital of the empire to Damascus. So began the dynastic period of the Umayyads.

The Umayyads secured control of the Islamic Empire that now stretched over a vast area of land from India in the east to the Atlantic Ocean in the west. With the death of Mu'awiya, the struggle continued between his son Yazid and the Caliph Ali's son (and the Prophet's grandson), Hussein. Finally, in a bloody massacre on the banks of the Euphrates near the town of Kerbala in 680, Hussein was beheaded by a soldier of the Umayyad army. The date of his martyrdom, the 10th of the Muslim lunar month of Muharram, is known as 'Āshūra (from the Arabic word for 'ten': 'ashra) and is an important day of mourning for all Shi'a Muslims.

The Umayyads were nothing if not pragmatic. Through the rapid initial conquests of the Caliph Umar, they had inherited the sophisticated administrative and financial infrastructure of the Persians and Byzantines. Most of this they kept unchanged, apart of course from replacing the Pahlavi (Persian) and Greek languages of these two empires with Arabic, a process that took some time to complete. Taxes and expanding trade strengthened the caliphs, who grew wealthy and powerful.

The most influential of the Umayyads was Abd al-Malik, who ruled for twenty years between 685 and 705. During his reign he reorganized and strengthened governmental administration and oversaw a further expansion of the empire with the continued Islamization of Asia and North Africa. He was a master politician and a powerful and autocratic ruler. Abandoning the traditional policy of consulting with a council of advisers, he reserved all major decisions for himself. He was also capable of great cruelty against his enemies when necessary, which seems to have been fairly often.

Abd al-Malik had to deal with internal resistance from a range of different groups opposed to Umayyad rule and it took him many years to quell all rebellions and revolts across northern Syria, Iraq, Persia and Arabia. He carried out campaigns against the Byzantines in Anatolia in 692, and continued with the conquest of North Africa, where he had to defeat both the native Berbers and the Byzantines. A major victory came in 697 when his army captured Carthage, one of the most important cities along the North African coast.

In contrast to this warmongering, Abd al-Malik was also more pious than any of his Umayyad predecessors and is probably best known today for the Dome of the Rock in Jerusalem, the oldest extant Islamic monument, which he built during the first years of his reign. The rock on which this holy shrine sits is still sacred to both Muslims and Jews today.

During the last decade of the seventh century he made the bold decision to establish a common currency for all his dominions. He created the first Islamic royal mint between 693 and 697, modelling the new coinage on those of the Greeks and Persians, but with Arabic Qur'anic inscriptions replacing the traditional images of kings. Abd al-Malik charged Muslim alchemists with experimenting with the best materials to use for the new coins, which were made mainly from gold, silver, copper and alloys of these and other metals.

Other than alchemy, the Umayyads showed little interest in the sciences. Apart from their passion for grand architectural projects, they were also not very interested in culture and learning, in part because of their preoccupation with securing and expanding their borders, and quelling the constant unrest within. And in stark contrast with the later Abbāsids, who relied heavily on the experience and knowledge of the sophisticated Persians to help them rule – a sharing of affairs of state that was to have crucial knock-on effects in initiating the golden age of science – the Umayyads excluded all non-Arabs from positions of power and influence, even if they were Muslim converts.[3]

So it was that, exactly one hundred years after the Arabs marched out of Arabia, they reached the furthest point in their expansion. In the famous battle of Tours in 732, the Muslim armies of the Umayyad dynasty, having conquered half of France, finally ran out of steam and were defeated by the Franks under Charles Martel. By this time the Islamic Empire covered an area larger in expanse than either the Roman Empire at its height or all the lands conquered and ruled by Alexander the Great. In fact, for the first time since Alexander, the lands of Egypt, the Fertile Crescent of the Middle East, Persia and India were reunited, allowing each to grow and prosper through mutual trade and relatively peaceful coexistence in ways that none had quite been able to do for a thousand years beset with wars, divisions and rivalry.

Despite their vast empire and great prosperity, the Umayyads lasted just ninety years and, towards the end of their dynasty, had to face increasingly difficult revolts and uprisings, particularly from the disaffected Shi'a based in the Iraqi city of Kūfa. But the most serious of these began in the Persian region of Khurasan in the east, where a blend of Arab and Persian culture was catalysing the growth of a substantial religious and political movement claiming its right to power as descendants of the Prophet's uncle al-Abbās. Its army moved westwards and, in a series of bloody battles, finally defeated the Umayyad army in 750. Immediately, a new caliph, Abū al-Abbās, was declared in Kūfa. A descendant of the Prophet's uncle,[4] he became the first of a long line of Abbāsid caliphs that would last for a remarkable five hundred years.

Having defeated the Umayyads in battle, but concerned that they might attempt to seize power again, the ruthless Abū al-Abbās tricked all the members of the Umayyad family into attending a conciliatory dinner party where he instead had them killed. The only survivor, a young prince named Abd al-Rahmān, escaped to Spain, where the Umayyad dynasty would endure for a further three centuries.

After his victory over the Umayyads, Abū al-Abbās's reign was marked by efforts to consolidate and rebuild the caliphate, with a new government made up of Arabs, Persians, Christians and Jews. However, after his early promises, he turned his back on the Shi'a community who had supported him. He died of smallpox in 754, only four years after deposing the Umayyads. His brother al-Mansūr took over as caliph of this vast new empire, and its influence would reach far beyond its own limits.

Two and a half thousand miles to the west, Offa, son of Thingfrith, had been crowned the Christian King of Mercia (Middle England) in 757 and ruled for nearly forty years. Many historians regard him as the most powerful Anglo-Saxon king before Alfred the Great. In the 780s he extended his power over most of southern England. One of the most remarkable extant artefacts from King Offa's reign is a gold coin that is kept in the British Museum. On one side it carries the inscription OFFA REX (Offa the King). But, turn it over and you are in for a surprise, for in badly copied Arabic are the words *La Illaha Illa Allah* ('There is no god but Allah alone'). This coin is a copy of an Abbāsid dinar from the reign of al-Mansūr, dating to 773, and was most probably used by Anglo-Saxon traders. It would have been known even in Anglo-Saxon England that Islamic gold dinars were the most important coinage in the world at that time and Offa's coin looked enough like the original that it would have been readily accepted abroad.

Back in Kūfa, the Caliph al-Mansūr needed a new imperial capital and so set about looking for the best place to build it.

Like the city of Alexandria, founded a thousand years earlier by Alexander the Great, Baghdad grew from nothing to become the world's largest city just fifty years after the first brick was laid. And just like Alexandria, it became a centre for culture, scholarship and enlightenment that attracted the world's greatest minds. Before its foundation, the two largest urban conurbations in Iraq were the garrison cities of Kūfa and Basra, which had both been founded by the early caliphs during the long war with the Sasanians.

Al-Mansūr chose the exact site for his new city carefully. It is told that among the many people offering advice were several Christian monks he met in what is now central Iraq, who claimed that their ancient texts documented how a great king would one day build his new city on the site next to their monastery.[5] This happened to be a farm called *al-Mubāraka* ('the Blessed') and it suited the caliph perfectly, situated as it was on the west bank of the Tigris close to several thriving market villages.

A ninth-century Persian historian by the name of al-Tabari (c. 839–923), who wrote enormous compendiums of early Islamic history, describes in his *Annals of the Prophets and Kings* how al-Mansūr chose the site:

> He came to the area of the bridge and crossed at the present site of Qasr al-Salām. He then prayed the afternoon prayer. It was summer, and at the site of the palace there was then a priest's church. He spent the night there, and awoke the next morning having passed the sweetest and gentlest night on earth. He stayed, and everything he saw pleased him. He then said, 'This is the site on which I shall build. Things can arrive here by way of the Euphrates, Tigris, and a network of canals. Only a place like this will support the army and the general populace.' So he finalised the plans and assigned monies for its construction.[6]

Before laying his new city's foundations, al-Mansūr had asked three of his most respected astrologers to cast a horoscope for him. These wise men were an Arab, al-Fazāri, a Persian, Nawbakht, and a Jew, Mashā'allah, who between them agreed on the most favourable hour on the most favourable day for the first stone to be set in place: 30 July 762.

Four years in the building, the Round City was based on the plans of traditional Roman military camps and designed with security

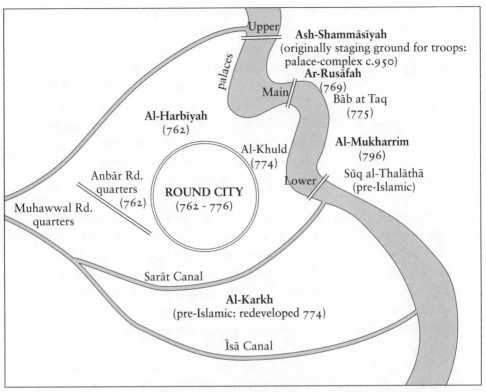

Schematic map of early Abbāsid Baghdad showing the location of
al-Mansūr's original Round City on the west bank of the Tigris.

uppermost in al-Mansūr's mind. It was surrounded by a double set of
immense brick walls, the outer one about 6 miles in circumference,
and then by a broad moat that was fed by the Tigris. Four gates
pierced these fortifications, from which roads radiated to the far cor-
ners of the empire. The Khurasan Gate in the north-east was the
gateway to Persia, while the Basra Gate in the south-east, the Kūfa
Gate in the south-west and the Damascus Gate in the north-west each
led to the city after which it was named. Each gate had also been carefully designed so as to secure the inner city against invasion, with a
complex series of curved passageways, ramps and chambers. A large
chamber was built high into each gate, roofed with a dome that was
in turn crested, 100 feet up, by a grand weathervane.

Within the city, roads ran from each gate to the centre, first through an outer ring of buildings that housed the caliph's family, staff and servants, then through an inner ring of buildings housing the arsenal, the treasury and the government, until they reached a grand, wide esplanade on which stood the headquarters of the palace guard, the mosque and the grand palace itself, known as *Qasr Bāb al-Thahab* (the Golden Door Palace).

Because of its surrounding fortifications and comparable size, one cannot help but compare al-Mansūr's Round City with the US-controlled Green Zone set up in 2003 after the fall of Saddam's regime, just a few miles down the river: a contrast that is both powerful and apt.

The Round City itself was not much more than an enormous palace-complex, which combined the caliph's residence with the administrative buildings of government. While it alone would have been equal in size to most other imperial cities in the world, it was very different from any other city, for the general populace all lived outside its walls. Its construction brought thousands of labourers and troops from far and wide to swell the population of the surrounding districts.

Long before Islam, huge markets had flourished on both banks of the Tigris to serve the villages and farming communities in the areas surrounding the Round City, which would soon be subsumed within the greater metropolis of Baghdad. To its south was the vast market district of al-Karkh (a name that was later used to mean the whole of the city of Baghdad on the west side of the Tigris) and, on the east bank, the bustling *Sūq al-Thalāthā'* ('Tuesday Market'). Soon after al-Mansūr had completed the Round City, al-Karkh in particular quickly became congested, struggling to meet the demands of the new influx of inhabitants, and so underwent extensive development, including the construction of new commercial facilities and the widening of the major roads. Other districts, such as al-Harbiyya north of the Round City, were newly built and quickly grew to rival al-Karkh in size and importance. The name *Harbiyya* derives from the word *Harb*, meaning 'war', for this district was originally the residence of the many thousands of troops who served the caliph.[7] Each one of these boroughs would have been large enough to require its own sprawling markets, wide avenues, mosques and municipal buildings.

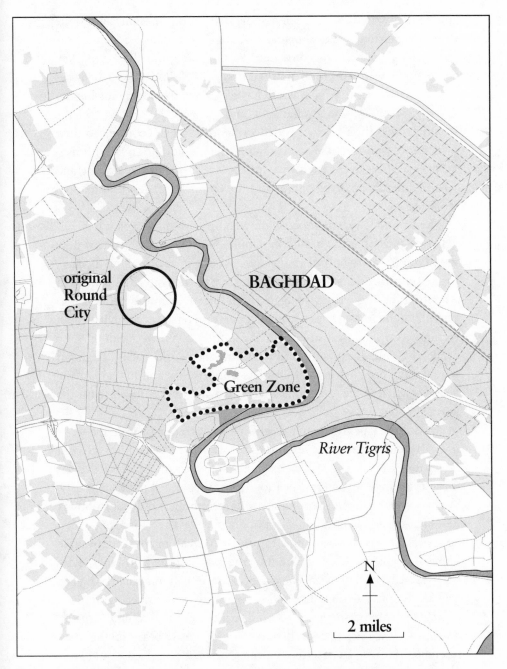

original
Round
City

BAGHDAD

Green Zone

River Tigris

N

2 miles

Round City projected onto a map of modern Baghdad contrasting its size
and location with that of the US controlled Green Zone set up in 2003.

And each would have been subdivided into different and quite distinct quarters. The shoemakers' market might lead onto the booksellers' market; the bird market alongside and flower market. Then there were the food markets (*Sūq al-Ma'kūlat*) and bakeries (*Sūq al-Khabbāzīn*), which would have been set apart from the higher-class goldsmiths, moneychangers and elegant boutiques for the wealthy. Even the traders' residences were divided according to their professions and status in society: perfumers would not mix with fish-mongers. There were exclusive streets where the more elegant and wealthy merchants lived apart from the common traders and manual workers.

The Round City was soon swallowed up within an expanding con-urbation of more than a million people. Not only was Baghdad now the administrative hub of the Islamic world, it also became a centre for art, culture and trade; and with the rest of the empire embroiled in a continuous and bloody struggle (both internally and with its neigh-bours), Baghdad must have seemed a peaceful oasis by comparison. In fact, it was originally also known as *Madinat al-Salam*, meaning 'City of Peace'. And like many cities around the world today, Baghdad would have been a world of limitless opportunity and luxury for the wealthy while at the same time a wretched and miserable place for the poor.

Al-Mansūr quickly began to feel somewhat trapped within the walls of his Round City and for reasons of security abandoned it for a brand new palace outside the walls. This might at first seem paradoxical given the comfortingly strong fortifications that surrounded the Round City, but he regarded his close proximity to large numbers of loyal troops as more reassuring than the claustrophobia of the palace-complex, which he continued to use for administration. Al-Mansūr moved into his new home, the fabulous Qasr al-Khuld on the banks of the Tigris, in 774. Its precise location had been chosen because it was on slightly higher ground than its surroundings and so relatively free of river mosquitoes during the summer nights. Al-Khuld, which means 'Eternity', was so named because the palace gardens were said to be so beautiful that they resembled Heaven as described in the Qur'an. The palace would later become famous for having held the magnificent and lavish wedding party of al-Rashīd and Zubayda.

The cultural climate in the new capital would have been very different from what was familiar to the indigenous rural population, and was unlike anything ever seen before. It brought together a multicultural society of Muslim and Christian Arabs, Muslim converts from among other races in the indigenous population, as well as Jews, Sabians, Zoroastrians and pagans. The predominant way of life would not have been too different from that of the Persian Empire which the Muslims had conquered and which had ruled these lands for hundreds of years, but the new mix of mutually tolerant religions and cultures would have made for a fascinatingly colourful society.

Despite the Abbāsids' problems of consolidating power and their need to build coalitions with the Persians who had helped bring about their victory over the Umayyads, the first century of Abbāsid rule was a period of huge prosperity and impressive achievements. It had taken a new Islamic Empire to achieve the necessary unity between different peoples and cultures, but it was this empire's multicultural and multi-faith tolerance that fostered a real sense of expectancy and optimism, and this would usher in a golden age of enlightenment and intellectual progress.

Initially, emphasis among most Abbāsid men of learning was placed on the interpretation of the words in the Qur'an. After all, this was the very first book to be written in the Arabic language. Grammar, syntax, punctuation and calligraphy had all to be agreed and refined. But this in turn encouraged a certain devotion to scholarship that, once started, took on a life of its own. One cannot, therefore, understand Arabic science without considering the extent to which Islam influenced scientific and philosophical thought. Arabic science was, throughout its golden age, inextricably linked to religion. Clearly, the scientific revolution of the Abbāsids would not have taken place if it were not for Islam, in contrast to the spread of Christianity over the preceding centuries, which had nothing like the same effect in stimulating and encouraging original scientific thinking.

But the spread of Islam was not in itself sufficient to light the touch paper of scientific enquiry. There is no evidence of any original scientific activity taking place during the preceding Umayyad dynasty beyond the isolated efforts already being made by Jewish and Christian scholars in the region. It was, instead, a fresh cultural attitude towards scholarship, which the Abbāsids inherited from the Persians, coupled with the newfound wealth and power of the caliphs of the expanding Islamic Empire that was to help foster an interest in academic enquiry lost since the glory days of Greek Alexandria. The age of Arabic science only began, however, once a quite separate period of almost frantic activity had built up a head of steam. This took place mostly in Baghdad and was known as the translation movement.

3

Translation

The significance of the Greco-Arabic Translation Movement lies in that it demonstrated for the first time in history that scientific and philosophical thought are international, not bound to a specific language or culture.

Dimitri Gutas, *Greek Thought, Arab Culture*

Why did the golden age of Arabic science that blossomed so suddenly during the reign of the early Abbāsid caliphs begin? And why did it eventually come to an end?

It is always assumed that the answer to the second question is the more difficult to articulate and certainly the more contentious, for there were many different contributing factors to the decline of the Islamic Empire, and the most important turn out not to be the most obvious. But that is for later in our story; for now, we shall explore the answer to the first question. At first glance it seems straightforward. The common view is that the exciting advances made in mathematics, astronomy, physics and engineering, the industrialization of chemistry, the great progress in medicine and the flourishing of philosophy that took place, first in Baghdad and then elsewhere in the Islamic Empire, all began thanks to the success of a spectacularly massive translation movement – a process that lasted for two centuries – during which much of the wisdom of the earlier civilizations of the Greeks, Persians and Indians was translated into Arabic. Then, once a culture of scholarship had taken hold within the Islamic Empire, it quickly became self-sustaining, leading to a grand synthesis of scientific knowledge that grew to far outstrip the sum of what had come before.

But while the Abbāsids did indeed sponsor and encourage a massive translation movement, which brought together essentially all world knowledge under one roof, this only pushes the enigma a stage further back. Why did the translation movement itself take place? Or, more to the point, what was it about the Abbāsid mindset – for the beginning of the translation movement does indeed coincide with the arrival on the scene of the Abbāsids – that differed from earlier civilizations in that part of the world, such as the Persian Sasanians, the Byzantines, and even the Muslim Umayyads of Damascus? Militarily powerful though these great empires were, none had shown any real intention of resuscitating the earlier glories of Alexandria that had flourished in the early centuries after the birth of Christianity.

With the arrival of the Abbāsids, all that suddenly changed. The translation movement began in the mid-eighth century, and before too long all levels of elite Abbāsid society in Baghdad were involved, for this was not simply the pet project of the caliph. A huge amount of money was laid out by a large number of wealthy patrons to subsidize and pay for this movement, and translation quickly became a lucrative business. The patrons supported the movement in part for the practical benefits it brought them in finance, agriculture, engineering projects and medicine, and in part because this patronage quickly turned into a de rigueur cultural activity that defined their standing in society. And everyone was involved. As one historian puts it: 'It was no eccentric whim or fashionable affectation of a few wealthy patrons seeking to invest in a philanthropic or self-aggrandising cause.'[1] The translation movement was not, therefore, a separate process that led on to a subsequent golden age of science. It should be seen instead as an integral early part of the golden age itself. Once it got going, it became part of a wider quest for knowledge. By the mid-ninth century it had evolved into a new tradition of original scientific and philosophical scholarship that further fuelled the demand for more translations, both in quantity and quality.

So why is this incredible Graeco-Arabic movement not a well-known chapter in world cultural history, alongside other similarly seismic events? Baghdad between the eighth and tenth centuries should be spoken of in the same breath as the golden age of Athens during the time of Pericles in the fifth century BCE, or Alexandria of the Ptolemies a few hundred years later, or Renaissance Florence of the Medici family in the fifteenth century. Even if the translation movement were all we have to thank the Abbāsids for, this would and should still be regarded as a major epoch in history. But it was not all we have to thank them for; it marked just the beginning of the golden age. So before we explore exactly what was translated and by whom we have to look carefully at why it took place at all.

As with the reasons for the eventual decline of the golden age, it turns out that it owes its origins to a variety of factors, not all of them obvious. Many historians are now making compelling arguments for these and are belatedly overturning years of an over-simplistic historiographical view.

Let us first consider the three standard reasons usually held up as having enabled and brought about the translation movement.

The first is that it began on the whim of one or two enlightened caliphs, as might be deduced from al-Ma'mūn's famous dream about Aristotle, which instantly ignited within him a lifelong obsession with Greek scholarship. However, the translation movement began much earlier than the reign of al-Ma'mūn – under his great-grandfather and the founder of Baghdad, al-Mansūr – and was in full swing by the time al-Ma'mūn had his dream. In fact, if the dream story is true, it would have been entirely in keeping with the cultural atmosphere he was an integral part of. So one can more correctly say that the dream was the *result* of the translation movement and the intellectual climate that brought it about, rather than the other way round.

The funding of the movement came from right across Baghdad's society. Along with the caliphate, it included their courtiers, military leaders, officials of state, administrators, even the leading scholars who had become wealthy as they rose through the ranks as translators themselves. During al-Ma'mūn's reign the most famous of these scholars – men such as Hunayn ibn Ishāq – did not work in isolation, but employed teams of students, translators and scribes.

Without the patronage and encouragement of the caliphs themselves, the translation movement that blossomed and flourished in

Baghdad simply would not have taken place on anything like the same scale. But the enthusiasm and commitment to scholarship of the early caliphs was just part of this wider intellectual movement.

A second reason for the start of the translation movement that is often heard is the spread of Islam itself; that since it is the religious duty of all Muslims to search for knowledge and enlightenment, this inevitably led them to seek out the secular Greek texts on science and philosophy and have them translated into Arabic. While it is certainly true that early Islam encouraged a general spirit of enquiry and a curiosity about the world that was less evident in Christianity and Judaism, we are still left with the issue of why the translation movement started when it did and not earlier, during the Umayyads.

Moreover, the translation movement transcended religious boundaries. A large number of the translators were Christians, and they would not have played such an important role if the main motive behind the movement had been religious, following the teachings of the Qur'an or the advice of the Prophet (the *Hadith*). The all-important patronage of the movement also cut across society to include non-Muslims. The fact that the teachings of the Qur'an and *Hadith* encouraged the seeking of knowledge was certainly a necessary factor in the development of original schools of thought in theology, philosophy and even the exact sciences. But these started somewhat later than the translation movement.

Which leads us to the third widely perceived origin for the movement; that it was Greek-speaking Christians living in the lands previously part of the Byzantine Empire and well versed in Greek science, who should be thanked for transmitting this knowledge on to the Abbāsids. The reality is somewhat different. The study of the work of Greek philosophers like Aristotle and Plato, as well as some medical and astronomical texts, was, it is true, going on within Byzantine centres such as Antioch and Edessa in northern Syria, where a modest Graeco-Syriac (a dialect of Aramaic, the ancient Semitic language that evolved into Arabic and Hebrew) translation movement was taking place. But it could be argued that these translations tended to be of poorer quality than what was to come later and were not subject to the rigorous demands of accuracy nor the depths of intellectual understanding.

With the spread of Islam throughout the region, political and religious barriers that had existed between the various sects and denominations became less important. Thus, while religious tensions continued, such as Christian Iconoclasm, Karaite versus Talmudic Judaism and sectarian arguments within Islam itself, Christian and Jewish scholars were now freer to share their knowledge in a spirit of more open collaboration. But this openness of early Islam to other faiths does not entirely explain why relatively few translations took place during the hundred years of Umayyad rule, yet increased dramatically in number as soon as the Abbāsids took over, when many of the most influential and skilled Christian and Jewish translators travelled to Baghdad seeking fame and fortune.

So, if it was not the spread of Islam, enlightened caliphs or Christian scholars carrying the torch of ancient Greek science and philosophy in the Islamic world, what was it? How, for instance, did al-Ma'mūn know of Aristotle in the first place? More generally, why should the Arabs, those uncultured nomads of the desert, suddenly become interested in Greek philosophy? The answer is that they did not – not until *after* the start of the translation movement, anyway. It was only then that we begin to see translations of the medical texts of Galen, the philosophy of Aristotle, the geometry of Euclid and the astronomy of Ptolemy. The first translation of a Greek text would often be into Syriac, then from Syriac into Arabic. Subsequent more careful and accurate translations were made directly from Greek to Arabic only as understanding of both the Greek language and the scientific content of the original texts improved.

What then were the true reasons for the translation movement? Before the arrival of the Abbāsids, we witness what historians refer to as smaller-scale 'translation activities' rather than a full-blown movement. These involved the translation of astronomical and medical texts from Indian to Pahlavi in the Sasanian Empire and from Greek to Syriac in the Byzantine, Sasanian and Umayyad empires. Then, around the time of the Caliph al-Mansūr in 754, a quite sudden and dramatic change took place. I believe three important factors helped trigger the translation movement. Not all three happened at once and no one factor was sufficient to explain what happened. But together, they offer a compelling argument.

39

Unlike the Umayyad dynasty, whose capital, Damascus, had been part of the Greek-speaking Byzantine Empire, the Abbāsids had moved the whole operation further east into the heart of what had been part of the Persian Empire of the Sasanians. This was no accident. Powerful Persian clans such as the Barmakis and the Nawbakhts had helped them to power and continued to maintain a strong influence in government for many generations. The Abbāsids, in turn, needed the support of this Persian nobility and encouraged the interweaving of Arab and Persian cultures and identities.

But Arabic was now the official language of the empire, and there was immediately seen to be a need for translation of Pahlavi texts into Arabic, and full caliphal support was offered to the project. Some of these texts were Persian in origin; others, such as many medical, mathematical and astronomical works, had been originally translated into Pahlavi from Greek and Indian and were in use in cities such as Gondēshāpūr (called Jundaysābūr in Arabic).[2] So the first and most important factor in bringing about the translation movement was this Abbāsid obsession with Persian culture. This was typified by one translator who, when asked why he searched for Persian books to translate into Arabic, is supposed to have replied: 'we [the Arabs] have all the words, but they [the Persians] have all the ideas.'[3] This need for translation was at the outset almost entirely for practical purposes; it had to be seen as useful and necessary.

This is where the second factor comes in: an obsession with astrology. Sasanian ideology, based on Zoroastrian myth, was very appealing to the Caliph al-Mansūr, who developed a deep personal interest in astrology. He also knew he needed the support of the influential Persian aristocracy, most of whom were still Zoroastrian and had not converted to Islam. His interest in astrology, therefore, while wholehearted and genuine, can also be seen to have a shrewd political motive. Astrology, as distinct from astronomy, was embedded in Persian culture and played a fundamental role in Persian daily life, in stark contrast to the Arabs, who saw it as being against the teachings of Islam with its links to fortune-telling and divination. But such was the influence of Sasanian culture on the Abbāsids that astrology underwent a revival in the second half of the eighth century. Astrologers were employed in the caliph's court to cast horoscopes, offer advice and glorify his achievements. We have already seen how al-Mansūr employed his three top astrologers to advise him on the right day to start building his new capital.

It is not surprising therefore that the first 'scientific' discipline to be systematically translated from Pahlavi into Arabic was astrology. One of the earliest texts was the hugely influential five-part astrological work of the prophet Zoroaster, *The Book of Nativities*, which was first translated into Arabic between 747 and 754.[4] Astrology, the art of plotting the positions of the stars for horoscopes, had become a perfectly acceptable branch of knowledge. Known as *'ilm al-nujūm* (the science of the stars), it was indistinguishable from mathematics and astronomy (*'ilm al-falak*) and those interested in astrological texts were keen to get hold of star charts and mathematical tables. So this early Abbāsid interest in astrology naturally led to the search for astronomical texts already available in Pahlavi or still in Sanskrit, the language of the Indian mathematicians and astronomers.

Al-Fazāri, one of the astrologers who advised al-Mansūr, and the man credited with building the first astrolabe in the Muslim world, is also associated with translating several astronomical texts from Sanskrit into Arabic. It has even been claimed that he was the first to translate the *Siddhanta*, written by the greatest Indian mathematician and astronomer, Brahmagupta (598–668), into Arabic. This was arguably the very first time that the Abbāsids encountered Hindu astronomy, but the date and authorship of the translation are uncertain owing to confusion surrounding several contemporary scholars, all called al-Fazāri.[5]

The word *Siddhanta* is a Sanskrit term meaning 'The Doctrine' or 'The Tradition'. It was originally written, as was the tradition among Indian mathematicians, completely in verse. But frustratingly, Brahmagupta provided no proofs of the many mathematical theorems it contains. The Arabic translation of this text is known as the *Sindhind* and, along with Ptolemy's *Almagest* and Euclid's *Elements*, it was destined to have a huge influence on the scholars of Baghdad. It appears likely that the *Siddhanta* had originally been translated into Pahlavi, possibly in the Persian city of Gondēshāpūr, which had been a great centre of Sasanid scholarship. The book contained not only tables and star charts, but mathematics and crude trigonometry. However, it was notoriously obscure and difficult to follow.

There is a dubious apocryphal story which, if true, not only dates the translation of the *Sindhind* to the time of al-Mansūr but explains the reason for its lack of clarity. The story describes how Arabs first conquered then settled in the land of Sindh (today one of the provinces of Pakistan) in the early days of Islam. When the Abbāsids came to power these settlers seized the opportunity to declare themselves independent. But al-Mansūr would not tolerate this and sent an army to quell the uprising. After his victory, a delegation from the defeated Sindh came to Baghdad. In the party was an Indian sage named Kankah, who spoke no Arabic or Persian, and his speech, describing the wonders of Indian astronomy and mathematics had to be translated first into Persian by an interpreter, and then into Arabic by a second interpreter, a process which rendered the final form of his instruction very involved and abstruse. What he had been describing was Brahmagupta's *Siddhanta*.

Later Islamic scholars such as the polymath al-Bīrūni in the eleventh century dismiss this story as highly unlikely, claiming that a more likely scenario was that the *Sindhind* was a translation of a Persian version already in use in Gondēshāpūr. The only likely truth in the story is therefore that the *Siddhanta* did indeed pass through two translations on its way to the Arabs.

It is not until well into the ninth century that we see among Islamic scientists and philosophers an emerging confidence in a new rational and scientific world-view that led many to criticize astrology as not having a place alongside true sciences like mathematics and astronomy. Some, however, continued to dabble in it, including the mathematician al-Khwārizmi. Others, even centuries later, would recognize its importance in convincing their less-enlightened rulers to continue funding their astronomical projects. One such scholar was the Persian al-Tūsi, who had to feign an interest in astrology to persuade the Mongol ruler Hūlāgū Khān to fund his new observatory in Marāgha in north-west Persia in the mid-thirteenth century.

But back in the eighth century it was this early widespread obsession with astrology that helped ignite interest in translating the predominantly Greek works in the other sciences.

The third factor that played a role in establishing and accelerating the translation movement was the serendipity of emerging technologies. A knowledge of subjects like geometry was required for engineering projects[6] such as arched stone bridges, waterwheels and canals; accurate astronomical data were needed to predict the phases of the moon for timekeeping; and arithmetic was vital for accountancy. All these played an important role; but all would have been equally important to earlier civilizations and so do not explain the sudden acceleration in the volume of translations. However, it was the arrival of one technology in particular that made all the difference in the world.

The first paper mill in the Abbāsid Empire was built in the city of Samarkand in Central Asia on the silk route between China and the West. The city was already one of the greatest in the Persian Empire many centuries before the Islamic conquest and was to continue as a centre of learning and scholarship well into the Middle Ages. The Muslim army defeated the Chinese in 751 on the banks of the river Talas several hundred miles north-west of Samarkand in modern Kyrgyzstan. This Abbāsid victory marked not only the furthest expansion of the Chinese Tang dynasty westwards but the furthest east into Asia that the Islamic Empire would venture. Pertinent to our story is that among the Chinese prisoners of war were those who had knowledge of papermaking – an invention of the Chinese in the second century CE – who were taken back to Samarkand. There, their knowledge was crucial in the building of the first paper mill, helped by the abundance of raw materials like flax and hemp crops in the region. The first paper mills in Baghdad began to appear in the last decade of the eighth century.

Parallel with this was a rise in technologies associated with the production of books: the development of dyes, inks, glues, leather and book-binding techniques,[7] all of which exploded on the scene within a very short time. Paper quickly became far cheaper as a writing material than papyrus and parchment, and multiple copies of texts would often be produced by a whole team of scribes working side by side.

Prior to this, the codex (in which sheets are bound together as books between covers, usually wooden) had replaced the scroll much earlier than the invention of paper itself. First used by the Romans and Hellenistic Greeks, codices were originally made of papyrus and parchment. In fact, it is claimed that during the Prophet Muhammad's lifetime, the pages of the Qur'an were kept as a codex between wooden boards.

So the translation movement owes its beginnings to the appeal of Persian culture, and astrology in particular, to the Abbāsids, along with the development of paper-making technology they had learned from the Chinese. But once it began, this obsession with translating ancient texts sparked the beginning of a golden age of scientific progress.

A sharp increase in the number of translations took place during the reign (786–809) of Harūn al-Rashīd. Medical, astronomical and mathematical texts began to be translated from Greek, Syriac, Persian and Indian. But at this relatively early stage, scholars were careful in their choice of manuscripts to translate. The importance of any scholarly scientific work is said to be measured by the extent to which it renders all earlier ones on the same subject superfluous. It was quickly realized that many Persian works on science were themselves translations from the original Greek. Soon those Greek originals were being sought. By this time, Islamic scholars and patrons of the translation movement had moved on from an interest in purely practical subjects like astrology, medicine and agriculture to mathematics and astronomy. What is missing from this early list of disciplines is philosophy, as exemplified by the work of the two Greek giants: Plato and Aristotle. The later translation movement from Greek and Arabic into Latin *began* with philosophy because of a desire to understand these great works. But interest in this field among Islamic scholars came relatively late in Baghdad's translation movement and finally took off for a quite touching reason: Muslim scholars felt somewhat lacking in their reasoning and debating skills on matters of theology alongside their Christian and Jewish counterparts already familiar with Aristotle and Plato and therefore more experienced in such logical disputations.

It is interesting to note that while a number of significant Jewish philosophers and scientists made invaluable contributions to the intellectual culture of Baghdad, their work was almost entirely in Arabic rather than Hebrew. A good example lies with the work of Sahl Rabbān al-Tabari (c. 786–845), who came to Baghdad and is said to have made one of the first translations of Ptolemy's *Almagest* into Arabic. This Jewish astronomer and physician, whose name literally means 'the son of the rabbi of Tabaristan' – by reference to a province in northern Iran – settled in Baghdad during the time of al-Rashīd. His son, Ali (*c.* 838–70), who converted to Islam, wrote the first Arabic encyclopedia of medicine and would tutor a boy named Muhammad ibn Zakariyya al-Rāzi, who was destined to become one of the greatest clinicians who ever lived.

Some historians have claimed that despite the Abbāsids' admiration of all things Persian and, by association, their link to Indian science and culture in the East, the whole of the translation movement was built on what was originally Greek science.[8] To some extent this is true. The expansion of Alexander the Great's empire as far east as India, many centuries before Islam, carried the fruits of Greek science far beyond its home shores – although we should not forget the sea trade routes from Egypt as a separate avenue of transmission. This knowledge, one can argue, eventually made the circuitous journey from its Greek origins, via India, back to the palace courts of Abbāsid Baghdad. Much of Greek knowledge also reached the Arabic world through the great Christian cities of Antioch and Edessa where, to a lesser extent, a translation tradition from Greek to Syriac had flourished in the centuries before Islam's arrival.

Certainly in the fields of medicine and philosophy, where Hippocrates, Galen, Plato and Aristotle were peerless, the Arabs had the Greeks to thank for almost the entirety of their knowledge. In geometry, too, the Indians and Persians could claim little expertise. But it is unfair to dismiss their contribution to the development of Arabic science completely during the translation movement. For without its exposure to Indian mathematics, the Muslim world would not have had the decimal numbering notation, or the kick-start in trigonometry that was to prove so useful in astronomy. Similarly, Arabic astronomy is seen as a continuation of the work of the Persian observatories, which itself would not have flourished without Indian mathematics.

An alternative and erroneous view, more sympathetic to Persian culture and history, is based on an interesting myth that is worth recounting here. In 333 BCE, Alexander the Great conquered the

Persian Empire and deposed its last king, Darius III. Alexander marched on the Persian capital at Persepolis, where he found writings on the various sciences and branches of knowledge regarded by Persians as divine in origin, passed down by the prophet Zoroaster himself. Alexander had all texts translated from Persian into Greek, after which he destroyed the originals. Hundreds of years later, Sasanian kings ordered the collection of all Greek works and their retranslation back into Persian. In this way, Persians justified their use of Greek knowledge in medicine, astronomy and astrology, since they claimed that it was all stolen Persian knowledge anyway.

As a scholar and a poet himself, al-Rashīd was a great patron of the arts and it was under his rule that Muslim scholars began to study the great works of the Greeks and the Indians in earnest, and to assimilate that knowledge into Arabic culture. Al-Rashīd's court in Baghdad was full of artists, musicians, poets and theologians from far and wide. But it was his second-in-command and tutor of the young Ma'mūn, the vizier Ja'far al-Barmaki, who oversaw many of the early translation activities. The Barmakis, who had sponsored and supported the Abbāsids' rise to power and whose loyalty was rewarded by their hereditary appointment as grand viziers (and occasional execution), found they had tremendous power in the day-to-day running of the state. They were, moreover, strong supporters of the translation movement and were able to infuse the caliph's court with their Persian cultural heritage.

Another prominent Persian family who sponsored the translation movement was the Bukhtishūs. Several members of this family personally commissioned the translation of medical texts into Arabic. Even before the arrival of the Abbāsids, Persian physicians would already have been familiar with many of the medical texts of Hippocrates and Galen, whose teachings had been practised in Gondēshāpūr. Their chief beneficiary when it came to medical texts was the Christian physician and translator Hunayn ibn Ishāq, who was destined to become the most famous and prolific translator of the age.

Another scholar of Baghdad to benefit from their generous support was Thābit ibn Qurra (c. 836–901), a pagan from the city of Harrān in north-west Mesopotamia (now in Turkey) who began his working life as a market moneychanger before discovering philosophy. Thābit translated the mathematical work of Euclid, Archimedes, Apollonius and Ptolemy. He also prepared summaries of the works of Aristotle. But he was a brilliant mathematician in his own right and wrote original works on geometry, statics, magic squares and the theory of numbers. He even covered astronomy and, towards the end of his life, was appointed court astronomer by the Abbāsid Caliph al-Mu'tadid. Several of his works were themselves later translated into Latin and were highly influential in the West.

Another prominent Christian translator in ninth-century Baghdad was a Byzantine Greek by the name of Qusta ibn Luqqa (d. *c.* 912). Like many of the top translators, he was a polymath who understood mathematics, medicine, astronomy and philosophy. He came originally from the town of Baalbek (Heliopolis) in the Bekaa valley in Lebanon. Like Hunayn ibn Ishāq, he was urged to convert to Islam but never did so. Among the books he translated from Greek to Arabic were those of Diophantus the mathematician, Aristarchus (the first astronomer to propose a heliocentric model of the solar system) and Galen. Qusta wrote many original works on medicine and geometry, and even a treatise on the astrolabe, the most important astronomical device before the telescope (see Plate 7).[9]

As Arabic scholarship began in earnest during the first half of the ninth century, with an increasing amount of original writing being commissioned in astronomy, geography, mathematics and medicine, so inevitably did original research in those subjects, generating the need for further texts to be translated, or more careful and accurate translations of Greek texts already existing in Arabic. The knowledge gained from these texts inspired many to dedicate their lives to those subjects. For example, it was part of every scholar's education in al-Ma'mūn's Baghdad to study Ptolemy's *Almagest*, and it was the knowledge they gained from this important text that led to the first observatories being built in the Islamic Empire, in Baghdad and Damascus during al-Ma'mūn's reign. He appointed astronomers, who began a systematic programme of careful observations to check the accuracy of Ptolemy's star charts. This marked the beginning of seven hundred years of Arabic astronomy and provided the bridge from the Greeks to the Copernican revolution in Europe and the birth of modern astronomy.

Many of the most important Greek texts were translated into Arabic several times. A good example is Euclid's *Elements*, which had a huge impact on Islamic mathematics. This was first translated by al-Hajjāj ibn Yūsuf during the reign of al-Rashīd at the beginning of the ninth century. The same man was later to produce a new translation for al-Ma'mūn. But the text was also translated by Hunayn ibn Ishāq, and his version was then revised by Thābit ibn Qurra. Finally, a further revision was made by the astronomer al-Tūsi almost four centuries later. The work probably first became known in Europe through Latin translations of this later version. It has even been claimed that the *Elements* was known to the Caliph al-Mansūr, who had heard of it from Christian priests and had requested a copy from the Byzantine emperor.[10] But the quality of any Arabic translation of the *Elements* made for al-Mansūr is debatable, as is its usefulness to any of the early Abbāsid mathematicians.

The translation movement finally came to an end in the second half of the tenth century, not because of a decline in or a loss of interest in scholarship but because it had naturally reached a stage when it was no longer required. All the great works had been translated, retranslated, studied and commented upon and were by this point being replaced by original Arabic works that took the sciences further. Indeed, some of the very greatest Greek texts, such as Ptolemy's *Almagest*, were no longer seen as 'state of the art' and had been superseded by more sophisticated astronomical works. By this time, the collective scientific enterprise was embedded in Baghdad's cultural atmosphere of scholarly patronage and competition.

The first great scientist of Islam, however, predates this period by a generation. His life and achievements are shrouded in mystery and controversy. He is known in the West as Geber the Alchemist.

4

The Lonely Alchemist

We may ask ourselves what men like Gauss or Faraday would have done if they had been born in the eighth or ninth century instead of being able to take advantage of another millennium of human effort.

George Sarton

Many of the great scientists of the golden age were not Arabs but Persian, even though they wrote all their work in Arabic, the official language of the empire. This is a source of considerable sensitivity to Iranians and other Central Asian Muslims, who understandably dislike their great heroes being mistaken for Arabs (particularly when the Arabic definite article 'al' is attached to their names). To stress to you how difficult it can sometimes be to disentangle the roots and origins of many of these men it might be useful for me to share with you my own somewhat blurred ethnic background.

The al-Khalīlis (Al-Khalilis)[1] are a Shi'a clan from the cities of Najaf and Kūfa in Iraq with strong Persian roots that go back over two hundred years. Around the end of the eighteenth century, my great-great-great-grandfather, Merza Khalil, a prominent physician from Tehran who had originally studied in the city of Qum to become an imam and after whom the Al-Khalili family is named, was on a pilgrimage to Mecca. His trip coincided with that of the Ottoman wali of Baghdad, the administrative ruler of a large chunk of today's Iraq, who fell ill. Khalil was called upon to treat him with the appropriate herbal remedies that he was an authority on. After recovering, the wali invited him back to Iraq to settle, which he did in 1799. Of

49

his six sons, the eldest, Muhammad, remained in Iran to achieve even greater distinction in medicine than his father by becoming the personal physician to the shah, Nasr al-Dīn Qajar (1831–96), earning him the title of *Fakhr al-Atibbā'* ('The Pride of Physicians'). Naturally, this is a source of great pride to the Al-Khalili clan, even today, for Shah Nasr al-Dīn was one of the greatest rulers in Persian history. A great reformist, he introduced in Iran the postal service, the rail system and newspaper publishing. On a visit to Britain in 1873, accompanied by my great-great-great-uncle Muhammad, the shah was appointed by Queen Victoria a Knight of the Order of the Garter, the highest English order of chivalry.

I am descended from two of Khalil's other sons, Bāqir on my grandfather's side and Merza Hussein on my grandmother's side. The latter, I always find fascinating to recount, was a spiritual leader of millions of Shi'a Muslims in Ottoman Iraq, Persia, Lebanon and India at the end of the nineteenth century. Based in the city of Najaf, he belonged to the group of *mujtahids* (clergy with the authority to interpret the Qur'an) and played an important role in the mobilization of public pressure across the Persian border against the excessive corruption and pro-Russian policies of the last of the Qajar rulers prior to Iran's constitutional revolution of 1905. After the death of the supreme leader Merza Shirazi in Najaf in 1895, Merza Hussein Al-Khalili became the absolute leader of the Shi'a clergy of Najaf. He was responsible for a number of public works, including the building of a canal between Kūfa and Najaf. By the beginning of the twentieth century this great-great-grandfather of mine was given the loftier title of Ayatollah.

I am thus in the fourth generation of Al-Khalilis to have been born in Iraq. Despite this, Saddam Hussein certainly did not regard the Al-Khalilis as true Iraqis, and many of my relatives were executed during the height of hostilities with Iran in the 1980s for having what were perceived to be divided loyalties. When my father came to Britain to study engineering in the 1950s and met my mother he became the first of the Al-Khalilis to marry outside the clan. It could therefore be argued on ethnic grounds that I have no Arab blood in me at all! Does any of this matter? My point is that while Arabs and Persians are technically different races (Semitic and Arian), the inhabitants of Iraq today are of such a racial mix – Arabs living alongside Assyrians, Kurds, Persians, Armenians and Turkomans – that it is rather pointless to try to lay claim to particular figures in history as belonging to any one race.

Baghdad was in fact the second capital of the Abbāsids. For a number of years before its foundation they had taken Kūfa, the city of my father's birth, as their capital. Today, Kūfa is no more than a suburb of the much larger city of Najaf. But in the mid-eighth century, even after the move to Baghdad, Kūfa retained its importance both as a centre of scholarship and the spiritual home of the Shi'a movement that had helped bring the Abbāsids to power. It is in this city that my story of Arabic science really takes off.

If there is one scientific discipline that can truly be said to have begun in the medieval Islamic world, it is chemistry. And to a large extent this was due to the achievements of one Muslim scholar, working alone in Kūfa in the eighth century.

Or at least that is one version of history.

For reasons that will soon become clear, I shall begin by examining the term 'alchemy'. There is no ambiguity about its meaning today as an irrational, pseudo-scientific belief that base metals can be transmuted into silver and gold, with its origins rooted in myth, legend and superstition. It is commonly thought that, just as astronomy can be shown to have grown out of the much older and non-scientific practice of astrology, so also the science of chemistry emerged from alchemy. This is wrong.

The first attempts to understand and manipulate matter go back long before Islam. The Egyptians, Babylonians, Greeks, Indians and Chinese all practised and developed a crude form of applied chemistry: in metallurgy, in the production of paints, salts and dyes, and even in the fermentation of alcoholic beverages. Quite independently of such practical concerns, the Greek philosophers were interested in developing theories and rudimentary classifications of the material world, such as the four elements of Empedocles: earth, air, water and fire.[2] Aristotle subscribed broadly to this idea but believed that all four were different aspects of the same 'primary substance' or *protylē*, which contains within it the potential to take on all four different forms. This potential is expressed in the effects of the four fundamental qualities of heat, coldness, dryness and humidity. Aristotle also postulated the existence of a fifth element, the aether, which was immutable and imperishable.

Similar theories appeared around the same time in China, where it was believed that there were five fundamental elements (earth, water, fire, metal and wood) and in India (earth, water, fire, air and space). The question is whether this combination of the philosophy of matter on the one hand and applied chemical processes on the other constitutes what we might define as real chemistry. I would say not; chemistry is a science and as such must satisfy the rigorous requirements of the scientific method. It is more appropriate to call these ancient practices and notions, going back many thousands of years, 'protochemistry';[3] the pursuit of alchemy can be regarded as a subfield of this protochemistry.

But what of this Muslim scholar to whom I claim we owe so much? Geber the Alchemist is without doubt one of the most fascinating and enigmatic figures in the history of Arabic science. His real name is Jābir ibn Hayyān (c. 721–c. 815) and he lived before the reign of al-Ma'mūn. I shall be making the case that he be regarded as the father of chemistry, but there are two problems that must be addressed if I am to offer a convincing argument. First, Jābir himself did not help his case by combining in his work some remarkable laboratory chemistry with mystical and bizarre notions and obscure writing that is often extremely hard to follow. In fact, the origin of the word 'gibberish', which goes back to the early sixteenth century, refers to any obscure language 'such as that used by Gibber (or Jābir)'. Secondly, a huge mythology has grown around his work, fuelled by later Islamic and Christian scholars who wrote under his name, making it hard to determine just what is authentic and what is not. Digging through the vast literature on the subject has been for me both hugely enjoyable and somewhat frustrating, and the debate about Jābir's place in history still rages.

Jābir was a Yemeni Arab in origin and the son of an apothecary. He was born in Khurasan in eastern Persia, where the Abbāsid revolution began. But with the founding of the new empire, he moved with his family to Kūfa where he began practising medicine. His father had been politically very closely allied with the Persian Barmaki family and so Jābir came to be regarded by them as a loyal and trustworthy character. He received their generous patronage, in particular that of Ja'far, the grand vizier of al-Rashīd.

It is thought that Jābir had a Baghdad residence near the Damascus Gate, but most of his time seems to have been spent in Kūfa, because of the 'healthiness of the climate' there. When, in 802, al-Rashīd had his vizier Ja'far executed in order to curtail the influence of the Barmaki family, Jābir, now an old man, lost his elevated status in the caliph's court and spent his remaining years under house arrest.

To his many followers, Jābir was known as *al-Sūfi* (the Mystic) and certainly much of his work was tied in with mysticism and magic. But a number of contemporary historians have downplayed the alchemical side of his work and point to this quotation from the prologue of one of his most famous books, *Kitab al-Rahma al-Kabīr* (*The Great Book of Mercy*), where Jābir is critical of those who practise the 'art' of transmutation:

> I have seen people giving themselves over to the search for the art of transmuting gold and silver, in ignorance and without consideration, and I have seen that they are of two types, the deceivers and the deceived. I am filled with feelings of mercy and compassion because they waste their money and weary their bodies in a fruitless search.[4]

It is unclear here whether he is critical of *any* attempts to transmute metals into gold and silver or just of those who did not have his knowledge of the mystical art and were therefore frauds. What we do know from his writings, however, is that he was far less interested in transmutation than in the even grander quest for the creation of artificial life in the laboratory – what was known as *takwīn* – and fancied himself as a medieval Dr Frankenstein.

Despite this, Jābir did much to free up chemistry from its origins in superstition and turn it into an experimental science. In his own words: 'The first essential in chemistry is that thou should perform practical work and conduct experiments, for he who performs not practical work nor makes experiments will never attain to the least degree of mastery.'[5] He was closely associated with Ja'far al-Sādiq (d. 765), the sixth Imam of Shi'ism, who tutored him on theology.

And many Shi'a today still proclaim Jābir himself as a spiritual leader and one of the great figures of Islam because of his association with the Imam. Jābir himself, out of respect for his mentor, claimed that his scientific theories were no more than the knowledge passed down to him from Imam Ja'far, which had been transmitted all the way from the Prophet via his son-in-law Ali.

Intriguingly, a number of Muslim alchemists who came after Jābir and who studied his work seem to have tried hard to keep his status and work secret. The tenth-century Baghdadi historian Ibn al-Nadīm, who had no doubts about Jābir's important place in history, wrote that one group of scholars had told him Jābir had never even existed, and that even if he had he would have written only one book (*The Great Book of Mercy*); the rest were written by other, later scholars. Al-Nadīm finds this conspiracy to rewrite history hard to believe:

> But I assert that if an excellent man sits down and toils to compile a book which comprises two thousand leaves, fatiguing his genius and intelligence in producing it, while wearying his hand and body in transcribing it, and then attributes it to someone else, whether existent or non-existent, it is a form of folly . . . What profit would there be in this, or what advantage?[6]

That Jābir is regarded in the West as having been 'just an alchemist' probably has more to do with the prejudices of the early European translators of his work than with his own scientific leanings. Some of his most influential books were translated into Latin in the twelfth century, at a time when alchemy was still considered a respectable pursuit in Europe (it would continue to be so, well into the Renaissance). Even Isaac Newton was a devoted alchemist later in life and is sometimes referred to as the last of the magicians rather than the first scientist of the age of reason – and he lived nine hundred years after Jābir.

One distinction that was made between the two disciplines is that while chemistry was regarded as the *science* of matter, alchemy involved the *philosophy* of matter. But where was this line in the sand between science and philosophy, especially as alchemy also involved scientific notions of experimentation, observation and theory? Perhaps, since Jābir was far more interested in this empiricism than in philosophy, he should be regarded more as a chemist than an alchemist.

Of course, one cannot deny that much of the work of Jābir ibn Hayyān was firmly rooted in superstition and magic, which was not uncommon during those times, and many bizarre and colourful notions can be found in his writing: that impregnating a woman with bird sperm would produce a human child with wings; that putrefied hair generates serpents; and that statues can be used to trap demons within them. But it is the pompous certainty with which some authors have laid claim to their arguments, either denying Jābir's very existence or simply belittling the impact of his and other medieval chemists' work, regarding it as mere alchemy, that I wish to address. So, let us explore how this split between alchemy and chemistry first came about.

Unlike its sister science, physics, which arose from natural philosophy, chemistry is a much older discipline and has its origins in practical applications like metallurgy. Indeed, the Greek word *chymeia* proba-bly came from the word *cheein*, to smelt metals.[7] This *chymeia* was passed on to become the transliterated Arabic word *kīmiyā'*. It was used to denote all laboratory operations with materials – in fact, what we would still regard as experimental chemistry today. Another intri-guing possible origin of the word (suggested to me by an Iraqi colleague and professor of chemical engineering, Adel Sharif) is that *kīmiyā'* originated with the work of Jābir himself, who may not have been familiar with the Greek *chymeia*, but instead called it 'the science of quantities' (*'ilm al-kammiya*) because of the importance he placed on the precision of measuring the various amounts of substances he mixed together.

The desire to transmute base metals into gold was not seen as a separate field and so there was no need for a different word to define it – although it was often referred to in ancient times simply as the 'Art'. In Arabic, the definite article *al* was attached to the word *kīmiyā'* to make it *al-kīmiyā'*. To this day, the Arabic word for 'chemistry' is either *kīmiyā'* or *al-kīmiyā'* and there is no distinction between them other than a grammatical one. It is the latter that then became the

Latin word *alchymia* (or *alchemia* and *alchimia*), which appears frequently in medieval Latin. Some Europeans, however, understanding its origin, stripped off the *al* to return closer to the original Greek and referred to it simply as *chymia*. The important point is that, even in Latin, both words were used interchangeably. Thus Jābir's seminal book *Kitab al-Kīmiyā'* (*The Book of Chemistry*) was originally translated from Arabic into Latin by the Englishman Robert of Chester in 1144 as *Liber de compositione alchimiae*. But as we shall see shortly, it was six hundred years before the word *alchimia* became 'alchemy' and came to have its modern meaning of transmutation.

A number of historians have until recently been lazy in pinpointing the origin of this distinction. Their mistake has been to push the notion that there was a clear and well-understood difference between alchemy and chemistry all the way back to the Islamic golden age. However, even after Europeans began using two different words, 'chemistry' and 'alchemy', they still did not distinguish between the two. A practitioner was referred to either as a 'chemist' or an 'alchemist' (the prefix 'al' being the only difference, even in modern English, between the two words). Sometimes their meanings were even reversed: before the seventeenth century, transmutation was often referred to as 'chemistry' and those who practised laboratory chemistry were referred to as 'alchemists'. For example, the book *Alchemia* by Andreas Libavius in 1597 describes many of the standard chemical techniques such as distillation, crystallization and the production of salts and acids, but makes no mention of transmutation of metals into gold.

It was only in the mid-eighteenth century that authors began to apply separate meanings to the two words. Thus, the entry in Diderot's *Encyclopédie* (first published in 1751 and one of the great works of the Enlightenment) defines *alchimie* as 'the art of transmuting metals', whereas *chimie* is 'the science which concerns separation and unifications of the principles making up bodies'.[8] It is this distinction that has reached us today.

Some historians of science, sympathetic to the achievements of early Muslim chemists such as Jābir or the great al-Rāzi (who was better known as a physician), argue that these men knew the distinction between chemistry and alchemy and that they, and other enlightened Islamic rationalists such as the philosophers al-Kindi and Ibn Sīna, even dismissed alchemy, much as they shunned astrological beliefs in favour of serious astronomical observations. While this is true for some of these later Islamic scholars,[9] it is not quite so clear in the case of Jābir. In any case, I do not see that such a stance is necessary in order to legitimize the achievements of Jābir in chemistry. After all, was Aristotle a fool for believing in the four elements theory of matter? Was Plato any less of a genius for his adherence to the intromission theory of vision (that claimed we see objects by emitting light from our eyes)? Indeed, was Isaac Newton less worthy of the mantle of the greatest scientist who ever lived for his own obsession with alchemy? Hindsight is wonderful, but we should not project back our modern scientific ideas and values onto a very different time. Referring to Jābir ibn Hayyān as an alchemist rather than a chemist (according to our modern definitions of the two words) is rather like referring to the great Alexandrian astronomer Ptolemy as an astrologer.

To take one example, Jābir believed that all metals are composed of sulphur and mercury in different proportions. While every school-child now knows this notion to be quite wrong, Jābir's motives for studying the nature of matter, as well as many of the experimental techniques he perfected, are still just as valid today. Similarly, Ptolemy believed in the geocentric model of the universe with the stars and planets fixed to rotating spheres around a central earth, which we today know to be a completely discredited notion. This does not diminish Ptolemy's place in history. Science advances, and Jābir's rudimentary chemistry evolved, just as Ptolemy's astronomy did.

Chemistry and alchemy were therefore not separate disciplines during the time of Jābir. One did not evolve into the other – they did not even run in parallel. Part of chemistry dealt with the occult and mysticism, other parts dealt with practical applications in industry, and yet others with a genuine attempt to understand, categorize and classify substances based on careful experimentation. All were present in the early work of Jābir ibn Hayyān. While the final shift from the occult to a real experimental science took place a little after Jābir, he was without doubt the first scientist to go beyond the theories of the Greeks, and he revolutionized the way science was carried out. He stressed careful observation, controlled experiments and accurate records, in contrast with much of Greek chemistry that was either based on hypotheses and metaphysical notions or scientifically sterile practical applications.[10]

Jābir's writing covered a vast range of subjects. He was interested not only in the theory and practice of chemical processes and the classification of substances, but in pharmacology, medicine, philosophy, cosmology, logic, music and numerology – in a way very similar to the broad interests of many of the Greek philosophers a thousand years before him. Much of his writing was of a religious character, and his work on alchemy does tend to be shrouded in secrecy, with warnings from his mentor and religious master Imam Ja'far that it should not fall into the hands of the unworthy. Much later, when the work had been translated into Latin, European scholars managed to wrap it up in even more mystery and confusion. Historians have even questioned whether this labyrinth of chemical and alchemical writing (known as the Jabirian Corpus) is completely authentic.

And there is a more serious problem than simply one of provenance. The French historian Paul Kraus showed in the 1940s that the almost three thousand works attributed to Jābir ibn Hayyān could not possibly have been written by one man, for they contain too much disparity in both style and content. This issue has been subject to conflicting opinion and speculation by historians over the past century and is referred to in academic circles as the 'Jābir Problem'. The issue is not so much the obscurity of the writing as whether Jābir was in fact the true author of this huge body of work. For instance, it is argued that the Jabirian Corpus displays numerous indications linking it to the much later Isma'īli movement of Fātimid times, implying that most of the works attributed to Jābir in the eighth century were probably written between the ninth and eleventh centuries. Other parts of the Corpus survive only in Latin and no evidence has been found of any earlier Arabic versions, possibly implying that there never were any, and that they were first composed by European scholars in Latin in the twelfth or thirteenth centuries. Even during early Islamic times, controversies raged. A philosopher by the name of al-Mantiqī wrote in 970 CE, less than two centuries after Jābir's death, that the

Jabirian works were apocryphal and that the true author was a personal friend of his by the name of al-Hassan al-Mawsilī (not a view many take seriously).

However, the sheer volume and breadth of the Corpus that has reached us has convinced scholars that there had to be at least one other much later author, who is referred to as Pseudo-Geber. The most famous work attributed to this mysterious scholar is the *Summa perfectionis magisterii*, an alchemical treatise probably written in the thirteenth century. For many years, Pseudo-Geber could not be associated with any historical personality, although it was commonly agreed that he was probably Italian. Relatively recently,[11] it has been suggested that he was a Franciscan monk named Paul of Taranto, who lectured in the monastery of the Friars Minor in Assisi during the second half of the thirteenth century. Even if this is true, it is nevertheless quite likely that Paul of Taranto relied in his *Summa* on a Latin version of a work originally composed in Arabic by al-Rāzi as well as on the Latin translation, *Liber de septuaginta*, of Jābir's *The Book of Seventy* (*Kitab al-Sab'īn*). So while much of the Jabirian Corpus may not have been directly written by Jābir himself, he certainly influenced these later scholars.

It was in the 1920s that the debate really raged about the credibility of Jābir and his achievements in chemistry. While I am mindful I must not allow this discussion to sink too far into the intellectual quicksands of academic debate, I have to admit that I have found it fascinating to explore the way historians of science have argued both for and against Jābir's place in history. Below is an extract from a typical scholarly paper written in 1922 that argues that Jābir ibn Hayyān's chemistry was so advanced that it could not possibly be credited to him:

A notable perversion of history was the appearance in about 1300 A.D. of certain writings important in the history of chemistry purporting to be the work of the Arabian Geber, which was the Latinized name of Djaber [Jābir ibn Hayyān]. The real Djaber lived probably about the eighth century, and little is known of his personality. He is, however, considered by later Arabian alchemists as of high repute in the art ...
The works appearing under the name of Geber were very notable, and made a great impression in the fourteenth century. They were manifestly

the work of an experienced and capable chemist familiar with and describing well the methods of distillation, sublimation and the preparation and purification of many metallic salts and solutions. They contained our first definite information concerning the preparation and use of mineral acids – or corrosive 'waters'. The credulous Middle Ages accepted generally without question the authenticity of these works as being by the eighth-century Geber, and the early historians of chemistry accepted this interpretation . . . It remained for M. Berthelot to establish beyond doubt the pseudonymous character of these writings. In the libraries of Europe he located and had translated a number of works, manuscripts in Arabic credited to the original Geber. None of these works bore any resemblance in style or contents to the work of the Pseudo-Geber. They are indeed much more like the early Greek alchemical writings upon which they are manifestly based. The acceptance of these thirteenth- or fourteenth-century writings as of Arabian origin in the eighth century up to very recent times has had the result of early Arabian chemists receiving credit for an advanced knowledge of chemistry which has not been evidenced by any Arabian literature known at the present time. This advanced knowledge is rather to be credited to some European chemists, probably both Muhammedans and Christians, of the latter part of the thirteenth century, and the Pseudo-Geber was probably not himself Arabian but a Latin-writing Spaniard or at any rate from some other country of southern Europe conversant with the development of Spanish-Arabian chemistry of that period.[12]

Here is the problem with this viewpoint: the historian Berthelot referred to in the quote was a chemist and not an Arabist. Indeed, he spoke no Arabic and had to rely on a translator, who was not a chemist. Unfortunately, this division of labour led to a number of misinterpretations and many mistranslations of technical terms, rendering the whole study discredited.[13]

Despite such misgivings over the reliability of certain analyses of the Jabirian Corpus, there still remains the serious issue of its sheer size and the mysterious circumstances under which some of it purported to have been written. The primary reason for many historians' belief in the later dating of the Corpus and its multiple authorship is that there were simply too many treatises for one man to have written. But in fact the huge figure of three thousand separate works in the Corpus is exaggerated and there are actually fewer than one thousand.[14] Many 'books' are really just one-page manuscripts, and there are gaps in the numbering of the catalogue. Of course, even a conservative estimate of five hundred books is still a huge legacy for one man.

In a sense, the authenticity of the entirety of the Corpus is not really a problem. Just because later authors attributed their work to Jābir does not invalidate or diminish his own contribution. The consensus today is that it is safe to assume the existence of an authentic core of writing dating back to Jābir in the eighth century, but that much of the Corpus grew around this core and was added later. It seems that a large number of texts appeared originally in Latin and have no Arabic origin, but were falsely attributed to Jābir to lend credibility to their authors.[15]

What is more interesting is the quite separate issue of the constant reference to Greek texts in parts of the Corpus. It has been argued that this is proof that it could not have been the work of Jābir. The translations from Greek into Arabic, and hence an appreciation of the work of Aristotle and others, did not really take place until after Jābir's death. But we have seen how these translations, either first into Syriac and then Arabic, or directly into Arabic, were made several times, each version correcting errors in previous translations with a better understanding of the content. A nice example is Aristotle's *Categories*, a hugely important philosophical work, which was thought to have been first translated into Arabic by Ishāq ibn Hunayn, son of the more famous Hunayn ibn Ishāq, in the mid-ninth century. But an account of this text in the Jabirian Corpus is very different from Ishāq's version. There is good reason to believe, from the archaic style of the language, terminology and structure, that it could have initially been translated before Ishāq's time, and that Jābir could therefore have been aware of it.[16] If true, this hints not only at the impressive extent of Jābir's knowledge, but at an earlier date for the first translations of many more of the Greek texts than is commonly thought.

So what of the contents of the Corpus itself, or at least those parts of it that we can be confident were written by Jābir himself? He is known to have developed and perfected numerous chemical techniques, such as crystallization, distillation, evaporation, calcination (the thermal treatment of ores and minerals to separate out certain substances from them) and sublimation (the process by which a solid is heated directly to a vapour, then collected as sediment), all of which are standard fare in any chemical laboratory today. We also have him to thank for introducing the word 'alkali' into our vocabulary, a term which originates from the Arabic *al-qāli*, meaning 'from ashes' (because one of the most important alkali metals, potassium, came from the ashes of fires, which are mostly potassium carbonate). His use of sal ammoniac (as described in his *Sandūk al-Hikma*, *The Chest of Wisdom*) is also noteworthy because it is here that we first see the beginnings of the use of applied organic chemistry.

Jābir used his chemical knowledge in a number of practical processes, such as the prevention of rusting, the use of manganese dioxide in glass-making and the tanning of leather. Many of his descriptions are of industrial processes, such as furnaces for distillation, producing coloured glass, smelting and refining metals, as well as techniques for glazing ceramic tiles, preparing steel, and making dyes and varnishes. He also developed apparatuses like alembics (which, as you might guess from the first two letters, comes from the Arabic *al-inbīq*, itself derived from the Greek *ambix*, meaning 'cup'). It is a vessel with a beaked cap that is part of the apparatus used in distilling. Its modern descendant is the pot still (which is used for distilling whisky).

Other new industrial processes, such as those associated with book-making (paper, inks and glues), as well as perfumes and pharmaceuticals, also grew around this time. All this activity points to a bustling economy demanding innovation and new technologies. Some of this industrialization would have also been seen in earlier civilizations from the Roman Empire to China, but it is no coincidence that many of the chemical words in use today derive from the Arabic: alcohol, alkali, alembic, amalgam, benzoic, borax, camphor, elixir and realgar. Of course, several of these words can be traced further back, to Greek, Persian or Indian origins.

A great example of applied chemistry was the manufacture of soap. Solid bars were barely known in northern Europe until the thirteenth century when they began to be imported from Islamic Spain and North Africa. By that time soap-making in the Islamic world had been industrialized: the town of Fez in Spain had some twenty-seven soap-makers, while cities like Nablus, Damascus and Aleppo became famous for the quality of their soaps.

I am referring of course only to solid soap bars and not suggesting that the Arabs invented soap itself. The use of substances as detergent goes back to the ancient Babylonians, who used boiled animal fats, wood ashes, even stale urine, which contains ammonia. The Greeks and Romans, too, used a form of soap, and Galen even records a recipe for boiling animal fats, oils and caustic soda.[17] But it is the industrialization of the manufacture of soap bars that is new. This was at a time when Europe had descended into the filth and grime of its Dark Ages, during which cleanliness was not high on the agenda; in the Muslim world it was a religious requirement.

The chemists' understanding of the properties of alkalis and other chemicals gave the glass-making industry a lift, too. They discovered that the colour of glass could be changed using new chemicals like manganese and newly discovered metallic oxides, and with their industrial furnaces, some several storeys high, they were able to manufacture coloured glass in huge quantities. The use of new pigments within ceramic tiles allowed them to decorate mosques in a glorious range of colours and designs.

What all the medieval Arabic texts on chemistry have in common is great attention to detail based on careful experimentation. The techniques that were developed drove a thriving and successful industry, but we also see in the work of Jābir the beginning of chemistry as an empirical science motivated by a desire to understand how the world is made up.

The periodic table one finds on the wall of every school science laboratory was conceived by the Russian chemist Dmitri Mendeleev in 1869. Its key idea is to group together substances with similar properties, as well as arranging them according to their atomic weight. On one side, for instance, are the inert gases and, on the other, the volatile metals. It is a triumph of classification, giving scientists a way of organizing their knowledge of the material world, something mankind has been striving to do since the dawn of time. But the very earliest attempts at this classification go back much further than is commonly assumed, and can be traced all the way back to medieval times and chemists such as Jābir.

When we develop ideas about how the natural world behaves we try to give it a kind of schema allowing us to organize its ingredients into categories so that we can make more sense of it, and this can in turn lead to further insights. The Greeks' belief in the four fundamental elements of air, earth, fire and water was a purely philosophical idea with little practical value. Chemists in the Islamic Empire changed that, for they were the first to use experimental observations to classify the substances they knew.

Unlike later chemists, Jābir ibn Hayyān was still very much wedded to the same mystical and metaphysical mindset of his ancient Greek predecessors. He too believed that matter was ultimately composed of the four 'natures' or 'primary' characteristics of hot, cold, moist and dry, described by Aristotle. But the process of combining such abstract theories with experimentation was beginning to take form in his work. While still somewhat controversial, he is credited with the discovery of many chemical compounds, such as sulphuric acid – also known as vitriol – and hydrochloric acid (by mixing vitriol with salt). The scepticism of many historians over this particular claim is due to their assertion that the earliest known written recipes for these acids date from only the thirteenth century, particularly in the writings attributed to Pseudo-Geber.[18] But we know, for instance, that the first clear instructions for the preparation of nitric acid can be found in Jābir's treatise The Chest of Wisdom.[19] There is also strong evidence[20] that he was the first to make aqua regia, a mix of nitric and hydrochloric acids that dissolved gold – and therefore a vital solution for alchemists in their search for the philosopher's stone. The discovery of inorganic acids such as these was hugely important in the development of chemistry.

Before I end this chapter, it is useful to say something about the man to whom Jābir passed the chemical baton; for the other great figure in medieval Islamic chemistry was Abū Bakr Muhammad ibn Zakariyya al-Rāzi (c. 854–c. 925). Known in the West as Rhazes, he was to become far more famous for his work in medicine and is regarded as the greatest physician of the medieval world. In chemistry, he extended and built on the work of Jābir and established the subject more firmly as a true experimental science based on careful and accurate observation.

One of al-Rāzi's greatest achievements in chemistry was his classification scheme, which illustrated a level of sophistication far beyond that of Jābir. In his *Book of Secrets* (*Kitab al-Asrār*), written around the year 900 and essentially a treatise of alchemical secrets, he classified all substances into four groups: animal, vegetable, mineral and derivatives of these three. His minerals were in turn tabulated into six categories according to their chemical properties rather than superficial appearance, the same guiding principle that lies behind the modern periodic table. They were: spirits (such as quicksilver and sulphur), metals, stones, atriments, boraces and salts. Each group had a chemical property profoundly different from all the others: spirits were flammable, metals were shiny and malleable, salts dissolved in water, and so on. While these classifications are not the way we organize chemicals today, the point is that, for the first time, al-Rāzi was grouping substances on the basis of experimental observations, not philosophical musings.

So to those who still suggest that chemistry did not truly come of age until Renaissance Europeans such as Robert Boyle (1627–91) and Antoine Lavoisier (1743–94), I would argue that their definition of chemistry as a proper experimental science is too rigid. Of course the Islamic chemists were way off beam with many of their theories. But science does not begin with the latest, most accurate, theories. For how then should we treat Newton's law of gravitation? We now know it to be based on the erroneous belief that the gravitational force acts instantaneously between bodies, however far apart they are. This magical 'action at a distance' was replaced by the more accurate description of gravity as a curvature of space-time in Einstein's General Theory of Relativity. But no one claims that Newton's work on gravity is not science. Indeed, it is rightly considered as one of the very greatest scientific discoveries in history.

At the opposite extreme, we can all agree that the alchemical magic and spells of the ancients are not part of science. The question is where we draw the line in the work of Jābir ibn Hayyān. This is where we appeal to the quite clear definition of the scientific method: it is the investigation of phenomena, acquiring of new knowledge, and correcting and integrating previous knowledge, based on the gathering of data through observation and measurement. Wherever it is being practised, that is where real science is being done. So was Jābir doing real science? Not quite. Some of the ingredients of the scientific method were not yet in place. But I am more than happy to refer to him as a scientist. What is more, he was the very first of the great scientists of the golden age, even though he did not live to see the creation of al-Ma'mūn's great academy in Baghdad, the place where we see the golden age truly beginning. It was known as the House of Wisdom and its light would radiate across the empire, and beyond.

5

The House of Wisdom

The teacher who is indeed wise does not bid you to enter the house of his wisdom but rather leads you to the threshold of your mind.

Khalil Gibrān

Court astrologers, physicians, engineers, architects and mathematicians have played an important role in many societies going back millennia before the Abbāsids, serving the practical needs of government, whether it was casting horoscopes, treating the sick, designing temples, palaces, bridges and canals, developing ever more sophisticated weapons, or devising new and easier methods for calculating taxes or dividing estates. But with the arrival of Islam, new responsibilities began to appear. For instance, astronomers and mathematicians were required to determine the times of prayer and the direction of Mecca, and to track the phases of the moon, all of which required increasingly sophisticated and advanced scientific know-how.

It was only during al-Ma'mūn's reign, however, that a huge and sudden shift in emphasis took place, from the purely practical employment of these men of learning (*'ulamā'*) to a culture that encouraged free and creative thinking across a wide range of disciplines.

Whether or not al-Ma'mūn dreamt of Aristotle while still in Merv, he was certainly inspired enough to initiate regular discussion sessions and seminars among experts in *kalām*, the art of philosophical debate – a custom he had learnt from his Persian tutor Ja'far. He would invite religious experts and literary scholars to his palace from far and wide to present their ideas to him in an open intellectual atmosphere. Following his triumphant return to Baghdad in 819, this custom continued and grew. He offered lucrative financial incentives and generous hospitality to a wide range of scholars. Every week, guests were invited to the palace, wined and dined, and then would begin to discuss with the caliph all manner of scholarly subjects, from theology to mathematics.[1]

Al-Ma'mūn was not satisfied with simply listening to what these learned men had to say. He was well aware of the treasures to be found in the ancient texts of the Greek philosophers, some of which had already begun to be translated for the Abbāsid caliphs before him. He would send emissaries great distances to get hold of these scientific texts. Often, foreign rulers defeated in battle would be required to settle the terms of surrender to him with books from their libraries rather than in gold. Al-Ma'mūn was almost fanatical in his desire to collect all the world's books under one roof, translate them into Arabic and have his scholars study them. The institution he created to realize his dream epitomizes more than anything else the blossoming of the scientific golden age. It became known throughout the world as the House of Wisdom (*Bayt al-Hikma*). Or so the story goes.

Before we look at the activities and main characters in al-Ma'mūn's Baghdad, I should make clear from the outset that no physical trace remains of the House of Wisdom today so we cannot be sure where it was located or what it looked like, or the range of activities carried out there. In fact, some historians argue against exaggerated claims about its scope and purpose and the role of al-Ma'mūn in setting it up.[2] They warn against the 'fanciful and sometimes wishful projections of modern institutions and research projects back into the ninth century';[3] and argue that the House of Wisdom was nothing like as grand as it became in the eyes of many once the activities of the scholars in al-Ma'mūn's court had become the stuff of legend. This, they believe, is the only reliable way of interpreting what little we have to go on from the historical records left to us.

Many also make the quite legitimate point that to focus on one, possibly mythical, institution detracts from the sheer scale of original scholarship that was carried out all over al-Ma'mūn's Baghdad, for there would probably have been hundreds of private libraries around the city. So rather than trying to collect up many diverse activities under one roof, we should really be talking about the whole of Baghdad as the *Medinat al-Hikma* ('City of Wisdom').

However, this over-caution smacks a little of babies and bathwater, for the absence of evidence should not be too hastily interpreted as evidence of absence. We should certainly therefore examine the subject more carefully. Perhaps the House of Wisdom was indeed no grander than a palace library, modelled on older Persian libraries. So why should we regard it as being any more special than these other, earlier libraries?

The notion of a repository of written records goes back long before Islam. Probably the most famous of the ancient world was the great Library of Alexandria, but few records survive as to the size and layout of this academy either. It is known to have contained many thousands of 'books', each comprising several papyrus scrolls. Like al-Ma'mūn's House of Wisdom, the legacy of the Library of Alexandria has reached mythical proportions, the most famous concerning its ultimate fate. One story is that it was destroyed in a fire in 48 BCE by Julius Caesar's army; that this took place during his occupation of Alexandria while 'resolving' the civil war in Egypt between King Ptolemy XIII and his sister Cleopatra. Another, because there are extant records of the library from much later, is that it survived well into the late third century CE, when it was destroyed in another war over the control of Egypt between the Roman Emperor Aurelian and the great Syrian Queen Zenobia, who ruled over Egypt at the time. There is even a mythical account of the library being sacked by the Arabs after their conquest of Alexandria in 641 under the Caliph Omar. Most likely of all, however, is that it was destroyed in the late fourth century by Alexandrian Christian followers of the Coptic Pope Theophilus in a revolt against the pagans of the city and for whom the library was a powerful symbol of Greek pagan teaching.

I recently visited the new Bibliotheca Alexandrina, built on the original site of the old library and completed in 2002. This huge and hugely impressive modern architectural edifice is today a cultural centre containing manuscript archives, museums, art exhibitions, even a planetarium. Visitors are struck by the sheer scale of the building, with its vast, well-lit open halls, but it still has a long way to go to fill its shelves with the eight million books there is space for.

The first systematically organized library in the world, much older than the one in Alexandria, had flourished in northern Iraq. The great Assyrian library of Nineveh was built by King Ashurbanipal (r. 668–627 BCE), and contained more than twenty thousand clay tablets with cuneiform texts. Just as in Alexandria, this remarkable library was destroyed by fire, but an advantage of clay over papyrus, parchment or paper is of course that it is immune to flames and the tablets were simply baked hard. So we have available a huge body of information from that library about the life not only of the Assyrians, but of the Babylonians before them whose culture they inherited.

The origin of Islamic libraries actually goes back to the Umayyad Caliph Mu'awiya (r. 661–80) in Damascus, who housed a collection of books in what has also been referred to as a Bayt al-Hikma.[4] So libraries were not new concepts to the Abbāsids. There is also little doubt that their early libraries were modelled on those of Damascus as well as on Persian libraries in cities such as Isfahan and Gondēshāpūr. Since the Abbāsid dynasty was built through a fusion of Arabic and Islamic administration and Zoroastrian and Sasanian culture, the Persian influence is seen everywhere: copying the Sasanians' model of a library was only natural.

There is good evidence that an early Abbāsid Bayt al-Hikma existed during the time of al-Ma'mūn's father Harūn al-Rashīd and another, fifty years earlier, during the reign of al-Mansūr. The medieval historian Ibn al-Qifti refers to the library of Harūn al-Rashīd as *Khizānat Kutub al-Hikma*, which translates as the 'Storehouse of the Books of Wisdom'. Was the historian making a point of distinguishing this earlier library from the more impressive institution of al-Ma'mūn by downgrading it with a more modest name? Far more likely in my view is that the library, or repository of books (*khizāna*), that was set up by the early caliphs was indeed distinct from al-Ma'mūn's academy, and that the medieval Arabic historians knew this. Their work preceded the destruction of the House of Wisdom at the hands of the Mongols, and they were likely to have had access to more evidence than is extant today. So it is quite possible that while there were indeed *khizānāt* belonging to al-Mansūr and al-Rashīd, it was not until al-Ma'mūn's time that we get the 'real deal'.

It is also possible that al-Rashīd's library was already doubling as a translation house. One of its directors was a man we know only by the name of Salm,[5] who was asked to oversee the translation of Ptolemy's *Almagest* from Persian into Arabic for a member of the Barmaki family around the turn of the ninth century. However, there is no evidence that any translations actually took place in the library itself.

Better known was another translator, by the name of al-Fadl ibn Nawbakht, the son of al-Mansūr's astrologer. Al-Fadl was responsible for the translation of a number of texts from Persian into Arabic. According to reliable records, he is referred to as being associated with al-Rashīd's Bayt al-Hikma,[6] but he died before al-Ma'mūn's return to Baghdad. This early Bayt al-Hikma would have most likely been situated within al-Rashīd's palace, Qasr al-Khuld. Al-Ma'mūn's palace, Qasr al-Ja'fariyya, was on the opposite side of the river to those of his predecessors, so it might seem reasonable that he would have moved his father's library, along with any translation activity it might have contained, into his own palace complex when he arrived in Baghdad.

Al-Ma'mūn is said to have sent a number of men to Constantinople to obtain Greek texts from the Emperor Leo V (Leo the Armenian). But since this emperor died in 820, this must have taken place soon after al-Ma'mūn's return to Baghdad. One of the men he sent, Salmān, was the then director of the House of Wisdom.[7] We also hear of another scholar, by the name of Sahl ibn Hārūn, a Persian nationalist, poet and astrologer, who is referred to as the chief librarian at the House of Wisdom.[8]

The library itself grew rapidly, with the acquisition of many texts from Greece, Persia and India, and with the addition of the Arabic translations of these texts, a process that was already becoming an industry in Baghdad. This growth would have gathered pace with the use of paper, as a new and cheaper writing material, replacing papyrus and parchment. The translators would each have had scribes recording their work and producing multiple copies of each text. By the middle of the ninth century the House of Wisdom would have become the largest repository of books in the world.

Not only does the translation movement dramatically pick up pace at this time, encouraged by a passionate caliph and the ever more generous patronage of Abbāsid society, but we also witness the arrival in Baghdad of some of the greatest minds in Islamic history, men who would help change the face of science for ever. Baghdad became a hub for scientific and intellectual activity, attracting the very best of Arab and Persian philosophers and scientists for several centuries to come.

In Arabic, both words, *bayt* and *hikma*, are still in common usage today. *Hikma* means 'wisdom', 'knowledge' or 'reasoning', and derived from it are such common words as *hakīm*, meaning 'wise'. But it is likely that the meaning of *hikma* in the context of the House of Wisdom refers more specifically to natural sciences such as astronomy, physics and mathematics rather than wisdom in general, and so a more honest translation might be 'House of Science'. A later academy, built in eleventh-century Cairo, known as *Dar al-Hikma* (where the word *dar* implies a grander residence than *bayt*), was even referred to as *Dar al-'Ilm* (where *'ilm* means 'knowledge' or 'science').

By the time of al-Ma'mūn, the translation movement had matured beyond its narrow fixation with Persian astrological texts and the few famous texts of Euclid, Aristotle and Ptolemy. Now that it was in full swing, not only were some of the more important Greek works already on their second or third translation, each more careful and detailed than the previous one as the scholars themselves gained a better understanding of the subject, but the net was cast ever more widely in an attempt to collect all Greek knowledge. We also see the arrival of scholars who were far more than mere translators: men such as the physician Hunayn ibn Ishāq[9] (809–77) and the philosopher al-Kindi (*c.* 800–*c.* 873) not only translated the great works of Greek philosophers such as Galen and Aristotle, but reinterpreted, commented on and extended them.

And then there was al-Khwārizmi. One of the world's most famous historians of science, George Sarton, is best known for a multivolume reference book called *Introduction to the History of Science*. In it, he divides up world history going back to the sixth century BCE into half-century chapters, each named after the most important scientist of that age, anywhere in the world. The period between 800 and 850 is referred to as 'The Time of al-Khwārizmi'.[10]

Muhammad ibn Mūsa al-Khwārizmi was born around 780 and died around 850. And in line with the habit of the day, his name suggests that he was originally from Khwārism (or 'Khorezm', a province of Uzbekistan in Central Asia). Little is known about his life, but we do know that al-Ma'mūn employed him in his House of Wisdom, where he worked not as a translator but as a mathematician and astronomer. He was instrumental in introducing the Arabs to Hindu numerals and he carried out important work in geography. But his greatest legacy is his extraordinary book on algebra. Indeed the word 'algebra' is derived from the title of this book: *Kitab al-Jebr*, in which he lays out for the very first time the rules and steps of solving algebraic equations. This is known today as an 'algorithm', a term in common usage in computing and derived from the Latinized version of al-Khwārizmi's name: Algorithmus. Al-Khwārizmi is regarded as the father of the field of algebra, and I shall explore this claim in greater detail in Chapter 8.

Three colourful characters associated with the House of Wisdom who were hugely influential in ninth-century Baghdad were the Banū Mūsa (Sons of Moses) brothers. Muhammad, Ahmed and Hassan were all born around the first decade of the ninth century and had considerable power and wealth in the caliph's court. As well as being remarkably talented mathematicians and engineers in their own right, they were also the most famous and influential of all the Abbāsid patrons of the translation movement, paying good money to the top translators in Baghdad (a 500-dinar monthly salary) for books on a range of subjects from medicine to astronomy.

Their father, Mūsa ibn Shākir, had worked as al-Ma'mūn's astrologer in Merv but died when the brothers were still young. As a consequence, al-Ma'mūn himself ensured that the three boys gained the very best possible education, and they were part of his entourage on his return to Baghdad in 819. Soon, they were being tutored by the very best scholars in the world and would become an integral part of the House of Wisdom. Growing up in this environment and sticking together as a close-knit family, they built up a powerbase within the circle of Baghdad scholars.

Individually, the brothers were brilliant scientists and wrote a number of treatises on mechanics and geometry. The eldest, Muhammad, is said to have been the first person to suggest that celestial bodies such as the moon and planets were subject to the same laws of physics as on earth – which marked a clear break from the received opinion of his day. Indeed, his book *Astral Motion and the Force of Attraction* shows clear signs that he had a crude qualitative notion not so far from Newton's law of gravitation.[11] But the brothers are probably best known for their wonderful inventions and engineering projects. Two of them, Muhammad and Ahmed, were put in charge of canal projects to provide water for the still growing cities of Baghdad and Sāmarra to its north.

Most famous of all was their *Book of Ingenious Devices* (*Kitab al-Hiyāl*), published in 850. This was a large illustrated work on mechanical devices that included automata, puzzles and magic tricks as well as what we would today refer to as 'executive toys'. Many involved complicated water devices making use of clever valves and levers that remind me of the sort of imaginative contraptions devised by the American cartoonist Rube Goldberg (and, certainly for those of my generation, most likely to have been encountered in the Hanna-Barbera cartoon *The Perils of Penelope Pitstop*, in which the villain, the Hooded Claw, always insisted on trying to kill the heroine through some highly complex series of mechanical steps). It is quite fascinating to think that similar – and not always quite so pointless – devices were invented in Baghdad almost twelve centuries ago (see Plate 18).

One of the most impressive devices described in the book is also possibly the earliest example of a programmable machine: a robotic flute player. Known as 'The Instrument that Plays by Itself', it produced its different sounds by using small variations in air and water pressure by means of conical valves as automatic regulators. Pins on a rotating drum open, via tiny levers, one or more of the nine holes of a flute, which is positioned parallel to the drum. The wind for the flute is generated by water that fills a reservoir and forces the air to escape, and the whole drum is driven by a waterwheel.[12]

The most famous of all the Baghdad translators, Hunayn ibn Ishāq, was just a young boy when al-Ma'mūn dreamt of Aristotle. Despite never converting to Islam, Hunayn remained active over a period spanning the rule of no fewer than nine caliphs. He was born in the ancient Christian city of Hīra, just south of Kūfa, in the year of al-Rashīd's death, and went on to train as a physician under the tutelage of the court physician Yuhanna ibn Māsawayh. He quickly became an expert in ancient Greek and began translating texts into both Syriac and Arabic. He would spend many years travelling around the world in his search for Greek manuscripts, and is known to have translated the philosophical works of Plato and Aristotle. It is the medical work of Galen that is his most important legacy, however, for not only did it open up the Islamic world to this great treasure, but it is only through these Arabic translations that much of Galen's work reaches us today.

The precocious young Hunayn had originally been introduced to al-Ma'mūn by the Banū Mūsa brothers and was only 17 years old when he completed the translation of Galen's *On the Natural Faculties* in 826.[13] He went on to translate many of the most important works by Galen, such as *On the Anatomy of Veins and Arteries* and *On the Anatomy of Nerves*. He also added to his translations much of his own original findings, such as one of the very first known drawings of the anatomy of the human eye in his *Ten Treatises on the Eye*, written around 860 and regarded as the first systematic textbook of ophthalmology (see Plate 6).[14] He would soon rise to the position of head of translations in the House of Wisdom itself (although there is no reliable primary source evidence of this), with his own circle of translators and scribes. Some historical accounts have al-Ma'mūn putting Hunayn in charge of the whole of the House of Wisdom, replacing the previous director, Sahl ibn Hārūn, in 830.

Another person employed in the House of Wisdom by al-Ma'mūn was a man whose name is still familiar in the Arab world today and is known simply as 'the Philosopher of the Arabs'. His name was al-Kindi (Latinized as Alkindus) and he is regarded as the first of the Abbāsid polymaths, a character so important that I shall devote an entire chapter to him later on. He was an excellent mathematician and, together with al-Khwārizmi, was instrumental in introducing the Islamic world to the Hindu decimal system. He famously studied cryptanalysis and was the first great theoretician of music in the Islamic Empire. But he is most famous for being the first to introduce the philosophy of Aristotle to the Arabic-speaking world, making it both accessible and acceptable to a Muslim audience. Central to al-Kindi's work was the way his writing fused Aristotelian philosophy with Islamic theology, thereby creating an intellectual platform for a debate between philosophers and theologians that would run for four hundred years.

A contemporary of al-Kindi at the House of Wisdom and fellow expert on Aristotle was an Arab of East African descent named Abū Uthmān al-Jāhith, who was born in Basra around 776 but spent most of his life in Baghdad. His name *Jāhith* translates as 'Goggle-Eyed', referring to his wide, staring eyes, which are reputed to have made him rather frightening to behold – to such an extent that no sooner had al-Ma'mūn employed him as a personal tutor for his children than he had to dismiss him because they were so disturbed by his appearance.

Al-Jāhith was one of the most influential figures in Arabic literature and was well known for his many works of fiction. But he was also one of the few Muslim scholars to show an interest in biology. In his *Book of Animals* (*Kitab al-Haywān*), al-Jāhith speculated on the influence of the environment on animals and the way they adapt to suit their surroundings, in much the same way that Aristotle did in his *History of Animals*. Aristotle believed in the fixity of species and denied that acquired characteristics could be inherited, an idea that Jean-Baptiste Lamarck would develop in the eighteenth century and which would subsequently be replaced by Darwinian evolution. It is worth mentioning, however, that al-Jāhith went beyond Aristotelian ideas to propose a rudimentary theory of Lamarckist evolution. For instance, he argued that the similarity in features and characteristics of animals like dogs, foxes and wolves mean that they must have descended from a common ancestor.[15] Many of his ideas were of course a mixture of rudimentary zoology, theology and folklore. He stated that 'the people of the Maghreb (north-west Africa) have different features to us [in Baghdad] possibly due to the "spoilt" air or the nature of the water and food there'.[16] He also spoke of those people who incur God's wrath as being thereby transformed into *miskh*[17] (beings that are half human, half animal) – an example of divine, reverse evolution!

Like al-Kindi, al-Jāhith was a strong advocate for the caliph's creed of Mu'tazilism, the rationalist philosophy opposed to the literalist interpreters of the Qur'an. The writings of both these scholars radiate an attitude of openness and freshness that is very typical of this age.

Of course, we shall never really know what life was like within the House of Wisdom, or how many of the Baghdad scholars actually worked there, and it is a source of great frustration that what little evidence and information we do have can be interpreted so differently by different historians.

We do know two things for certain, however. First, there was indeed an establishment known as the House of Wisdom that was founded – or at the very least expanded dramatically in scope from mere palace library – during the reign of al-Ma'mūn, and that became a centre for original scientific scholarship. The association with the House of Wisdom of men such as al-Khwārizmi, with his work in mathematics, astronomy and geography, and the Banū Mūsa brothers and their remarkable achievements in engineering, is for me strong evidence that it was closer to a true academy, in the mould of the Library of Alexandria, than just a repository of translated books.

Secondly, its enduring mythological status is testament to the extraordinary nature of those scientific discoveries and their wider impact. What should matter to us is not the precise details of where or when the House of Wisdom was created or what went on there. Far more interesting is the history of the scientific ideas themselves and how they developed as a result of it. Take al-Khwārizmi's *Kitab al-Jebr* as an example. Whether he produced this great mathematical text while in a library, a private study within the caliph's palace or surrounded by the greatest minds of the empire in a hive of intellectual activity is the stuff of legend and to some extent irrelevant. What is important is how a single book, quite modest in its mission, could lead to the birth of the new discipline of algebra. And we have al-Ma'mūn and his patronage of al-Khwārizmi and his associates in the House of Wisdom to thank for this, whatever the place looked like.

It is well established and uncontroversial that the much earlier academy in Alexandria was similarly more than just a library, for it not only brought together under one roof much of the world's accumulated knowledge, but acted as a magnet, attracting many of the world's greatest thinkers and scholars. The patronage of the Egyptian

Ptolemaic dynasty that provided travel, lodging and stipends to those men is not so different from the government research grants that university academics around the world today receive to carry out their research. And so the Library of Alexandria became a place where original scholarship across many disciplines was carried out.

If this backward projection of our idea of a research institution works for the Library of Alexandria then, I argue, it is just as valid in the case of Baghdad's House of Wisdom. Despite what little information we have about the House of Wisdom, the magnificent reputation it and its scholars acquired is completely justified. It became the seed from which sprouted all the subsequent achievements of the golden age of Arabic science, from Uzbekistan in the East to Spain in the West.

Al-Ma'mūn himself was not satisfied with setting up this seat of learning, or even to collect together, at no small expense, the world's most important scientific texts. He also built the first astronomical observatories in the Islamic world and was the first ruler personally to fund and follow the progress of major research projects involving the collaboration of whole teams of scholars and scientists. His true legacy to science, therefore, is that he was the first to fund 'big science'. He commissioned careful astronomical observations to check many of the values obtained by the Greek astronomer Ptolemy, commissioned the drawing of a new map of the world and, most ambitious of all, charged his best scientists to devise a new way of measuring the circumference of the earth.

6

Big Science

Sleepless, I watch the heavens turn
Propelled by the motions of the spheres;
Those stars spell out (I don't know how)
The weal and woe of future years.
If I flew up to the starry vault
And joined the heavens' westward flow
I would learn, as I travelled the sky
The fate of all things here below.

The Caliph al-Ma'mūn

To counter the naive Eurocentric arguments of those who claim that the Abbāsids did nothing more than translate and assimilate existing Greek knowledge, historians tend to point out that once the translation movement was in full swing, the scholars of Baghdad began to question, extend and improve upon the knowledge they had acquired. While this is certainly true, it hardly smacks of a scientific revolution on the scale of what would later take place in Europe at the hands of Copernicus, Kepler and Galileo. So, while it is certainly vital to highlight the achievements and originality of a genius like al-Khwārizmi, it is equally important to understand what was so special about this time and place; what were the various ingredients that came together – whether due to complex socio-geopolitico-religious reasons or just serendipity – to produce something exceptional? We have already explored these in connection with the translation movement and, to some extent, the knock-on effects this had on the attitude of al-Ma'mūn and his contemporaries in Baghdad towards science in general. But there is another consequence of this that was revolutionary: they fundamentally changed the way scientific research was carried out.

What took place during the reign of al-Ma'mūn was something quite new in scholarship. A consequence of bringing together for the first time a wide range of different scientific traditions from around the world was that the scholars of Baghdad had at their disposal a far broader world-view than anyone before them. Differences in the translations of Persian, Indian and Greek astronomical texts, for instance, each with its own cosmological model, set of measurements and tables of astronomical values, not always in agreement with each other, meant they could not all be right. Of course these different scientific cultures had not developed in isolation. Cross-fertilization of ideas had taken place on many occasions and for different reasons in ancient times, with the Greeks acquiring the medical knowledge of the Egyptians and the mathematics and astronomy of the Babylonians, and the conquests of Alexander the Great in Central Asia leading to a two-way exchange of ideas and scientific knowledge with India. There was even a Babylonian 'brain drain' to Greece in the third and second centuries BCE.

But the scholars of Baghdad were starting their education from scratch. For the astronomers in particular, to be able to compare and comment objectively on the many texts they had translated with fresh eyes and open minds must have been gloriously exciting. Questions started to be asked and doubts raised. Clearly, discrepancies needed to be resolved, and it soon became apparent that there was an urgent need for a new set of comprehensive astronomical measurements to be made. But this was too big a task to be undertaken by just one scholar, and al-Ma'mūn was an impatient man.

Some time during the second decade of the ninth century, and associated with his new House of Wisdom, al-Ma'mūn ordered the building of the first astronomical observatory in Baghdad. This was the only way to check the accuracy of one of the greatest texts at the disposal of his scholars, which was, by then, translated and studied in Arabic: Ptolemy's *Almagest*. Indeed, Ptolemy is rightly regarded as one of the greatest scientists in history because of his lasting influence on science for a millennium and a half.

Not much is known about the life of Ptolemy, other than that he flourished in Alexandria from 121 to 151 CE. However, his fame is due almost entirely to the publication of his masterpiece of ancient astronomy, the *Mathematical Treatise*. The title it is known by today derives from the Arabic *al-Kitab al-Majisti* ('The Great Book'). This huge text brought together all Greek astronomical knowledge, such as the extensive work of that other great Greek astronomer Hipparchus three hundred years earlier, who had in turn been influenced by Babylonian astronomy. Books I and II of the *Almagest* deal with the different kinds of celestial motion, Books III–VI with solar and lunar theories, Books VII and VIII are catalogues of the stars, and finally Books IX–XII with the theory of the planets. Together with Euclid's *Elements*, the *Almagest* was regarded as the most important scientific book to be translated into the Arabic language. But despite this incredible legacy, Ptolemy made surprisingly few astronomical observations himself – unlike Hipparchus – and what he did make he often failed to report correctly.[1]

The observatory that al-Ma'mūn commissioned in Baghdad to check many of the Greek observations reported in the *Almagest* was probably the world's first state-funded large-scale science project. Modern science often involves the participation of thousands of scientists in multinational, multi-billion-dollar projects such as the Large Hadron Collider at CERN in Geneva. What al-Ma'mūn achieved, albeit on a far more modest scale, would produce no less spectacular results. He put together an impressive team of mathematicians, astronomers and geographers to work on three major projects that would have been impossible for one man working alone.

Sanad ibn Ali al-Yahūdi was an ambitious young man who moved in the right circles of high society in Baghdad. The son of a Jewish astrologer who very probably worked in the caliph's court, Sanad realized that he would have to convert to Islam if he really wanted to make a name for himself in the caliph's circle. Like many bright young minds of his generation he studied the *Almagest*, but he felt that he needed to be part of the 'in' crowd of illustrious scholars associated with al-Ma'mūn to pursue his science further. One man in particular was to play an influential role in Sanad's life. Already highly regarded and a few years older than Sanad, al-Abbās al-Jawhari held regular meetings in his home with a group of scholars. According to one account, the young Sanad convinced al-Jawhari of his impressive understanding of the *Almagest* and was welcomed into the circle.[2] Al-Jawhari also then put in a good word on his behalf with the caliph, and Sanad was soon given work in the new House of Wisdom.

The senior astronomer in al-Ma'mūn's court was a Persian by the name of Yahya ibn abi Mansūr, who was associated with the early days of the House of Wisdom and who is said to have been one of the tutors of the Banū Mūsa brothers.[3] When al-Ma'mūn was convinced of the need to repeat the astronomical observation and measurements quoted in the *Almagest*, the two men he turned to were the wise old Yahya and the enterprising young Sanad. They were charged with building and heading up the new observatory in the year 828. While the notion of an observatory was certainly not new – although this would have been the first in the Islamic world – never before had one been created as a genuine scientific institution. The site chosen was in the north-east of the city, in a district known as al-Shammāsiyya. Some historians have referred to it by its name of the Mumtahan observatory,[4] but it is often just called the Shammāsiyya. Historians cannot be sure about the types of instruments used at the observatory, but there would have been a sundial with brass gnomon to determine the height of the sun from the length of shadow it cast, as well as astrolabes and, most importantly, a mural quadrant (an instrument like a giant protractor from a school geometry set, cut in half to make a quarter of a circle and placed on its edge in order to measure the precise position in the sky of an object along a sighting rod or tube, known as a dioptra arm). In order to carry out this ambitious astronomical project, al-Ma'mūn also called upon al-Jawhari and, not surprisingly, also enlisted the help of the great al-Khwārizmi.

One other astronomer was also drafted in to help. He was not quite as highly regarded at the time as al-Khwārizmi or Yahya ibn abi Mansūr, but was destined to be among the many Islamic astronomers to influence the European Renaissance. His name was al-Farghāni and his main claim to fame, apart from a widely circulated compendium of Ptolemy's *Almagest* (a deep knowledge of the *Almagest* was one's minimal entry ticket into this exciting collaboration), was his association with a device built to measure the water level of the Nile some years later called the Nilometer, which still exists to this day in central Cairo. His legacy also endures through the great Italian writer and poet Dante (1265–1321), who derived most of the astronomical knowledge he included in his *Divine Comedy* from the writings of al-Farghāni (whom he referred to by his Latin name, Alfraganus). Another famous Italian, Christopher Columbus, also used al-Farghāni's value for the circumference of the earth in order to persuade his backers to fund his famous voyage. But al-Farghāni's contribution to the Shammāsiyya project seems to have been his expertise with astronomical instruments. His treatise on the astrolabe still survives and provides the mathematical principles of astrolabe construction.[5]

In addition to writing the *Almagest*, Ptolemy had also produced a set of astronomical tables that proved to be a very useful tool for many astronomical calculations. They were known as the *Handy Tables* and contained all the data needed to compute the positions of the sun, moon and planets, the rising and setting of the stars as well as eclipses of the sun and moon, all far more rapidly and conveniently than similar tables he included in the more comprehensive *Almagest*. His *Handy Tables* became, with various modifications, the model for the later Arabic astronomical table, or star chart, known as the *zīj*.[6]

And so it was that over a period of a year or so in 828–9, the first critical appraisal of Ptolemy and his astronomy began in earnest when the earliest systematic astronomical observations in the Islamic world were made at Shammāsiyya. During this time, many observations of the sun and moon were made, mainly by Yahya ibn abi Mansūr and overseen by al-Khwārizmi, and a table with longitudes and latitudes of twenty-four fixed stars is recorded as having been drawn up at this time. Al-Ma'mūn then ordered the creation of a second observatory to carry out further measurements, this time at the Dayr Murrān monastery on the slopes of Mount Qasyūn overlooking Damascus.

His senior astronomer, Yahya ibn abi Mansūr, died in the early summer of 830 and so the work at the new observatory was overseen by Khālid al-Marwarrūdhi, who designed several new instruments to be used there. He also built a 16-foot mural quadrant to measure solar angles. It was made of brass and mounted on a marble base built into the side of the mountain and aligned with the meridian. With his instruments in place, al-Marwarrūdhi led another series of solar and lunar observations during 832–3 to compliment those made at

Shammāsiyya. However, it seems he encountered some difficulties with the warping and expansion of the metal instruments in the summer heat.[7]

On completion of all the observations, a new *zīj* was produced for al-Ma'mūn, with a compilation of all the results from the two observatories. It is known as *al-Zīj al-Mumtahan*,[8] which translates as 'The Verified Tables'. The name of Yahya ibn abi Mansūr is often associated with this *zīj* but, since he was not involved with the Syrian observatory measurements, it clearly could not have been down to him alone. In fact, this endeavour was equivalent to a modern-day scientific paper with multiple authors, and the group of astronomers involved in producing it were referred to as *Asshāb al-Mumtahan* ('Companions of the Verified Tables') – hence the alternative name of Shammāsiyya as the Mumtahan observatory.

A widespread misconception is that until Christopher Columbus discovered America everyone believed the earth to be flat. However, even the ancient Greeks had figured out that our world is a sphere. For Pythagoras in the sixth century BCE, this was obvious from a purely aesthetic point of view: surely the gods would have created the earth as a perfect sphere, the most pleasing of mathematical forms. This model was later endorsed by Plato, Aristotle and Archimedes, based on more practical evidence. A flat earth, for example, could not explain how the Pole Star is seen lower in the sky as one travels further south, but a curved surface could. They had even gone so far as to make crude guesses about the size of the earth. For instance, Aristotle had cited a value for its circumference of 400,000 stadia, while Archimedes estimated 300,000 stadia. Since one stadion equates to roughly a tenth of a mile, these figures correspond to 40,000 and 30,000 miles, respectively – not far off the correct value of just under 25,000 miles. Even Plato, whom I do not regard as having been as good a scientist as either Aristotle or Archimedes, provides a remarkable description of our planet as a large sphere floating in space: 'First of all the true earth, if one views it from above, is said to look like those twelve-piece leather balls, variegated, a patchwork of colours, of which our colours here are, as it were, samples that painters use.'[9] Not only did Plato know that the earth was spherical but his description of its surface as having a 'patchwork of colours' evokes the images we are so familiar with today of our planet viewed from space with its weather patterns swirling above seas, deserts and snow-capped mountains.

As for its size, another Greek scholar decided he could go one better than educated guesswork. He believed he could actually measure it. His name was Eratosthenes (c. 275–195 BCE) and he was the chief librarian of Alexandria, as well as being a brilliant astronomer and mathematician. His method for working out the size of the world was, like so many great ideas in science, beautifully simple: if he could measure the distance along the surface of the earth corresponding to just one of the 360 degrees around its circumference, then all he would have to do is multiply this distance by 360.

He knew that on the longest day of the summer solstice the midday sun shone vertically down to the bottom of a well in Syene (modern Aswan) in southern Egypt. But on that same day each year, he had observed that the sun was not directly overhead in Alexandria in the north; instead, its rays shone down at an angle equal to one-fiftieth of a full circle (that is, one-fiftieth of 360 degrees, or 7.2 degrees). He assumed that Syene was directly south of Alexandria, so if he knew the distance between the two cities, then multiplying this distance by fifty would give him the complete circumference of the earth. There are no details about exactly how this was done but apparently he had someone walk from Alexandria to Syene, counting paces! The distance reported back to him was precisely 5,000 stadia (about 500 miles). This gave a value of 250,000 stadia, or 25,000 miles, for the circumference of the world – a value so close to the modern measurement of 24,900 miles that it would seem churlish and pedantic to find any fault with it.

But the truth is that Eratosthenes was very lucky to have got so close. There were a number of serious errors, inaccuracies and crude guesses involved in his method that conspired by chance to give an answer close to the correct one. While the midday sun at the summer solstice is indeed directly overhead at the Tropic of Cancer, the city of Syene was not on the tropic but about 22 miles north; nor was it exactly due south of Alexandria. Most importantly, it would not have been possible to measure the distance between the cities with any degree of accuracy at all. Counting paces would have been unreliable and the path taken would in all likelihood have followed the meandering course of the Nile, including the complex Delta region around Alexandria. Lastly, we do not know the exact length of his unit of distance (the stadion); I said 'a tenth of a mile', but this is rather approximate. In any case, the fact that the number of paces came to exactly 5,000 stadia is suspicious and most modern historians do not believe Eratosthenes ever did have the distance measured in this way but had unwittingly used instead a value for the distance that itself had been calculated from an even earlier estimate of the earth's circumference;[10] a sort of circular logic whereby an estimate of the earth's circumference is used to deduce a distance that is then itself used to recalculate the circumference.

And so we move forward in time a thousand years to Abbāsid Baghdad and the band of astronomers working for al-Ma'mūn. They knew about Eratosthenes' method from the writings of Ptolemy. In fact, Ptolemy quoted a later, revised but incorrect value for the circumference of the earth of just 180,000 stadia by another Greek astronomer, by the name of Posidonius.[11] Ten years after his arrival in Baghdad, al-Ma'mūn wished to know what all this meant: exactly how long was one Greek stadion? No one could agree. This called for another project for the Companions of the Verified Tables.

Al-Ma'mūn dispatched a group that included his top astronomers, Sanad, Yahya, al-Jawhari and Khālid al-Marwarrūdhi, along with carpenters and metal-workers, to the north-west corner of Iraq in the flat plains of Sinjar, about 70 miles west of Mosul. There, the group split into two teams who headed out in opposite directions, due north and due south, counting paces as they went and placing arrows in the ground as markers along the way. They stopped when they had measured a 1-degree angle of the earth's curvature based on the positions of the stars. Both groups then turned around and re-measured the distance back to base. The average of the measurements was taken and found to be 56.6 Arabic miles. We know that an Arabic mile, or *mīl*, is about 20 per cent bigger than our modern-day 'statute' mile, so this distance is actually about 68 miles. Multiplying this number by 360 gives a figure of 24,500 miles, which is a more reliable figure than the one arrived at a thousand years earlier by Eratosthenes.

Good scientist that he was, al-Ma'mūn then commissioned another expedition to carry out a second measurement, this time in the Syrian desert. Starting from the city of Palmyra in central Syria, his astronomers measured the distance to the city of Raqqah to its north. They found the two cities separated by 1 degree of latitude and 66.6 *mīl*, giving a larger circumference of 24,000 *mīl*, or 28,700 statute miles.

Of course, while the whole project is admirable, all these numbers just added to the confusion. Everyone seems to have been in the right ballpark and it is probably pointless trying to credit those who arrived at the closest value. Al-Ma'mūn's astronomers will have had to contend with the same issues as Eratosthenes. For instance, al-Raqqah is in fact about 1.5 degrees of latitude north of Palmyra as well as being about a degree of longitude to the east. In any case, the true distance between the two cities is more than 100 miles (around 90 *mīl*). Many historians and geographers throughout history have quoted these numbers, none of them having an accurate idea of the exact length of a *stadion* or a *mīl*. Even Marco Polo and Christopher Columbus used them, but apart from confusion over units (these explorers were unaware of the difference between a Roman and Arabic mile), they were often unwittingly quoting al-Farghāni quoting Ptolemy quoting Posidonius quoting Eratosthenes.

But the remarkable Sanad ibn Ali had another trick up his sleeve. The great eleventh-century Muslim polymath al-Bīrūni reports in his famous treatise *The Determination of the Coordinates of Cities* (*Kitab Tahdīd al-Amākin*) that Sanad had proposed to al-Ma'mūn a far better way of measuring the circumference of the earth that did not involve trudging across hot deserts counting paces. While accompanying al-Ma'mūn on one of his campaigns[12] against the Byzantine Emperor Theophilus around 832, Sanad is supposed to have suggested the trick of climbing a mountain that overlooked the sea and measuring the angle of inclination to the horizon. This, along with knowledge of the height of the mountain, could be used, together with some rudimentary geometry, to determine, not the circumference of the earth, but its radius. Of course, it is then a simple matter of multiplying this figure by twice pi to obtain the circumference.

But al-Bīrūni was well known for his modesty in crediting others and we have no other record to suggest that Sanad actually carried out this experiment. Famously, it would take the even greater genius of al-Bīrūni himself to perform this measurement carefully and settle the argument about the size of the earth for good. But that story will have to wait until a later chapter.

The third spectacular project undertaken by al-Ma'mūn's group of scholars was the most ambitious of all. Another of the great works of Ptolemy was his *Geographia*. In this book, he included all that was known about the geography of the world at the time, much of it based on the work of an earlier geographer, Marinus of Tyre (70–130 CE), who had come up with the idea of coordinates involving latitudes and longitudes and had defined the line of longitude going down through the Canary Isles as his 'zero meridian' and the parallel of Rhodes for his measurements of latitude. Ptolemy's *Geographia* was translated into Arabic by a group of scholars in the House of Wisdom with the help of al-Khwārizmi and seems to have been the key text that triggered the early Islamic interest in geography. Here again, we see the audacity and self-belief of al-Ma'mūn. With two new observatories, confirmation of the circumference of the earth and his scholars' rapidly developing skills in geometry and algebra, he commanded the production of a new map of the world. After all, Ptolemy's map did not include important Islamic cities such as Mecca or Baghdad; the former had not been important enough and the latter had not existed then. Al-Ma'mūn's astronomers had worked out the distance between these two cities by taking measurements during a lunar eclipse and found it to be 712 *mīl*, which is less than 2 per cent off the actual distance.

Al-Ma'mūn's scholars began to recalculate the coordinates of many of the major landmarks in the known world and soon found discrepancies in Ptolemy's values. So a new map was produced which contained major improvements on Ptolemy's. It depicted the Atlantic and Indian oceans as open bodies of water, not landlocked seas as Ptolemy had suggested. While the Greeks had revealed a good knowledge of closed seas like the Mediterranean they showed little understanding of the vast ocean expanses beyond, something Arab traders were able to report back on by the time of al-Ma'mūn. The map also corrected Ptolemy's gross overestimate for the length of the Mediterranean Sea of 63 degrees of longitude and put it instead at 50 degrees, which was far closer to the correct value. Unfortunately, this Abbāsid map no longer exists, and it has been difficult to reconstruct it with any confidence. What is known about it has come mainly from a treatise produced at the same time entitled *Picture of the Earth* (*Sūrat al-Arth*). This treatise has been attributed to none other than al-Khwārizmi himself, who seems to have been central to the map project and is often regarded as the first geographer in Islam. However, it is more likely, from the sheer effort that went into it, that *Sūrat al-Arth* was, like the Verified Tables, a collective effort. It was modelled closely on the *Geographia* and completed in 833, the year of al-Ma'mūn's death. It contained tables of the latitudes and longitudes of more than five hundred cities and grouped locations under five general headings: towns, rivers, mountains, seas and islands, each in tables ordered from south to north, each with its precise coordinates in degrees and minutes of arc.

The oldest surviving world maps from the Islamic Empire are copies of earlier ones dating back to the early eleventh century and containing many references to al-Khwārizmi's tables. Several years ago, considerable excitement greeted what appeared to be a remarkable discovery. A renowned historian by the name of Fuat Sezgin based in Frankfurt claimed to have discovered a fourteenth-century representation of al-Ma'mūn's original map in the Topkapi Museum in Istanbul. But not everyone is convinced of its authenticity just yet.

Muslim cartography rapidly built on the work of al-Khwārizmi and his circle and the subject evolved into two different schools of cartography: those maps that followed a Baghdadi mapmaker by the name of al-Balkhi (850–934), which tended to be more like stylized diagrams than literal maps as we understand them (rather like the map of the London Underground), and those following the later style of a twelfth-century Andalusian cartographer by the name of al-Idrīsi. Other Muslim scholars who wrote on geography included Ibn Sīna (Avicenna) and al-Bīrūni in the eleventh century, along with the historian Ibn Khaldūn and the famous traveller Ibn Battūta in the fourteenth. But the important contribution of al-Ma'mūn's cartographers to the development of the field of mathematical geography cannot be overestimated.

*

There is one final area of scholarship that became something of an obsession for al-Ma'mūn, one that might sound surprising to us today. Indeed, it was something of a revelation to me when I first learnt about it: Egyptology.

The Pyramids of Gīza just outside Cairo date back to the middle of the third millennium BCE, making them already well over three thousand years old by the time of al-Ma'mūn. The ancient Egypt of the pharaohs was thus already a civilization lost in the mists of time by the time Islam arrived. Here is what the tenth-century historian al-Mas'ūdi has to say about the pyramids:

> The temples of Egypt are very curious structures . . . then there are the pyramids, which are very high and built in a remarkable way. Their sides are covered in all kinds of inscriptions, written in the scripts of ancient nations and of kingdoms that no longer exist. No one can read this writing or know what was intended by it. These inscriptions relate to the sciences, to the properties of things, to magic and to the secrets of nature.

Later he recounts:

> I have questioned the most learned Copts of Upper Egypt and other provinces on the meaning of the word 'pharaoh', but no one has been able to tell me anything about it, for this name does not exist in their language. Perhaps originally it was the general title of all their kings.
>
> You will find strange tales of the treasures and monuments of Egypt and the wealth which both its kings and other nations who ruled this land buried in the earth and which are sought even today.[13]

Al-Ma'mūn travelled to Egypt in 816 to quell an uprising and while there became fascinated with the Pyramids. It is said that he searched in vain for someone to explain their purpose to him. Medieval Arab fascination with accounts of ancient Egypt comes from several references made to it in the Qur'an, particularly in the story of Moses and the pharaohs, as well as what was gleaned from the translations of Greek classical writers such as Homer and Herodotus. But we can imagine the impact that actually seeing the Pyramids must have had on al-Ma'mūn.

His obsession with the translation of ancient texts extended naturally to his desire to decipher the hieroglyphic symbols on the walls of the tombs of Egypt. It was believed by the early Arab scholars that these symbols held ancient secrets associated with astrology and alchemy, as indeed many of them did. The alchemists closely associated with mystic Sufism were particularly fascinated with Egyptian scripts, the most prominent of these being none other than Jābir ibn Hayyān.

While in Egypt, al-Ma'mūn enlisted the services of a sage named Ayyūb ibn Maslama, who he hoped could translate hieroglyphs for him. After all, the Coptic language still spoken by many of the indigenous population there was itself a descendant of the old Egyptian language. Unfortunately, and to the disappointment of the caliph, Ayyūb was unable to make much sense of any of the inscriptions.

Al-Ma'mūn next ordered an excavation of the Great Pyramid of Khūfū. A team, accompanied by the caliph himself, managed to break their way in and found behind the opening a jar of gold, which al-Ma'mūn took with him back to Baghdad. Once inside, they discovered ascending and descending corridors. At the top, they came across a small chamber, in the middle of which was a sealed marble sarcophagus with the pharaoh's mummified remains still inside. At this point, al-Ma'mūn, not wishing to continue the desecration any further, ordered the excavation to stop.[14]

As a postscript to this account I cannot pass up the opportunity to tell how one Arab scholar who lived in Kūfa not long after al-Ma'mūn's reign did in fact succeed in cracking about half of all hieroglyphic symbols. I recently visited Saqqara, the ancient necropolis in Egypt dating back to the twenty-seventh century BCE, *before* the Pyramids of Gīza were built. I was shown around several tombs by London-based Egyptologist Okasha El Daly, who has made a comprehensive study of ancient Egypt in medieval Arabic writing. He makes a convincing case that a man by the name of Ibn Wahshiyya, who flourished in the ninth/tenth century, can rightly be regarded as the world's first real Egyptologist. So, whereas it is commonly assumed in the West that the hieroglyphic code was not cracked until 1822 when the Englishman Thomas Young and the Frenchman Jean-François Champollion deciphered the writings on the Rosetta Stone, I suddenly found myself marvelling at yet another little facet of the translation movement.

Ibn Wahshiyya's text on various ancient alphabets, *Kitab Shawq al-Mustaham*, gives a list of hieroglyphic symbols and their meaning, either as words or sounds, together with their Arabic equivalent; this nearly a millennium before Young and Champollion.

Let us return, though, to the House of Wisdom in Baghdad and al-Khwārizmi. For, as I have mentioned already, his greatest legacy to science was not in the field of geography, but in mathematics. The extent of the debt we owe to this man will become clear over the coming two chapters, when I explore the development of mathematics during the time of al-Ma'mūn.

7

Numbers

I will not say anything now of the sciences of the Hindus, who are not even Syrians, of their subtle discoveries in this science of astronomy, which are even more ingenious than those of the Greeks and Babylonians, and of the fluent methods of their calculations, which surpasses words. I want to say only that it is done with nine signs.

Severus Sebokht, Bishop of Syria

The 'five-bar gate' tally system, familiar in movies when scratched onto prison cell walls to mark off the days, is one way of counting that allows a running tally to be kept for a constantly updated number. This and other forms of tallies are also our most ancient way of counting, and go back many thousands of years. Cavemen during the Upper Paleolithic Age (40,000–10,000 years ago) first started using animal bones as tally sticks for counting. The earliest surviving example is probably the Lebombo bone, dating back 35,000 years, which was a small piece of the fibula of a baboon, marked with twenty-nine clearly defined notches, discovered within the Border Cave in the Lebombo Mountains of Swaziland.

Even before the invention of a sensible number system there would still have been a need to keep a tally – of the sheep in a flock, for instance. As each sheep passes through the farmer's gate out to graze in the morning, he cuts a notch in a stick. At nightfall, when the flock returns, he checks his sheep against the tally by running his finger along the notches, moving from notch to notch as each sheep passes. In this way he knows if any are missing without having to know the number of sheep in his flock. The tally stick served its purpose just as well as counting the flock serves the farmer today, and could be passed from one person to another just as easily as numbers are passed by word of mouth, or written down.

A simple modification of the primitive tally stick extended its scope to a remarkable degree. All that is needed is a second stick, which does more than simply double the space available for notches. This is how it works: one stick, called the standard, already has a number of notches on it, say twenty, while the other – the tally stick – is uncut apart from a dividing line splitting it into two sections. The farmer counts the sheep by moving his finger along the notches on the standard. As soon as he reaches the end of the standard he marks a notch on the bottom half of the tally stick, indicating one unit of twenty. He then starts again on the standard. Each time he reaches the twentieth notch he cuts a new one on the tally. When the last sheep has been recorded on the standard, he cuts that number of notches on the upper half of the tally stick – the units section. Now, if he has, say, four notches on the bottom half and seven on the top, his tally is $4 \times 20 + 7 = 87$. But of course he does not need to know this total as an actual number as he can reverse the process by marking off on both sticks when the sheep return.

The number of notches on the standard is, of course, quite arbitrary, and a standard of twenty has no special advantage. Nevertheless, counting sheep by way of making a score, or notch, on a tally stick for each unit of twenty is itself the origin of the word 'score' in Old English. In the Bible, the number seventy is written as 'threescore and ten', the word 'threescore' for sixty going back to the fourteenth century – as in 'Thre scoor and six daies' from John Wyclif's Bible, the very first translation from Latin into English.[1]

Such a base-20 counting system is known as vigesimal. Modern-day French numbering is still partially vigesimal: twenty (*vingt*) is used as a base in the names of numbers from sixty to ninety-nine. The French for eighty, for example, is *quatre-vingts*, which literally means 'four twenties', and *soixante-quinze* (literally 'sixty-fifteen') means seventy-five. This convention was introduced after the French Revolution in order to unify the various counting systems in existence at the time around France.

Other numeral systems have been used with different bases. A base of

1. Oil painting by Julius Koeckert (1827–1918)
of Abbasid Caliph Harūn al-Rashīd and King Charlemagne.

2. Hārūn al-Rashīd and the barber in a Turkish bath,
a fifteenth-century oil painting.

3. The eighth-century Abbāsid Palace of Ukhaidhir, south of Baghdad.

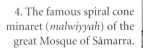

4. The famous spiral cone minaret (*malwiyyah*) of the great Mosque of Sāmarra.

5. The ruins of the tenth-century palace-city complex Medinat al-Zahrā', outside Córdoba.

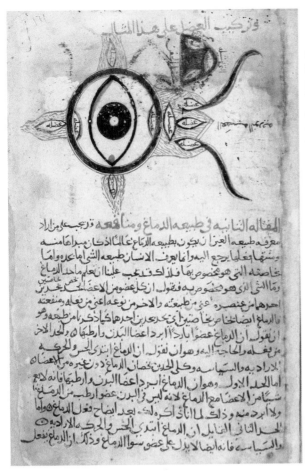

6. Description of the eye in Hunayn ibn Isḥāq's *Ten Treaties on the Eye*, originally composed around 860. This copy was made in Syria in 1197 and represents the earliest existing detailed drawing of the muscles of the eye.

7. A brass astrolabe from Saragossa, *c.* 1079–80.

8. A thirteenth-century painting depicting a trickster performing a 'cupping' in front of a curious crowd of people in eleventh-century Baghdad. The scene is described in al-Ḥarīri's popular *Maqāmāt* (*The Assemblies*).

9. A page from Ibn Sīna's *Canon of Medicine* showing his description of the human skeleton.

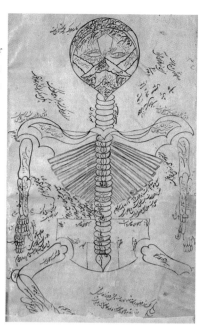

10. (*above*) Medieval Muslim surgical instruments, taken from a fifteenth-century copy of al-Zahrāwī's eleventh-century *Kitab al-Tasrīf.*

11. (*right*) A Balkhi style map of northern Iraq, marking cities along the Tigris and Euphrates rivers, in *Kitab al-Masālik wa al-Mamālik* (*Book of Routes and Provinces*), composed in the eleventh century by Abu Ishāq Ibrahim al-Istakhri.

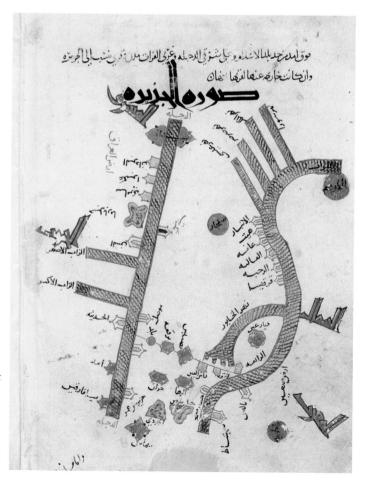

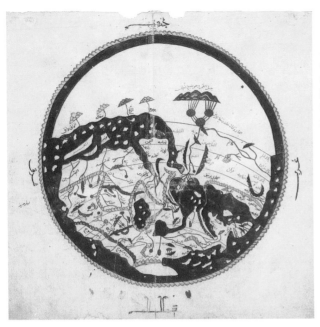

12. Al-Idrīsi's twelfth-century map of the world. It is shown, as was the convention, with the north at the bottom and therefore needs to be turned round in orderto take on a more familiar form.

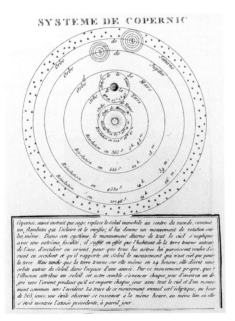

SYSTEME DE COPERNIC

13. Copernicus' heliocentric universe, with the sun replacing the earth at the centre. The moon correctly orbits the earth, but the stars still occupy the outermost orbit around the sun.

14. Ptolemy's geocentric universe as it appears in a Latin translation of the *Almagest*, with the earth in the middle and the sun, planets and stars arranged in their circular orbits outside that of the moon.

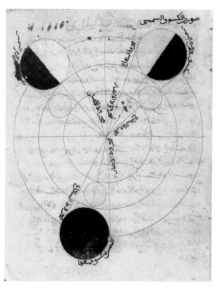

15. Diagram of a solar eclipse from
an eleventh-century manuscript of al-Karkhi
(also known as al-Karaji).

16. A map from the *Book of Routes and Provinces*,
composed by Abu Ishaq Ibrahim al-Istakhri,
showing Iraq, the Tigris river, Kufa, Baghdad
and Persian Gulf.

The Sundial

17. The little-known location of Ibn al-Shātir's sundial on an outside ledge
of one of the minarets of the Umayyad Mosque in Damascus.

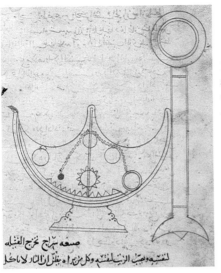

18. The Banū Mūsa brothers' self-trimming lamp, as described in their *Book of Ingenious Devices.*

19. The famous Elephant Clock of al-Jazari.

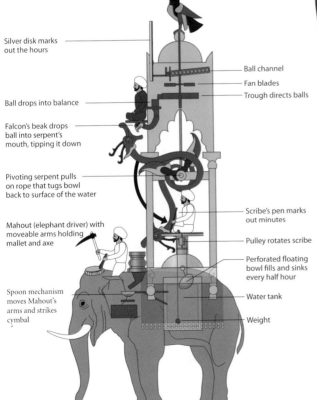

Silver disk marks out the hours

Ball drops into balance

Falcon's beak drops ball into serpent's mouth, tipping it down

Pivoting serpent pulls on rope that tugs bowl back to surface of the water

Mahout (elephant driver) with moveable arms holding mallet and axe

Spoon mechanism moves Mahout's arms and strikes cymbal

Ball channel

Fan blades

Trough directs balls

Scribe's pen marks out minutes

Pulley rotates scribe

Perforated floating bowl fills and sinks every half hour

Water tank

Weight

20. The inner workings of the Elephant Clock.

21. Diagram of a system for pumping water into a basin,
from the *Book of Knowledge of Ingenious Mechanical Devices*, by al-Jazari, 1206.

22. The newly opened campus of King Abdullah University
of Science and Technology (KAUST), in Jeddah.

twelve, known as the duodecimal system, is one of the earliest of these. Its use began perhaps because there are approximately twelve cycles of the moon (lunar months) in one year, and because the multiples and divisors of the number 12 are convenient: $12 = 2 \times 2 \times 3 = 3 \times 4 = 2 \times 6$, while $60 = 12 \times 5$ and $360 = 12 \times 30$, and so on. The use of twelve as a base number was widespread in Europe and the word 'dozen' comes from the old form of the French word *douzaine*, meaning 'a group of twelve'. The word 'gross', from the Latin *grossus* meaning 'large', was taken to represent the number 144, meaning a 'large dozen', or a dozen dozens.

Ultimately, though, the fact that humans have ten digits on their hands provided a standard so readily accessible and convenient that the base-10 (decimal) system has been adopted almost universally.

Pythagoras (*c.* 580–500 BCE) is rightly regarded as the first great mathematician in history and the school of thought that carried his name made huge advances, despite being more of a religious movement than a mathematical one. His philosophy was based on the notion that numbers were intimately connected with the reality of the universe; he regarded them as the abstract yet fundamental building blocks of physical matter. However, it should be noted that his life is shrouded in mystery and it has even been suggested by some historians that he never actually existed.

Even earlier than Pythagoras, around the eighteenth century BCE, the Babylonians used what is called a 'sexagesimal' numbering system, which, unlike the decimal system that changes units every ten, is based on sixtieths of the next highest unit. It is therefore from the Babylonians that we inherit the division of an hour into sixty minutes and a minute into sixty seconds. Similarly, the split of angles into degrees, minutes and seconds of arc is sexagesimal. The Babylonians had symbols for numbers up to 59, beyond which the next unit starts off as 1 again. Thus, to write our numbers in sexagesimal notation, we can divide the units by a comma. The number 61 would then be written as (1,1). Likewise, the number 123 is written as (2,3) since it is made up from $60 \times 2 + 3$. It follows that, for instance, the number 4321 would be written as (1,12,1), since $4321 = 3600 \times 1 + 60 \times 12 + 1$, and so on. This sexagesimal notation is continued into the fractions, where a semicolon can be used to separate integers from fractions. Thus, while (1,30) means the number 90 ($1 \times 60 + 30$), (1;30) means the number 1.5, as 30/60 is the same as ½. Likewise, (2;45) means 2.75, since 45/60 is the same as ¾.

There is a small Babylonian tablet (now at Yale University in the USA) showing a remarkably good approximation for the square root of 2. It is written in sexagesimal form involving fractions as (1;24,51,10). We can write this number in its full fraction form and add up all the fractions:

$$1 + \frac{24}{60} + \frac{51}{60 \times 60} + \frac{10}{60 \times 60 \times 60} = 1\frac{8947}{21600} = 1.414213\ldots$$

And given that the exact value is $\sqrt{2} = 1.414214\ldots$, we see that this is a startlingly good approximation. But this in itself is not what is really impressive. The Yale tablet, and many other known Babylonian tablets, prove (according to Otto Neugebauer, who, despite championing Babylonian science, was one of the most cautiously conservative scholars of the history of ancient science) that the Babylonians were well aware of the 'Pythagorean theorem': of determining the length of the diagonal of the square from the length of its side – this, one thousand years before Pythagoras![2] Thus, a square with sides equal to one unit has a diagonal that is the square root of the sum of the squares of the two sides. In a right-angled triangle it forms the hypotenuse:

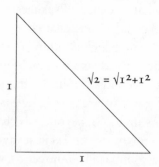

Ancient Indian mathematicians were also familiar with techniques for working out square roots, as can be found in a text known as the Bakhshali Manuscript, written on birchbark and found near the village of Bakhshali, in what is today Pakistan, in 1881. Dated between the second century BCE and the third century CE, it contains

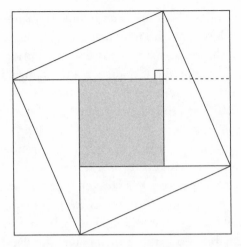

An ancient Chinese method for proving Pythagoras' theorem.
Consider the triangle in the top left of the square with its right angle
shown. Now see if you can make a connection between the areas of the
squares of its three sides.

techniques for solving a wide variety of mathematical problems, such
as a technique for working out square roots.[3]

Likewise, *The Arithmetical Classic of the Gnomon and the Circular Paths of Heaven*, by Zhou Bi Suan Jing, is an ancient Chinese
mathematical text that dates from the period of the Zhou dynasty
(1046–256 BCE). It is an anonymous collection of 246 mathematical
problems, each with detailed steps and answers, and contains one of
the first recorded proofs of the Pythagorean theorem, to which a later
Chinese mathematician, Chou Kung, provided an accompanying diagram (above), which is one of the simplest ways of seeing how the
area of the square of the hypotenuse equals the sum of the areas of the
squares of the other two sides.

Another example of mathematical prowess predating the ancient
Greeks shows honours shared between the Babylonians and the Egyptians and concerns the determination of the value of pi (the constant
ratio of a circle's circumference to its diameter). The value of pi is
what is known as an 'irrational number', one that cannot be written
exactly as a ratio of two whole numbers, which was a concept only
fully understood by Greek mathematicians. Thus, written in decimal

notation the exact value of pi is an infinite sequence of numbers. The extent to which we have been influenced by the Greek contribution to mathematics shows in many people's assumption that it was the Greeks who first figured out that such a fundamental constant exists. This is mainly because we universally use the Greek letter π as its symbol. It is also sometimes referred to as Archimedes' constant, after the Greek scientist who first estimated it rigorously by geometric means. But of course it was known long before the Greeks came on the scene. What is interesting is the way ancient mathematicians worked it out. Clearly to a very rough approximation, it has a value of 3. That is, the perimeter of any circle is three times the length of the line straight across the middle. For many purposes this might be good enough. But both the Babylonians and Egyptians needed to do better.

Rather than give this constant a name or even recognize its existence as a mathematical quantity, the ancients had it encoded within arithmetical rules for evaluating, for example, the area of a circle. We learn at school that this is given by π times the square of the radius, just as we learn that the circumference of a circle is π times twice the radius. The Babylonians often wrote that the area of a circle is given by one-twelfth of the square of the circumference. This may sound rather strange, but with a little not too complicated algebraic manipulation we see that this implies that they were using a value for π of exactly 3. One clay tablet dating back to the early second millennium BCE suggests the use of a more accurate value of $3\frac{1}{8}$, or 3.125, which is slightly smaller than the correct value of 3.1415...[4]

The Egyptians used a different formula, which stated that the area of a circle was given by the square of eight-ninths of the diameter. Again, a little re-jigging tells us that this is equivalent to their use of a value for π of 3.16, a little on the large side but still better than the rough value of 3.

On many other mathematical matters, the Babylonians, particularly during the Hammurabi dynasty (about 1780 BCE), made a number of advances, and we have thousands of cuneiform tablets that confirm this. For instance, their system of multiplication tables is so ingenious that it is far better than that of Ptolemy two thousand years later. Of course, I should not oversell the Babylonians' prowess and achievements in mathematics; while more advanced than the Egyptians, they were inevitably totally eclipsed by the Greeks, in particular by geniuses like Pythagoras, Archimedes and Euclid. It should be noted, however, that Ptolemy's *Almagest* used the Babylonian sexagesimal numbering system, although only for writing fractions. In common with all astronomical texts right up to Islamic times, integers were always written as letters very much like Roman numerals.

The Arabic alphabetic notation, copied from the Greek and Hebrew traditions, dates back to the early years of Islam. It was known as the *abjad* system since the first four numbers: 1, 2, 3, 4, were denoted by the first four letters of the alphabet: *alif* ('a'), *bā* ('b'), *jīm* ('j') and *dāl* ('d'). For instance, a number like 365, which Ptolemy would have written as τξε, would have been written by Islamic mathematicians as شسه. In each case, the three letters symbolize the numbers 300, 60 and 5. The point to note here is that these are very different from the decimal notation we use today, where just nine symbols, plus zero, are used for all numbers. Instead, the numbers 3, 30 and 300, for instance, would each be represented by a different letter.

Muslim mathematicians, even after inheriting the Indian decimal system, continued to use, and improve upon, Babylonian sexagesimal arithmetic, particularly in astronomical calculations, to such an extent that it was referred to as 'the astronomer's arithmetic'.

The prototypes of the number symbols we use today all come from India. They are found in the Ashoka inscriptions from the third century BCE, the Nana Ghat inscriptions about a century later and in the Nasik Caves from the first and second centuries CE – all in forms that have considerable resemblance to today's symbols.[5] For instance, the numbers 2 and 3 are well-recognized cursive derivations from the ancient = and ≡. However, none of these early Indian inscriptions contains any notion of place value or of a zero that would make modern place value possible. Hindu literature provides some evidence that the zero may have been known earlier, but there are no extant inscriptions from India with such a symbol before the ninth century.

A positional, or place-value, notation is a numeral system in which each position is related to the next by a constant multiplier called the base. Our decimal system of course has a base of ten and credit for its development can be traced back to two great medieval Indian mathematicians, Āryabhata (476–550), who developed the place-value notation itself, and Brahmagupta a century later.[6] More recent authors have argued that the oldest known authentic document containing the place-value system is the Jaina cosmological text *Lokavibhaga*, which was completed in 458.[7] By about 670 the system had reached northern Syria, where a bishop by the name of Severus Sebokht praised its Hindu inventors as discoverers of things more ingenious than those of the Greeks and spoke of their 'nine signs'. The zero was, it seems, unknown to him.

It is not clear when the Indian numerals would have become known to the scholars of Abbāsid Baghdad. It may have been as early as the time of al-Mansūr, when Brahmagupta's *Siddhanta* was first translated into Arabic, either directly from Sanskrit or from Persian. Two of the most famous Baghdadi scholars, the philosopher al-Kindi and the mathematician al-Khwārizmi, were certainly the most influential in transmitting Hindu numerals to the Muslim world. Both wrote books on the subject during al-Ma'mūn's reign, and it was their work that was translated into Latin and transmitted to the West,[8] thus introducing Europeans to the decimal system, which was known in the Middle Ages only as Arabic numerals. But it would be many centuries before it was widely accepted in Europe. One reason for this was sociological: decimal numbers were considered for a long time as symbols of the evil Muslim foe.

But there was a more important practical reason for the long delay. For most purposes in daily life, Roman numerals proved adequate and it was only with the emerging interest in science during the Renaissance that the importance of mathematics was understood and numbers appreciated as being at the heart of mathematics, and therefore the very foundation of modern science.

The Hindu-Arabic numbering system was finally popularized in Europe by the great mathematician Leonardo of Pisa (Fibonacci) (c. 1170–1250), who had travelled throughout the Mediterranean world to study under the leading Arabic mathematicians of the time. He returned from his travels around the year 1200 and within a couple of years, aged 32, wrote what he had learnt in the *Liber Abaci* (*Book of Abacus*, or *Book of Calculation*). However, the historian George Sarton makes the following point: 'A single example will suffice to indicate the

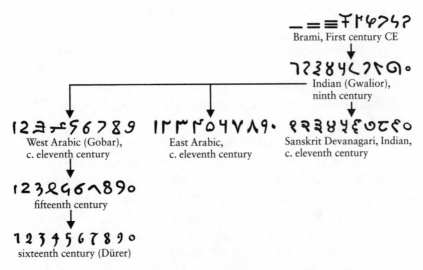

Brami, First century CE

Indian (Gwalior),
ninth century

West Arabic (Gobar),
c. eleventh century

East Arabic,
c. eleventh century

Sanskrit Devanagari, Indian,
c. eleventh century

fifteenth century

sixteenth century (Dürer)

The evolution of Hindu-Arabic numerals.

slowness of the integration of Hindu numerals in Western usage. As late as the eighteenth century the Cour des Comptes of France (the national Audit Office) was still using Roman numerals.'[9]

Considering the awkwardness of Roman numerals when performing arithmetic operations such as multiplication one would think that the Hindu-Arabic decimal system would have been embraced enthusiastically. But what is important about the system is of course not the symbols themselves used for the nine digits, or even that there were just nine of them (plus the zero). After all, just seven letters are needed to denote any integer up to a thousand in Roman numerals. What is crucial is the place-value system itself: that the Hindu-Arabic symbols could define any number up to infinity. They also allow numbers to be manipulated and combined far more efficiently than Roman numerals. Consider multiplying two numbers like 123 and 11. This is straightforward enough on paper for most of us and can even be done in your head if you are that way inclined. The answer is 1,353. But try doing the same multiplication using Roman numerals. You would have to multiply CXXIII by XI to give MCCCLIII. There is a method for doing this but it is somewhat cumbersome.[10] The technique was most likely originally discovered by accident in ancient Egypt and gradually refined as its practitioners became more adept.

Let us return though to the mathematicians of Baghdad who first inherited the Hindu decimal system. Al-Khwārizmi's great work on arithmetic, *The Book of Addition and Subtraction According to the Hindu Calculation*, written around 825, no longer exists in the original Arabic. Even this title is just a guess. It was probably the first book on the decimal system to be translated into Latin, under the title of *Liber Algorismi de Numero Indorum*, and begins with the words *Dixit algorismi* (or 'Al-Khwārizmi says'). It goes on to describe the procedures for various computational instructions and is the origin of the word 'algorithm', derived from the Latinized name of al-Khwārizmi. This and other early translations of his work met with much opposition in Europe and were referred to as dangerous Saracen magic.

But the Muslim world was very reluctant to abandon its old ways too. Despite being introduced to the Hindu decimal notation by al-Kindi and al-Khwārizmi, Arabic mathematicians preferred to stick with what they knew best: either the Babylonian sexagesimal system or the Greek and Roman tradition of using letters of the alphabet to denote numbers.[11] This is what was done routinely in astronomical tables, and continued the tradition they had learnt from texts such as Ptolemy's *Almagest*. Five centuries *after* al-Khwārizmi, the decimal system remained no more than a curiosity, and the Babylonian sexagesimal system continued to be used widely. Consider the example of the monograph on geography of the polymath al-Bīrūni: *The Determination of the Coordinates of Cities*, which was completed in 1025. In it, mathematical formulae are carefully derived, and then worked examples are shown, such as the coordinates of Ghazna, the city in central Afghanistan where al-Bīrūni lived, which are determined relative to both Baghdad and Mecca. Latitude determinations presented no difficulties to a genius like al-Bīrūni and computations were carried out according to the primitive technique of converting all sexagesimals into decimal integers. But for the longitude computations, which were more difficult at the time, all operations were performed with sexagesimals directly in the Babylonian manner.[12]

This custom was to continue for hundreds of years. The mathematical, astronomical and geographical tables published in Arabic during the Middle Ages contain hardly any decimal numbers. This can be seen as late as the fourteenth century in the tables of longitudes and latitudes compiled by the geographer Abū al-Fidā (1273–1331). So one can hardly criticize the Europeans for rejecting Hindu-Arabic numerals for so long when the Muslim world did not embrace them either.

Amid the considerable historical confusion surrounding the origin of many scientific ideas and, in the context of Arabic science, the broad span of opinions ranging from 'they did nothing more than pass on the knowledge of the Greeks and Indians' to 'we owe everything we know to them', one of the most problematic yet fascinating has been over the origin of zero.

The reason for this is not so much because of conflicting evidence, or the lack of it, to support a particular claim, but rather because the question: 'Who first discovered zero?' can mean several different things, and the answer is different in each case. So, let me be more precise:

Is the question: when was the very first use of a symbol, or mark, to indicate a blank placeholder within a number?

Or, more specifically: when was a symbol for such a placeholder used within our current decimal system, such as to distinguish between, say, the numbers 11 and 101?

Does it allude to the first appreciation of zero as a philosophical concept that symbolizes the absence of anything (emptiness, the void)?

Or does it mean the earliest reference to zero as a proper number in its own right, having the same status as any other and sitting on the boundary between positive and negative numbers?

There are clearly different levels of sophistication in understanding the concept of zero. We are not looking for a mathematician who simply woke up one morning and thought 'I know what is missing from our number system that would make arithmetic much more versatile and useful: the zero.'

The crudest definition of zero is that of a positional notation within a number. The ancient Babylonians, in the early second millennium BCE, needed to be able to distinguish between numbers in their sexagesimal tabulations. They appreciated from the very beginning the ambiguity in the meaning of their numbers. For example, consider the number (1,20). This might denote any one of the following numbers:

(a) (1,20), which means 60 × 1 + 20 = 80
(b) (1,0,20), which means 3600 × 1 + 60 × 0 + 20 = 3620
(c) (1,20,0), which means 3600 × 1 + 60 × 20 + 0 = 4800.

If there is no zero placed in the appropriate unit box, how can we tell what the number is? The Babylonians got around the problem in two ways. The cuneiform symbols for 1 and 10 were T and ⟨, respectively. Hence 20 would be written as ⟨⟨, and the number 80, or (1,20), would be written as T⟨⟨. But to distinguish this from the number 3620, or (1,0,20), they would simply leave enough of a gap between the symbols to denote the zero, or empty slot: T ⟨⟨. Of course this still leaves the problem of how to write the number 4800 (1,20,0). For this, they would simply write T⟨⟨, just as they would for (1,20) and trust the context in which it was written to make clear that it is 4800 and not 80 that is implied.

Much later, the Seleucid Babylonians, who ruled over Mesopotamia as the successors of Alexander the Great, invented a symbol to replace this ambiguous 'gap' that the old Babylonians employed. Thus, the earliest known symbol for zero (⟍) is found on many Babylonian cuneiform clay tablets from around 300 BCE. But it was only ever used to keep apart other number symbols, no different from our use today of the zero to distinguish between, say, 25, 205 and 2005. Strangely, they continued the custom of the old Babylonians of never placing the symbol at the end of a number, only in between other symbols.

One can argue about the extent to which this first use of a zero symbol constitutes the real invention of zero. Interestingly, the empty positions requiring a zero symbol occur far less frequently in the sexagesimal system than they do in our base-10 decimal system. It is not needed at all for integers less than 60 and only 59 times for integers less than 3600 (compared with 917 occurrences of the nought in the decimal system). So the Babylonians did not feel such an urgent need for it.

A little later than the Babylonians and on the other side of the world, the Mayans of Central America developed their own vigesimal positional (base-20) number system using very few symbols (a dot for

1 and a bar for 5). This allowed them to have a combination of dots and bars up to 19, then they would move to the next units. And, just like the Babylonians, they used a symbol for zero as a placeholder. The earliest recorded example of this dates to around 36 BCE.

The Greeks, who were very strongly influenced by Babylonian astronomy and the associated sexagesimal system, used their letters for whole numbers but sexagesimal notation for fractions. For this they needed a zero symbol too and picked a Greek letter for this, *omicron* (like the English letter 'o'). But in all three cases – the Babylonians, Mayans and Greeks – this zero is not a number or even a concept in its own right. Nevertheless, it would be correct, in answer to the question 'who first invented the symbol for zero?' to say: the Babylonians.[13]

What about the concept of zero as representing nothingness? Of course philosophical references to the 'void' can be regarded in some sense as being on a par with the mathematical notion of zero. If so, then the ancient Greeks got there first. One prominent historian of mathematics, Carl Boyer, has argued that Aristotle was thinking and writing about zero as a mathematical concept in the fourth century BCE.[14] In his *Physica*, Aristotle describes the idea of the mathematical zero in relation to a point on a line. He also mentions the impossibility of dividing by zero in the context of the speed of an object being inversely proportional to the resistance (or density) of the medium through which it is moving. Thus the speed in a vacuum (or void) would be infinite as there is no resistance. This, argued Aristotle, proved the impossibility of the existence of the void. We therefore see that, at around the same time, the Babylonians invented a *symbol* for zero, while the Greeks first described the *concept* of zero.

We now come to the more sophisticated issue of treating zero as a number in its own right, which would necessarily bring together the ideas of the Greeks and Babylonians. Many historians have argued that this did not happen until relatively recently. Even al-Khwārizmi avoided ever having to equate his algebraic quantities to zero. Instead, he would always have non-zero quantities on both sides of the equation. To state this symbolically, he would never set up an equation like $x^2 + 3x - 10 = 0$, but rather as $x^2 + 3x = 10$. In both cases, the value of x is 2 and the difference between these two notations is a trivial rearranging of the number 10 (according to rules laid down by al-Khwārizmi himself). But the first equation would have been quite alien to him since the 'zero' was not yet considered a number that other numbers could combine together to give.

Despite this, it is commonly agreed that the symbol for zero arrived in Baghdad from India as part of the package with decimal notation. Certainly it seems that the Hindus looked upon zero as a real number, rather than just a symbol, as early as 505 CE.[15] Until that time, the Hindu numerals contained separate symbols for 10, 11 and so on, and it was the invention of zero that did away with the need for separate symbols for any numbers above 9. Soon, Indian mathematicians were carrying out arithmetical operations involving zero. Brahmagupta correctly stated in 628 CE that zero multiplied by a finite number gives zero, and he described the impossibility of the division of a number by zero. It was only much later, towards the end of the twelfth century, that another Indian, Bhaskara, argued correctly that the value of any finite number divided by zero is infinity.

But it is the use of zero in algebra that seems to have been missing in the work of Islamic mathematicians. For instance, consider the relation $x^2 = 2x$. This is an example of a simple quadratic equation and as such has two possible roots (x can have two values). Clearly, these are 0 and 2 – both values 'work' if you replace x by them in the equation. But the early Islamic mathematicians would not have recognized $x = 0$ as one of the solutions. This quite subtle conceptual leap did not take place until the seventeenth century with the work of the French mathematician Albert Girard.[16]

Finally, as for the origin of the word 'zero', this can be traced back to the Indian word *sunya*, meaning the 'void', which was translated into Arabic as *sifr*, or 'nothing', and the word is still in use in the Arabic language today. Around the early thirteenth century its Latinized form became *zephirum* and this gradually evolved into the word 'zero'. But in Western Europe, a further detour was made: the Arabic *sifr* became the Latin *cifra* and the English *cipher*. And instead of denoting zero it was taken to mean any of the Hindu-Arabic numerals. Later, it came to signify a secret symbol, obscure way of writing, or the key to unlocking it (hence the word decipher). Because of this confusion, the English eventually adopted the Italian word *zero*.

*

The Book of Chapters on Hindu Arithmetic (Kitab al-Fusūl fi al-Hisāb al-Hindī) is the earliest known text on arithmetic still extant in Arabic and contains the earliest known use of the decimal point. The only known copy of this remarkable book was written in Damascus in 952 and is kept in the Yeni Gami Library in Istanbul. It is hugely important in the history of mathematics, though probably not widely enough known. Apart from a few missing pages and three unfinished chapters (one on the description of a computing board for the blind), it comprises 230 pages of clearly written text and mathematical calculations. But its author is hardly a well-known figure. Indeed there is no mention of him in the usually reliable and comprehensive *Fihrist* of Ibn al-Nadīm, the tenth-century historian and biographer of Arabic scholars. His name was Abū al-Hassan al-Uqlīdisi, whose title refers to Uqlīdis (Euclid), implying an association with the great Greek mathematician. But it would appear that this connection was not so much from al-Uqlīdisi's great expertise and mastery of Euclid's geometry (although no one can be sure, of course) as from the way he is thought to have earned his living by making and selling copies of the Arabic translation of Euclid's *Elements*.

Al-Uqlīdisi is the very first mathematician we know of to use decimal fractions, and to suggest a symbol for the decimal point (an oblique dash over the number).[17] In the preface to his book, al-Uqlīdisi explains that he has taken great pains to describe the best arithmetical methods of manipulating and computing fractions of all previous writers. This makes it very hard to determine whether the notion of decimal fractions, or even the notation used, is his discovery or that of an earlier mathematician.[18] But since this was not something the Islamic world inherited from the Indians it can be said that, unlike decimal numbers or the zero, decimal fractions were almost certainly an invention of Arabic mathematicians.

Some modern historians have tried to downplay the impact of al-Uqlīdisi's work, arguing that, apart from certain quite specific examples in which he used decimals,[19] he did not fully appreciate just how powerful and important they are in arithmetic. It has even been suggested that poor al-Uqlīdisi's use of decimal fractions was no more than intuitive and accidental, and nowhere near as comprehensive in their application as that of later mathematicians. This is rather harsh,

The first use of a decimal point seen here in *The Book of Chapters on Hindu Arithmetic* by al-Uqlīdisi, written in the mid-tenth century CE. The box on the left shows the magnified text with his notation of a dash above the digit 9, implying that the digits to its right are decimal places. The number itself is written today as 179.685 and is arrived at when al-Uqlīdisi carries out the operation of adding a number (135) to its tenth, then the result to its tenth, etc., three times – in other words, multiplying 135 by the cube of 11/10.

but it is true that much more accomplished mathematicians than al-Uqlīdisi were to follow, such as al-Samaw'al (*c.* 1130–*c.* 1180),[20] the son of a Moroccan rabbi and a mathematical genius, who wrote a book on algebra at the age of 19 and developed the concept of proof by mathematical induction as well as an important contribution to the binomial theorem. For other historians, it is the great Persian mathematician al-Kāshi and his encyclopedic treatise *The Calculators' Key* (*Miftāh al-Hussāb*)[21] five centuries later, who is the first to write comprehensively about, and use, decimal fractions.[22]

Just to muddy the water further, it has also been argued that Chinese mathematicians, such as the great Lui Hui in the third century, were in fact the first to use decimal fractions, although there is no evidence that al-Uqlīdisi was familiar with Chinese mathematics. In any case, the most prominent of the Chinese mathematicians known to have worked with decimal fractions was Yang Hui in the thirteenth century (two centuries after al-Uqlīdisi), although he did not use a symbol for the decimal point.[23]

What is interesting is that al-Uqlīdisi's notation was very close to the one we use for the decimal point today.[24] He wrote the number 179.685 as 179$\overline{6}$85, with a dash over the unit number.[25] This contrasts with the later work of al-Kāshi, who would either write the decimal part of a number in a different colour ink or write his numbers within a table with the decimal part in a separate column. Even more cumbersome is the notation used by the sixteenth-century Flemish mathematician Simon Stevin (1548–1620), who would have written al-Uqlīdisi's number above as 179$_{⓪}$6$_{①}$8$_{②}$5$_{③}$, where the numbers in circles denote the units, tenths, hundredths and so on. Slightly earlier than Stevin, in fifteenth-century European texts, we also see the use of a stroke to separate units from decimals as 179|685. But I much prefer al-Uqlīdisi's very early notation.

The decimal system as a whole, we now see, must be jointly credited to both Indian and Arabic mathematicians. The Indians were the first to use the base-ten positional system of nine ciphers, or digits, plus the zero symbol, instead of the accumulated strokes of the Egyptians, Babylonians and Romans. However, they did not extend this system to fractions. Since that important addition came from the Arabic mathematicians (both Arabs and Persians who wrote in Arabic), we quite properly refer to these numbers as Hindu-Arabic. What is important, I feel, is to stress that the addition of 'Arabic' to the naming is more than simply a reference to the fact that the Indian numerals arrived in Europe via the Muslim world.

8

Algebra

Suppose that a man, in his illness, emancipates two slaves, the price of one being three hundred dirhems and that of the other five hundred dirhems; the one for three hundred dirhems dies, leaving a daughter; then the master dies, leaving a daughter likewise; and the slave leaves property to the amount of four hundred dirhems. With how much must everyone ransom himself?

Al-Khwārizmi

The above quotation comes from *al-Kitab al-Mukhtasar fi Hisāb al-Jebr wal-Muqābala*. That's easy for you to say, you might be thinking. The full translation of this title is: *The Compendium on Calculation by Restoration and Balancing,* and for reasons that will soon become clear, it is admissible to abbreviate this mouthful to just *al-Jebr.* Its author is that stalwart of al-Ma'mūn's House of Wisdom, Ibn Mūsa al-Khwārizmi, and in it he sets out for the first time the subject of algebra as a mathematical discipline in its own right rather than a branch of arithmetic or geometry. Indeed, the word 'algebra' originates from the *al-jebr* in the title.

Al-Khwārizmi came to Baghdad in the early ninth century from a region of Central Asia just south of the Aral Sea. He was originally a Zoroastrian who we think converted to Islam. On the very first page of *al-Jebr*, he begins with the line *Bism-Illāh al-Rahmān al-Rahīm* ('In the name of God, the most Gracious and Compassionate'), with which all books written by Muslims begin, even to this day. But it could of course be that al-Khwārizmi was simply following tradition and did not wish to offend the caliph whose patronage he enjoyed. We have already seen how al-Khwārizmi was one of the central characters in al-Ma'mūn's circle of scholars. In producing his famous *Picture of the Earth* treatise, in which he tabulated the coordinates of hundreds of cities in the known world and gave instructions for drawing a new map of the world, he secured his legacy as the first geographer of Islam. And by overseeing the astronomical work at the Shammāsiyya observatory in Baghdad and then producing a highly influential *zīj*, he marked himself out as one of its great astronomers. But he is primarily known as a mathematician, and his treatise on Hindu numerals introduced the Muslim world to the decimal number system. Yet all these achievements pale alongside his greatest claim to fame, which is without doubt his book on algebra. Interestingly, and unlike his famous contemporary, al-Kindi, he never ventured into philosophy; nor was he involved in translations, and had no knowledge of the Greek language.

It is not known in what year al-Khwārizmi completed his *al-Jebr*, but on the very first page he wrote a dedication to his patron, al-Ma'mūn. It is from these early passages that we learn of his motivation for writing it: 'That fondness for science, by which God has distinguished the Imam al-Ma'mūn, the Commander of the Faithful ... has encouraged me to compose a short work on calculating by (the rules of) completion and reduction.'[1] And here lies part of the real value of his work, for what al-Khwārizmi did was to bring together obscure mathematical rules, known only to the few, and turn them into an instruction manual for solving mathematical problems that crop up in a wide range of everyday situations.

Before delving into the details of his book, it might be useful to explore exactly what is meant by algebra. We all learn at school how to solve problems involving 'unknown' quantities, usually labelled as x and y. It is quite straightforward to demonstrate why algebra is so useful in solving many different kinds of problems in mathematics, science, engineering, finance and so on. As a quick refresher, let us begin with a trivial example. Writing the equation $x - 4 = 2$ means that there is a number, currently designated by the letter x, that has a value such that if we subtract 4 from it the answer will be 2. It is obvious then that x must be 6, and I could have dispensed with the trouble of writing a mathematical equation involving the symbol x and simply stated in words: what is the number that, if we subtract 2 from it, leaves 4?

But how about another problem, where a knowledge of algebra and its rules can come in useful (even though the problem itself is no more than a simple brainteaser)? Here it is. You and I each have a basket of eggs, but we do not know how many eggs either basket contains. We are informed that if I give you one of my eggs then we shall both have the same number. If, on the other hand, you were to give me one of your eggs then I would have twice as many as you. How many eggs does this mean we each had originally? Try thinking through this puzzle before reading on.

The standard response from most people when set this problem is to resort to 'trial and error', testing out pairs of numbers to see if they satisfy the two criteria. First, you should quickly surmise that I must have two more eggs than you, so that by giving you one, we end up with the same number (I lose one but you gain one). But this does not give us a unique answer, for I could have twelve and you ten, or I could have 150 and you 148. The second piece of information now needs to be taken into account, but without algebra you would just be trying pairs of numbers until you hit upon the correct combination. In fact, the answer is that I have seven eggs and you have five – giving you one of mine means we both end up with six, but you giving me one of yours results in you being left with four while I have eight – twice as many as you.

To set up the problem algebraically, we would begin by saying: let the larger number of eggs be x and the smaller number y. We can now generate two equations: $x - 1 = y + 1$ and $x + 1 = 2(y - 1)$. We would then have to know the rules of algebraic manipulation (rearranging and reorganizing the letters and numbers in the equations) in order to arrive at the answer: $x = 7$, $y = 5$. It was this set of rules that al-Khwārizmi describes in his *al-Jebr,* and he is therefore widely hailed as the 'father of algebra'.

But the matter turns out to be rather more complicated than this. We should be careful not to credit al-Khwārizmi with inventing a discipline just because the name we use for it today originated from the title of his book. After all, I did not credit Jābir ibn Hayyān with the title 'the father of chemistry' on the basis of etymology; or, more specifically, credit him with the discovery of alkalis just because that particular word has Arabic origins; for alkalis, known by various names, were in use many hundreds of years before Jābir. The same should apply to al-Khwārizmi, and such a distinction as the founder of a discipline will need to be backed up with a more careful investigation into the mathematical legacy he inherited.

This issue was highlighted for me several years ago when I gave a public lecture at the Royal Society in London on the contributions to science from the golden age of Islam. I glibly, and without really backing up my claim, credited al-Khwārizmi with the invention of algebra. At the end of the lecture, a member of the audience approached me and argued indignantly that in fact algebra went back long before al-Khwārizmi and that if anyone deserved the title of 'the father of algebra' then it was a Greek mathematician by the name of Diophantus. Not being an expert on this matter at that time, I had no strong counter-argument. Had I been too hasty in my praise of al-Khwārizmi? Worse still, had I been guilty of intellectually lazy bias towards the scholars of Islam by downplaying some of the great achievements of the ancient Greeks – something I unfortunately encounter regularly and which I was determined to avoid? I undertook to look into the matter more carefully and describe in what follows what I managed to uncover. It turns out to be a quite fascinating subject, one that I do not believe has been carefully explored outside academic circles.

One cannot help but admire the concerted effort on the part of the Arabic mathematicians who came after al-Khwārizmi to promote and seal his reputation, a PR job that was helped further because of the impact his book then had in Europe. It was translated into Latin in the twelfth century, not once but twice, by the Englishman Robert of Chester and the Italian Gerard of Cremona. His work was also known to Fibonacci, the greatest European mathematician of the Middle Ages, who quotes al-Khwārizmi in his *Liber Abaci* of 1202. In it he refers to the *Modum Algebre et Almuchabale* and its author *Maumeht*, the Latinized version of al-Khwārizmi's first name, Muhammad.

But given the ubiquity of mathematical problems that needed to be solved algebraically, whether involving working out areas of land for agriculture, or financial problems to do with inheritance or taxes, or purely for solving puzzles for recreational purposes, it is hardly surprising that some form of algebra existed long before Islam. The question is whether it really qualifies as algebra. An ancient Babylonian problem found in a cuneiform text reads: 'What is the number, when added to its reciprocal, gives a known number?' The way we would formulate this puzzle algebraically today is to write the unknown number as x and the known number as b. We can then express the problem as an equation:

$$x + \frac{1}{x} = b.$$

This equation can be recast in the form $x^2 - bx + 1 = 0$, which is what is known as a *quadratic equation* (one in which the highest power of the unknown quantity is 2, i.e. x^2). Similarly, a cubic equation is one in which the highest power is x^3, a quartic, x^4, and so on. The solution of the quadratic equation written above is given by a formula that every schoolchild gets drummed into them (even if only to be forgotten later in life). For this particular example it is of the form

$$x = \frac{b}{2} \pm \sqrt{\left(\frac{b}{2}\right)^2 - 1}.$$

This means that, if given the value of b, you can work out x. The Babylonians knew this formula, as did the Greeks. They did not write a general equation as I have done above, but instead solved particular examples for particular values of the known quantity b.

Here is one type of problem that I have set many times when teaching basic algebra. It can be found in Euclid's *Elements* (Book Two, Proposition Eleven): *Divide the straight line AC, which is of known length, into two unequal segments: AB and BC. What are the lengths of these segments such that a square of side AB will have the same area as a rectangle of sides AC and BC?* (see diagram on opposite page)

Euclid solved this problem geometrically by dividing up the shapes in the diagram into smaller parts and comparing the different areas. There is no doubt that the Greeks were both the founders and masters of geometry, with Euclid's *Elements* representing their crowning glory.

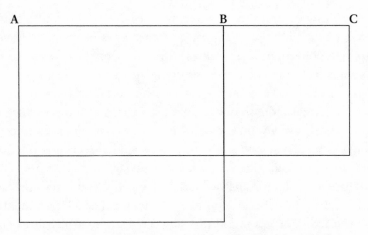

An example of a geometric problem requiring the solution of a
quadratic equation, taken from Euclid's *Elements* (Book Two,
Proposition Eleven). See text for details.

In fact, it was still the standard text taught at schools all over the
world until well into the twentieth century. However, far neater and
aesthetically more pleasing is to set this problem up algebraically. Call
one of the unknown lengths (AB, say) x. Then BC will be the full
length, L, less this length: $L - x$. We therefore know that the area of
the square is x^2, and that of the rectangle, L times $L - x$ and we have
the equation: $x^2 = L(L - x)$, which is another quadratic equation with
a solution for x that depends on the value of L.

If Greek and Babylonian mathematicians really were solving quadratic equations long before al-Khwārizmi – and he was certainly not
doing anything more complicated than that – then surely he cannot
be credited with founding the field of algebra. And what of the
contribution of Hindu mathematicians such as Brahmagupta? Most
importantly, who was this man Diophantus that my detractor argued
had the worthier claim to the title?

Little is known about the life of Diophantus other than that he
flourished in Alexandria in the third century CE. His most famous
work, the *Arithmetica,* in which he solves a large number of mathematical problems, is essentially a book about numbers. But as in
modern algebra, he uses a symbol for the unknown quantity as well
as for certain arithmetic operations like subtraction. Diophantus

explains how to multiply positive and negative terms and different powers of the unknown quantity, and then goes on to show how to simplify a collection of quantities to a more compact form. All this does suggest that Diophantus was doing algebra.

Most famously, Diophantus deals with a certain class of problems in which there is more than one unknown quantity and for which the solution is always an integer, or whole number. A simple example of this might be cast symbolically as $x + 1 = y$. Here, one possible solution is that $x = 1$, and so $y = 2$ or, alternatively, $x = 7$ and $y = 8$ and so on – there is no unique answer, and such an equation is referred to as indeterminate. It is also an example of what is called a linear equation since neither x nor y is raised to a power greater than 1. More generally, any equation involving two or more unknown quantities raised to any power, such that the solutions are always integer numbers, is called a Diophantine equation, even though Diophantus himself did not appreciate the richness of this field nor provide any general methods for solving such equations. The most famous Diophantine equation of all is the one highlighted by the great Pierre de Fermat (1601–65), the founder of modern number theory. In the margins of his personal copy of the *Arithmetica*, Fermat wrote various comments proposing solutions, corrections and generalizations of Diophantus' methods. The most famous of these remarks was the following: 'It is impossible to separate a cube into two cubes, or a fourth power into two fourth powers, or in general, any power higher than the second into two like powers. I have discovered a truly marvellous proof of this, which this margin is too narrow to contain.'[2] This is a statement of one of the most famous problems in the whole of mathematics and is known as Fermat's Last Theorem. In fact, for three and a half centuries it should have more correctly been called a 'conjecture' rather than a theorem. Stated mathematically, it says that there are no whole number values for x, y and z such that $x^n + y^n = z^n$, when n is greater than 2. For instance, there are no whole numbers for which the sum of the cubes of two integers equals the cube of another (unless they are all equal to zero, of course). A proof was finally found by the British mathematician Andrew Wiles in 1995, and I for one have no intention of checking his method, since it runs to more than a hundred pages and took him seven years to complete.

None of this should be credited to Diophantus, of course, but what it is meant to show is that his interest, like Fermat's, was more in the properties of numbers than in the algebraic manipulation of symbols.

In the seventh century the great Hindu mathematician Brahmagupta took up the challenge of tackling another Diophantine equation – what is known today as the Pell equation, which has the general form $x^2 - ay^2 = 1$. Brahmagupta posed the challenge of finding a value for each of x and y if $a = 92$. He suggested that anyone who could solve this problem within a year had earned the right to be called a mathematician. His solution was $x = 1151$ and $y = 120$. These days of course it is a simple matter, if you know how, to program a computer to search for the answer very quickly.

And so, back to ninth-century Baghdad. One thing we can be quite sure of is that al-Khwārizmi would not have been aware of Diophantus or his *Arithmetica,* for the first Arabic translation of this book was not made until several decades after al-Khwārizmi wrote *al-Jebr.* So where did he gain his mathematical education from?

One question, which seems not to have a clear answer, is whether al-Khwārizmi was familiar with Euclid's *Elements.* We know that he could have been – perhaps it is even fair to say that he 'should have been'. An early translation of the *Elements* was made by al-Hajjāj ibn Yūsuf, a contemporary of al-Khwārizmi, in the first years of the ninth century during the reign of al-Rashīd, and he would later produce an improved translation for al-Ma'mūn. It is not known which version of al-Hajjāj's translations, if either, would have been available to al-Khwārizmi. Some modern historians believe that al-Khwārizmi's use of geometric figures to supplement and justify his algebraic proofs suggests that he was familiar with the *Elements* and Euclid's geometrical methods for solving problems.[3]

Whether al-Khwārizmi had studied the *Elements* or not, the consensus now is that he was influenced by both Greek geometry and Hindu arithmetic. However, one twentieth-century scholar did not agree. Solomon Gandz was an Austrian-American historian of mathematics who claimed in a paper published in 1936 that al-Khwārizmi's *al-Jebr* was essentially a translation of an old Hebrew book on geometry called the *Mishnat ha Middot,* dating to around 150 CE.[4] Gandz argued that there was no trace or flavour of Euclid's *Elements* in al-Khwārizmi's work; that he must have been completely unaware of it since his text contained none of the definitions, axioms, postulates or demonstrations of proof that are such an integral part of the writing of Euclid. In fact, Gandz goes so far as to claim that al-Khwārizmi's work was a reaction *against* Greek mathematics. Many historians have disagreed with Gandz and some have explained any similarities between *Kitab al-Jebr* and *Mishnat ha Middot* as being because the *Mishnat* was actually written *after* al-Khwārizmi's time.[5]

Whatever the truth, those aspects of *al-Jebr* that are not original are not its important features. In particular, the geometrical diagrams showing a technique called 'completing the square' had been known since Babylonian times and were used by al-Khwārizmi only as a means of justifying the answers he arrived at algebraically.

I should clarify then what is meant by the two key words in the title of his book: *jebr* and *muqābala*. The former means 'completion' or 'restoration' – for instance the fixing, or setting, of broken bones. In mathematical terms it means moving a negative quantity from one side of an equation to the other and 'restoring' its sign to positive. Thus, if we have the equation $5x - 2 = 8$ then we can move the '2' that is subtracted from the $5x$ on the left over to the other side of the 'equals' sign so that it is added to the 8 instead: $5x = 8 + 2$, or $5x = 10$. The second word, *muqābala*, is the Arabic noun meaning the placing of something face to face with, or across from, or to compare. In mathematical terms, it means to balance an equation, or to do the same thing to both sides. Thus, if we have the expression $3x + 1 = y + 1$ then we can subtract the '1' from both sides to simplify the relation to $3x = y$.

These are two of the basic techniques in algebra and, along with several other rules al-Khwārizmi describes early on in his book, make it clear that this was intended as an instruction manual for manipulating quantities algebraically. But his motivation went beyond this. He describes at the start that the purpose of his book is to teach 'what is easiest and most useful in arithmetic, such as men constantly require in cases of inheritance, legacies, partition, lawsuits, and trade, and in all their dealings with one another, or where the measuring of lands, the digging of canals, geometrical computations, and other objects of various sorts and kinds are concerned.'[6] The book is divided into two halves. The first is of more interest to us, for this is where al-Khwārizmi lays down the rules of algebra and the sequences of steps (the algorithms) needed for solving different kinds of quadratic equations, each followed by a diagrammatic proof of his answer. The second half of the book is full of the applications of his methods and is where he tackles a wide range of everyday problems, as he describes in the quotation above.

He defines three kinds of quantities: the unknown (or what he calls the *shay'*, meaning 'the thing'), squares of the unknown (what he calls the *māl*) and numbers. He describes how a relationship involving these three types of quantities can be manipulated and rearranged so that we can find the value of the *shay'*. But it is the way he describes these steps and procedures that is remarkable. For this book is unlike any book on algebra one would find today. Rather than fill his pages with symbols and notations, he instead wrote entirely in prose. This did of course mean that it took him two pages to explain the steps necessary to compute a quantity, a process that could be stated in just a few lines using symbols in equations.

Now if I mention that the Hindus long before al-Khwārizmi, and even Diophantus, were using rudimentary symbols to describe their equations; that al-Khwārizmi in his *al-Jebr* never solved problems beyond the quadratic (x^2); that Diophantus tackled more complex problems; and that even the techniques al-Khwārizmi used, such as the method of 'completing the square' to solve a quadratic equation, were not new, then surely in the light of all this the argument championing his claim evaporates.

I have heard it said that the reason for al-Khwārizmi's reputation is simply because his was the first book that popularized the subject and set it in a form that could be followed by many people. But this is a feeble argument. One might just as well say that Stephen Hawking's reputation as one of the greatest scientists of the modern era is due to his best-selling *Brief History of Time*, rather than his pioneering work in cosmology and the theories of black holes.

So to settle the matter once and for all, I spoke to a mathematician friend of mine from the University of Warwick, Ian Stewart, who has a long-standing interest in the history of algebra. And, at last, the penny dropped. It turns out that it really has nothing to do with whether or not symbols are used, whether or not there are geometric proofs, the level of complexity of the equations, or the accessibility of the writing. What al-Khwārizmi did for the very first time and what sets him apart from all other mathematicians before him is subtle but crucial. He abandons the practice of solving particular problems, and instead provides a general series of principles and rules for dealing with (quadratic) equations, solving them in a set of steps: the algo-rithm. He thus made it possible for algebra to exist as a subject in its own right, rather than just a technique for manipulating numbers. In Stewart's words:

> It is the difference between on the one hand supplying lots of specific examples and leaving the reader to conclude that the same procedure works on similar ones and, on the other hand, explaining the procedure in general terms in its own right. So, when al-Khwārizmi says '*māl*' (meaning x^2), he doesn't refer to a specific square like 16, say. He means the square of his unknown, his *shay*', which does not represent any number in particular at all. He may use specific numbers that illus-trate the method later, but the method itself is conceived as a general procedure.

Thus, although al-Khwārizmi uses words rather than symbols as Diophantus did, he is in fact much closer to the sort of algebra we do today than the Greek is, because, for al-Khwārizmi, the unknown quantity (the *shay*') is a new kind of object which can be manipulated in its own right. For him, $2x + 3x = 5x$ is a statement about how to combine multiples of the unknown and not just a formula that works for certain values of x. The unknown has become a thing, not a place-holder for numbers. That is the true power of what al-Khwārizmi did, and that is real algebra.

Ultimately, Diophantus was more interested in the theory of num-bers and the relationships between them, just as Euclid's interest was geometry, whereas al-Khwārizmi's text teaches algebra for the very first time as a separate discipline from either arithmetic or geometry.

Many may still hold reservations about al-Khwārizmi's use of prose rather than symbols, so how relevant was this? One can categorize algebra broadly into three types. First, there is what is known as *rhet-orical algebra*, which contains no symbols at all and each step is described in words rather than equations. This was the tradition that al-Khwārizmi inherited and systematized. Next, there is *syncopated algebra*, which is mainly rhetorical but with a few notations and abbreviations included. This is the form of algebra used by Diophantus and it might appear at first sight to be more advanced than al-Khwārizmi's prose, but this is not the case, as I shall explain shortly. Finally, we have *symbolic algebra*, which was first developed in a crude form by the Hindus but would only develop into the modern form used in every language and culture around the world today in the hands of sixteenth-century European mathematicians.

Consider the following equation and how it might be presented in each of the three ways. Today we might write it symbolically as $3x^2 + 5x = 22$, but rhetorically this becomes 'three squares of the unknown added to five of the unknown equals twenty-two'. In syncopated algebra I will follow the notation that would have been used by Diophantus himself. He would have written it as $\Delta^v\bar{\gamma}\,\zeta\bar{\varepsilon}\,\iota\sigma\overset{\circ}{M}\overline{\kappa\beta}$, where ζ is the symbol he used for the unknown (his x) and Δ^v is its square. There is no symbol for '+' and the '=' sign is written as $\iota\sigma$ (the first two letters of the Greek word for 'equal'). The symbol $\overset{\circ}{M}$ defines the constant number. So Diophantus' notation was often nothing more than the first letter or two of the word describing the quantity or operation. For the numerals, he followed the standard tradition of the time in using letters of the Greek alphabet, with bars on top to distinguish them from the letters representing operations.

As we can see, using the notation of Diophantus does not make the task of solving equations any easier and this is very far from full symbolic algebra. In fact, it is no more powerful than the rhetorical algebra of al-Khwārizmi and the only advantage of such abbreviations would have been to save on Alexandrian papyrus. Furthermore, al-Khwārizmi's prose would have been far easier to follow, certainly for medieval translators.

The transition to symbolic notation in algebra was a slow and tortuous process, with many mathematicians inventing their own notation. There was even a concerted effort in Europe to resist the symbolization of mathematics on principle. One of the first books on algebra to contain equations and formulae was written by the English mathematician John Wallis in 1693. But another Englishman, the philosopher Thomas Hobbes (1588–1679), was highly critical of

Wallis and referred to the 'scab of symbols'. Needless to say, Wallis emerged the victor.

Al-Khwārizmi died around 850, but his status as the man who created a new sub-discipline of mathematics to sit alongside arithmetic and geometry had already been secured. Countless mathematicians throughout the Islamic world were inspired by his text and took on the subject's further development; men such as al-Mahani, Thābit ibn Qurra (the translator of Diophantus' *Arithmetica* into Arabic) and Abū Kāmil (known as 'the Egyptian Calculator') all extended al-Khwārizmi's work in the second half of the ninth century. Later, al-Karkhi, Ibn Tāhir and the great Ibn al-Haytham in the tenth/eleventh century took it further by considering cubic and quartic equations, followed by the Persian mathematician and poet Omar Khayyām in the eleventh century, the astronomer al-Tūsi and mathematician al-Fārisi in the thirteenth and al-Qalasādi in the fifteenth. All these men made wonderful contributions long before European Renaissance mathematicians really got going in the sixteenth and seventeenth centuries.

Before I leave the subject of algebra, I wish to pick out one man in particular from the illustrious list of mathematicians just mentioned. This is partly because I shall not return to him later in the book and he deserves mention. Better known for his poetry, it often surprises many to learn that Omar Khayyām (1048–1131) was one of the greatest of all medieval mathematicians. Unlike other Abbāsid scholars, he wrote in his native Persian rather than in Arabic and it is often suggested that he was a Sufi mystic, although it is far more likely that he was an agnostic Muslim.

Khayyām's greatest contribution was his work on cubic equations (in which the unknown quantity, x, can appear in powers up to x^3). In his famous *Treatise on Demonstration of Problems of Algebra*, he classifies thirteen different types of cubic equation and provides a general theory for their solution. He also developed both algebraic and geometric methods for solving them systematically and elegantly, using the method of conical sections (which involves slicing through a cone at different angles to produce different types of curves such as circles, ellipses, parabolas and hyperbolas).

While in his mid-twenties, Omar Khayyām made use of basic

instruments such as a sundial, a water clock and an astrolabe to measure the length of the solar year to a quite incredibly precise 365.24219858156 days, which is in agreement with the modern value to six decimal places. The difference, however, is not necessarily due to any inaccuracy on Khayyām's part, but rather because the earth's spin on its axis is gradually slowing down, so the length of a day is increasing (by 2 milliseconds every century). This means that the exact number of days in a year is decreasing. Compared with Khayyām's time, the length of the year will be 'out' in the sixth decimal place, or by two-hundredths of a second. Several years later Khayyām used this measurement to help devise a calendar[7] that was even more precise than today's Gregorian calendar, which is itself accurate to one day in just 3,330 years. The project, completed in 1079, was carried out by Khayyām and a group of astronomers who introduced several reforms to the existing Persian calendar, which was largely based on ideas from the Hindu calendar. It was named the Jalali calendar, after the Seljuk (in Arabic, Seljūq) sultan who had commissioned the work, and remained in use throughout Persia until the early decades of the twentieth century. In his *Treatise on Demonstration of Problems of Algebra*, Khayyām gives a remarkable insight into the prevailing attitude towards science among the wider public. One cannot help but wonder about the extent to which such attitudes have changed in a thousand years:

I was unable to devote myself to the learning of this algebra and the continued concentration upon it, because of obstacles in the vagaries of time which hindered me; for we have been deprived of all the people of knowledge save for a group, small in number, with many troubles, whose concern in life is to snatch the opportunity, when time is asleep, to devote themselves meanwhile to the investigation and perfection of a science; for the majority of people who imitate philosophers confuse the true with the false, and they do nothing but deceive and pretend knowledge, and they do not use what they know of the sciences except for base and material purposes; and if they see a certain person seeking for the right and preferring the truth, doing his best to refute the false and untrue and leaving aside hypocrisy and deceit, they make a fool of him and mock him.[8]

9

The Philosopher

We ought not to be embarrassed about appreciating the truth and obtaining it wherever it comes from, even if it comes from races distant and nations different from us. Nothing should be dearer to the seeker of truth than the truth itself, and there is no deterioration of the truth, nor belittling either of one who speaks it or conveys it.

Ya'qūb ibn Ishāq al-Kindi

One of several recurring phrases I have been using in this book has been the 'spirit of rational enquiry', describing the feeling that pervaded the intellectual atmosphere in al-Ma'mūn's Baghdad. I have also suggested that this spirit was to a large extent due to the widespread theological beliefs and doctrines of the *Mu'tazili*, or Mu'tazilites, who had originated in Basra some years before the arrival of the Abbāsids, but towards whom a number of the caliphs of Baghdad were sympathetic, including al-Ma'mūn. In this chapter I shall expand a little on their ideology and how it grew from earlier Christian scholars' interpretation of Greek philosophy, particularly the work of Aristotle. I find that many writers gloss over this issue without really explaining what the Mu'tazilites stood for beyond a cursory nod towards their rational, non-literalist interpretation of Islamic theology, and so give the impression that those opposed to them were somehow anti-scientific or irrational. This is rather simplistic and has contributed to the notion that the decline of the golden age coincided with a backlash from conservative Islam against Mu'tazilism. While this hostile response certainly took place, it had little to do with waning of the bright light of scientific progress in the Islamic world centuries later.

Conversely, many Muslims around the world have viewed Mu'tazilism and, by extension, the rationalist scientific world-view with a degree of hostility. This has been either due to their fundamentalist, or literalist, interpretation of the Qur'an, making them view all secular philosophy with suspicion, or because they have associated the theological views of the Mu'tazilites with al-Ma'mūn's unpopular inquisition (*mihna*) in which he tried to enforce his doctrinal beliefs on the general populace.

It is important to understand that the traditionalists who were opposed to the Mu'tazilite rationalists were by no means themselves *irrational* in their theological arguments. All theological schools of thought at the time operated on the basis of some form of synthesis between philosophy and theology – between reason and revelation. However, the Mu'tazilites were not just another sect among many, but rather the followers of a religious ideology that was seen as being aligned with the official doctrinal view of the caliphate. So it was politically sensible for those scholars who sought the patronage of the caliphate to align themselves with this movement.

The Mu'tazilites' primary ethos was to celebrate the power of reason and the human intellect. For them, it is this intellect that guides mankind towards a true knowledge of God, His attributes, and hence the basics of morality. In that sense, they were part of the wider new Islamic theological movement that arose from the early *kalām* debaters and their methods of argument. They were, of course, as has been true of most of the theological movements that have arisen within Islam since then, primarily driven by their desire to interpret the words of the Qur'an. Where they differed from the more conservative element was in their belief that such understanding could be achieved only through the seeking out of knowledge, a worthy ideology that has resonated with every scientist around the world ever since. This is the 'spirit of rational enquiry' I refer to.

More specifically, the Mu'tazilites resorted to metaphorical interpretations of those Qur'anic verses with anthropomorphic content, for they did not believe in an anthropomorphic God in any form. This allowed them, for instance, to reject certain literal interpretations of passages in the Qur'an that are described as the 'words of God'. God does not 'speak' in the way man does, they argued. Rather, His speech is something He brings into being and so, by extension, is the text of the Qur'an itself. This belief that the Qur'an was created by God rather than eternal is the best-known point of contention between the Mu'tazilites and the literalists. And while the theological debate surrounding the issue was extremely important to many scholars at the time, it is understandably somewhat academic as far as the everyday practice of Islam today is concerned.

A more serious difference between the Mu'tazilites and the literalists therefore – one that had a more direct and practical bearing on the nature of scientific progress – was the literalists' view that the text of the Qur'an and *Hadīth* (the recorded conversations of the Prophet) gave Muslims everything they would ever need to know about their faith, and so the sort of philosophical debate and reasoning as practised by the Mu'tazilites and the scholars of *kalām* was not only unnecessary, but un-Islamic. This view has since broadened in some quarters to the erroneous belief that all knowledge is contained in the Qur'an; that anything God felt it was worth mankind knowing, including the laws of nature and our place in the universe, can be found written in the Qur'an, so there is no point in scientific enquiry. Such a dangerous attitude is still held by some Muslims in the world today and is one reason for certain anti-scientific attitudes that have held back technological, economic and social progress in many Muslim countries.

Another early problem that confronted Islamic theology was the issue of free will. Since God is omnipotent, people have argued, everything must be pre-ordained and directed by God, and humans can logically therefore have no free will. However, the Mu'tazilites believed that the Qur'anic commands and prohibitions are in fact worded in such a way as to imply that we do have a choice over our actions, and so, since God is just, He will only punish those who were free to choose, but who made the wrong choices.

Facing the problem of the existence of evil in the world, the Mu'tazilites used their arguments concerning free will to define evil as something that stems from the errors in human acts. God does no evil, and does not demand of any human to do evil. For if man's evil acts had come from the will of God, punishment would have been mean-ingless. Mu'tazilites did not deny the existence of suffering that goes beyond human abuse and misuse of their free will granted to them by God. In order to explain this type of 'apparent' evil, they relied on the Islamic doctrine of *taklīf* – that life is a test for beings possessing free will, and hence the capacity for choice. None of these debates were new of course, as Christian and Jewish theologians had been discuss-ing issues such as free will and the nature of good and evil long before Islam.

Al-Ma'mūn grew up in this atmosphere and many of his tutors were prominent Mu'tazilites. In 827 he made clear his Mu'tazilite sympathies by declaring as official the doctrine that the Qur'an was created rather than eternal. This in itself was not a controversial view and was quite widespread among theologians at the time; it would be wrong to think that it was confined solely to the Mu'tazilites.[1] How-ever, just four months before his death in 833, al-Ma'mūn asserted his supreme authority in all religious matters by issuing his *mihna*, decree-ing that all Muslims should accept the doctrine of the createdness of the Qur'an. He regarded himself as not only the supreme political ruler of a vast Islamic Empire, but as the guardian of Islam itself, entrusted by God with ultimate truth. He believed it was his duty not only to protect the state politically from external forces, but to ensure its religious well-being. It was therefore necessary to educate his people and correct them on all theological matters.

It is unclear from the letters in which he set out his *mihna* what lengths he went to in order to ensure it was carried out. This dramatic event was seen by later historians as having tainted the whole Mu'tazilite movement. However, it was much more to do with al-Ma'mūn's attempts to enforce his personal theological views, which were in any case not at odds with most theologians' thinking at the time, than with his championing of an unpopular creed, let alone speaking for Mu'tazilism in general. The *mihna* would continue during the reign of the following two caliphs, his young brother al-Mu'tasim and his nephew al-Wāthiq, and was only abolished in 849 by the next caliph, al-Mutawakkil.

It was by no means just theologians who were debating such matters. The most important thinker of all during this time was a philosopher – the very first of Islam – and, as such, differing in a fundamental way from the Mu'tazilite *kalām* theologians. His name was Ya'qūb ibn Ishāq al-Kindi (*c.* 800–*c.* 873) – Alkindus to the West – and he was the first of the great Abbāsid polymaths as well as the last of al-Ma'mūn's great 'Hall of Fame' scholars that I want to introduce you to. Al-Kindi was an Arab from the powerful Kinda tribe, originally from Yemen but hugely influential in Arabia before and after the birth of Islam. He was born in Basra but probably spent some part of his childhood in Kūfa, where his father was governor. He is thought to have moved to Baghdad early in life and received his education there.[2] Having shown great early promise as a scholar of Greek philosophy he was recruited by al-Ma'mūn.

By this time the translation movement was at its height, amid what has been described as a fully fledged scramble for any Greek scientific or philosophical text that the scholars of Baghdad and their wealthy patrons could lay their hands on. At the centre of all this was al-Kindi, a man who would question everything around him, and who applied his impeccable logic to issues surrounding God and creation. As a devout Muslim, he showed sympathies towards the views of the Mu'tazilites, a stance that would certainly have helped him initially to gain favour in the caliph's court. But al-Kindi was no lackey, and he honed his views on purely logical, even mathematical, reasoning. This was a stance that would make him a number of enemies later in life and even bring him into direct conflict with rivals within the House of Wisdom itself.

During his early years, al-Kindi gathered around him a circle of scholars and translators, for he was not himself a translator and did not even read Greek. His strength was in assimilating, understanding and commenting on the translated work of the Greek philosophers that was presented to him. Eventually, the more prolific Hunayn ibn Ishāq would arrive in Baghdad and build up his own circle of translators. But what al-Kindi's circle lacked in sheer volume of translations, they made up for with the quality and choice of the Greek texts they picked to study, driven always by al-Kindi's own philosophical concerns and interests. His philosophy was a synthesis of ideas that were quite sophisticated for the time, based on the interpretation of revelation through reasoned argument, together with a rationalist, Aristotelian, view of the world around him, which fed directly back into his religious beliefs. He is thus rightly credited with being the scholar most responsible for bringing Greek philosophy into the Islamic world.

In order to understand this new synthesis of philosophy and Islamic theology, we need first to know a little about Aristotle himself and the philosophy on which al-Kindi based his ideas.

It is impossible to overestimate the impact that Aristotle (384–322 BCE) has had on mankind throughout history and across civilizations – and it is not surprising that he was the man that al-Ma'mūn met in his dream. In philosophy, he is peerless. Not only was he the greatest philosopher who ever lived, his ideas, through the work of al-Kindi, were to become the foundation on which early Islamic philosophy was built, even though many of the Aristotelian ideas would later be modified, extended and even rejected.

In many ways Aristotle represents the pinnacle of Greek knowledge and has been regarded by many as the greatest intellect of all time for his huge influence on so many thinkers over the next two thousand years. When one thinks of the greatest of the Greek philosophers, two other names also come to mind, however. Socrates[3] (470–399 BCE) was, in a way, almost anti-scientific in his views. For example, he disapproved of geometry as a discipline for its own sake and felt that it should only be taught as a practical tool in architecture, agriculture and where useful in mathematical calculations involving financial transactions. His was thus a positivist, pragmatist attitude towards knowledge. Plato (428–348 BCE), who bridged the fifth century of Socrates and the fourth century of Aristotle as a student of one and the teacher of the other, was more akin to what we would regard as a modern theoretical physicist than his mentor, Socrates. He believed that the universe was describable mathematically and that it was thus comprehensible. It was therefore the job of philosophy to make sense of the mysteries of the universe, such as the apparently irregular motion of stars and planets, in terms of regular mathematical laws. But Plato did very little in terms of contributing to knowledge beyond the abstract and metaphysical and is not regarded as being as great a *scientist* as Aristotle – or, for that matter, someone like Archimedes.

Aristotle became a student of Plato in Athens at the age of 18 and was later to take on the role of tutor to Alexander the Great. He founded his famous school in Athens, the Lyceum, in 335 BCE. As well as being a great philosopher, Aristotle made many advances in mathematics, physics and cosmology, and was even one of the first historians of science. But his greatest contribution was in the life sciences. He can rightly claim to be the 'father of biology', in the same way that Pythagoras was the 'father of mathematics' and Hippocrates the 'father of medicine'. Unlike Plato, who is known to have advised Greek astronomers to replace 'observation' with 'speculation', Aristotle based his approach on observation of the world around him and the gathering of data in order to build up empirical knowledge about nature – which is the way much of science is carried out today. Luckily, many of the greatest Greek 'experimental' scientists, such as Archimedes, Hipparchus and Galen, did not follow Plato's advice.

In physics, Aristotle was to put forward the idea that all motion is the realization of a body's potentiality to move. More generally, he argued that everything is subject to change. His term *kinēsis* refers to all kinds of change: alteration of the substance of an object, alteration of its size or shape, alteration of its quality and alteration of its position (motion). Thus the four types of *kinēsis* are represented by changes in quiddity, quantity, quality and position. An object falls because it 'naturally' wants to rejoin the earth from which it sprang, and fire rises so as to rejoin the sphere of fire above. Similarly, water and air find their natural levels. All other motion is not natural and requires the action of a force (which sounds remarkably like Newton's first law of motion: a body remains at rest or in constant motion unless acted upon by an external force). Of all the Greeks, Aristotle's work and teaching would have the greatest influence on Arabic scientists a thousand years later, and indeed on many later European thinkers.

Of interest here is Aristotle's cosmology. For him, the universe is finite in extent, but has existed for ever. He claimed that the stars in the heavens are made up of an indestructible substance called the aether and are eternal and unchanging. His cosmology thus described the first 'steady state' universe, an idea resurrected by the British scientist Fred Hoyle in the mid-twentieth century, but that has since fallen out of favour with the overwhelming evidence in support of the Big Bang theory.

The celestial bodies, including the sun, moon, planets and stars, were considered by Aristotle to be attached to rigid, crystalline spheres that revolve in perfect circles around the earth, which sits at the very centre of the universe. The other four fundamental elements – earth, water, air and fire – are subcelestial elements. He argued for a 'Prime Mover', a deity that is responsible for making the outermost sphere rotate at constant angular velocity, and imparting this motion from sphere to sphere, thus causing all the celestial spheres to rotate around the earth. This Prime Mover of Aristotle's universe became the God of Christian, Jewish and eventually Muslim theologians who studied his work, the outermost sphere of the Prime Mover became identified with Heaven, and the position of the earth at the centre of it all was understood in terms of the concern that God had for the affairs of mankind and their unique place in his creation.

Although al-Kindi was the first philosopher of Islam, he was certainly not unique in applying Aristotelian philosophy to religious thinking. Other, non-Muslim philosophers before him had also held that revelation in the monotheistic religions was about the discovery of absolute truths about God and man's place in God's universe, as discovered through logical philosophical enquiry.

Parallels can be drawn between al-Kindi and an earlier Alexandrian Christian philosopher named John Philoponus (490–570), an early critic of Aristotle and the first to combine scientific cosmology (the study of the nature of the universe) with the Christian doctrine of creation. The most important difference between Aristotle and Philoponus was that, for the latter, the universe is the single creation of a single God and therefore could not be eternal. Philoponus also held that the stars were not divine but in some sense had the same physical attributes as the earth.

Both al-Kindi and the Mu'tazilite theologians made use of Philoponus' arguments to establish their notions regarding the creation of the universe. The Mu'tazilites adopted the doctrine of creation *ex nihilo* ('out of nothing'), as did al-Kindi. And even beyond the Mu'tazilite circles, this was a common view among the scholars of Baghdad at the time, such as the Christian Job of Edessa (b. *c.* 760 CE) and the Jewish philosopher Saadia Gaon (882–942). So it is not that al-Kindi was a particularly close adherent of Mu'tazilite doctrine; rather, again, we see it as part of the general intellectual atmosphere of the time.

Al-Kindi's most important treatise, *On First Philosophy*, was an invitation to Muslim scholars to study Islam philosophically. Many theologians at the time and since have criticized him for this, thinking that he was attempting to replace revelation with rationalism. He was not. In the preface to *On First Philosophy*, he explains why the study of Greek philosophy is so important. He says that one should not neglect the achievements of previous scholars on the basis that they are of a different race, culture or creed and he accuses those who fail to appreciate the contribution of the Greeks of being narrow-minded, envious and lacking in pure faith in Islam:

> We should not be ashamed to recognise truth and assimilate it, from whatever quarter it may reach us, even though it may come from earlier generations and foreign peoples. For the seeker after truth there is nothing of more value than truth itself; it never cheapens or debases the seeker, but ennobles and elevates him.[4]

Since Aristotle's universe was eternal and uncreated, al-Kindi had to come up with a strongly reasoned logical argument to refute it. He thus adapted one of Philoponus' proofs of the creation of the universe based on the idea of the impossibility of infinity; namely, that the present moment could never have been reached if it were preceded by infinite time made up of a continuous and infinite sequence of events, which could not have been traversed to reach 'now'. Unlike Aristotle, al-Kindi demonstrated his ideas mathematically. Here is a neat summary of his argument. If one starts with an infinite quantity and subtracts from it a finite quantity, A, then the remainder, B, is either finite or infinite. If it is finite, then adding it back to A will always give another finite quantity, and not the original infinity. Therefore, B cannot be finite and must be infinite. But subtracting the finite quantity A from the original infinity means that B must be a smaller fraction of this infinity. And fractions, argues al-Kindi, must have limits. So it cannot be infinite. Therefore the whole notion of an infinite quantity is absurd.

Of course, we know in mathematics today that al-Kindi was wrong, since there are indeed infinities of different 'sizes'. We can even subtract one infinity from another with the remainder still being infinite. For example, take the infinity of all integer numbers and subtract from it the infinity of all even numbers. You are still left with the infinity of all odd numbers.

Al-Kindi's rationale about the impossibility of infinite quantities, including time, led him to the notion not only that the universe could not have existed for ever, but that time itself could not have existed before the creation of the universe and must have come into being together with the universe. This idea is remarkably close to our current understanding of modern cosmology based on the birth of space and time at the Big Bang billions of years ago, as described by Einstein's General Theory of Relativity. Furthermore, this finiteness of the universe allowed al-Kindi, in contrast to Aristotle, to call upon God as creator of the world who brings it into being out of nothing.

These philosophical ideas were essentially driven by theology, but al-Kindi was much more than a philosopher. If you thought al-Khwārizmi was versatile in spanning astronomy, geography and mathematics, you should be far more impressed with al-Kindi's résumé. For in addition to his philosophical writing he also made major contributions to mathematics, astronomy, optics, medicine, music and cryptography. And while it was quite common for scholars, almost up to the modern age, to cover a range of disciplines, few made such an impact across so many fields as al-Kindi. Like that of his contemporary al-Khwārizmi, it was al-Kindi's influence on future generations that marked him out as such an important figure in the history of science. In mathematics, for instance, both men played an important role in introducing Indian numerals to the Islamic and, later, Christian worlds. Like al-Khwārizmi, al-Kindi was to write an important treatise, *The Book on the Use of Indian Numerals* (*Kitab fi Isti'mal al-'Adad al-Hindi*), on the subject.

In cryptography, he famously devised new methods of code-making and -breaking – or at least provides the earliest known description – and he is credited with developing what is known as the frequency analysis method, whereby variations in the frequency of the occurrence of letters could be analysed and exploited to break ciphers. His work is detailed in a text rediscovered in 1987 in the Sulaimaniyya Ottoman Archive in Istanbul.[5] Fascinatingly, al-Kindi's motivation for developing his expertise in cryptanalysis seems to have arisen from his determination to decipher and translate texts from foreign languages unfamiliar to him. One can almost imagine him impatiently urging and cajoling his translators to speed up their work on important Greek treatises and, unable to wait, inventing ways of deciphering the unfamiliar text himself. Armed with the correct translation of just a few words, he would begin by determining the frequency with which different letters appeared in a particular text, and then progress to making associations between different letters and words until he had cracked the code of a language and whole sentences could be understood.

He was also the first great theoretician of music in the Arab-Islamic world. He surpassed the achievement of the Greek musicians in using the alphabetical annotation for one-eighth. He also realized the therapeutic value of music and attempted to cure a quadriplegic boy with music therapy. He is known to have written many texts on music theory, of which five have survived. In one, the word *mūsīqa*, from the Greek word *mousikē* (meaning 'art of the Muses'), was used for the first time in Arabic.

Al-Kindi carefully discriminated between what he saw as science and what he believed to be superstition. He regarded 'the art' (alchemy) as a deception and the whole notion of transmutation of base metals into gold as a sham, something he makes clear in his treatise *The Deceits of the Alchemists*.[6] But he believed in astrology unconditionally, although he at least tried to rationalize it scientifically and to distinguish it from its more populist association with horoscopes and fortune-telling. On the other hand, he accepted clairvoyance and divination by dreams as true, and attempted to understand dreams through a form of crude psychology. Before we are too dismissive of such backward notions, we should consider the number of people around the world today who still hold such views; even some of the giants of nineteenth-century science were themselves deeply committed to research into the paranormal.

Al-Kindi was still relatively young when al-Ma'mūn died, and he continued to serve under several caliphs, starting with al-Ma'mūn's successor, al-Mu'tasim (833–42), dedicating many of his most important treatises to him. But al-Mu'tasim and his son al-Wāthiq reigned for just nine and five years respectively. They were followed by al-Wāthiq's younger brother al-Mutawakkil (847–61), who, in stark contrast to all the previous Abbāsid caliphs, showed little interest in science and scholarship, and was to turn against rationalism in favour of a more literalist interpretation of the Qur'an and Hadīth that brought al-Ma'mūn's *mihna* to an end. We have no reason to believe that al-Kindi himself supported the *mihna*, of course. He was even critical of some of the ideas of Mu'tazilism itself, as can be found in the opening chapter of his *On First Philosophy*,[7] which he wrote during the reign of al-Mu'tasim.

In al-Mutawakkil, we see the first of a line of more conservative caliphs and the beginning of the backlash against the free-thinking and liberal theology of the Mu'tazilite movement. And al-Mutawakkil's often violent persecution of scholars whose views did not accord with his more fundamentalist version of Islam sees the theological pendulum swinging away from al-Ma'mūn's *mihna* to the other extreme; neither ruler endeared himself to those who did not share his views. Even al-Kindi was not spared. While not a Mu'tazilite himself, he broadly sympathized with their views and now suddenly found himself on the wrong side. He fell victim to what seems to have been a conspiracy led by the powerful Banū Mūsa brothers, who cultivated a mischievous streak bordering on the dangerous towards anyone who crossed their path.

The brothers had grown jealous of al-Kindi's extensive library and knew that the only way to lay their hands on it was to plot and scheme against him until they finally persuaded the caliph to expel him. Al-Kindi was physically beaten, his library confiscated and its contents granted to the brothers. But they did not keep them for long; having been requested by the caliph to build a canal, their engineer made such a shoddy job of the project that they begged a colleague, Sind ibn Ali, to put in a good word on their behalf with the caliph to get them off the hook. Sind appears to have agreed to do this on the proviso that they return al-Kindi's library.[8]

Despite having his library restored to him, al-Kindi lived his remaining years a lonely man. After his death, his philosophical work quickly fell into obscurity and many of his texts were lost even to later Islamic scholars and historians. A few have survived, however, in the form of Latin translations, while others have been rediscovered in Arabic manuscripts. Even so, all this amounts to only a fraction of his total output as cited in other sources. One reason for the loss of so much of his work may have been the Mongol destruction of the House of Wisdom library in 1258.[9]

Al-Kindi's legacy was not entirely forgotten, and the baton would eventually pass on to a philosopher in the tenth century of Turkish descent, by the name of al-Farābi, who would continue al-Kindi's mission of the Islamization of Greek philosophy, particularly the work of Aristotle. Al-Farābi's philosophy built on, extended and even eclipsed the work of al-Kindi. And while it was al-Kindi who first introduced philosophy as the handmaiden of theology, positioning him closer to a traditionalist version of Islam than al-Farābi, it was the latter who attempted a more serious and mature understanding of revelation and prophecy from a purely philosophical point of view. According to al-Kindi, the goal of metaphysics is the knowledge of God, for he believed that both philosophy and theology are concerned with the same subject. Al-Farābi strongly disagreed, and argued that metaphysics is actually concerned with what can be asserted about the proof of God's existence, but says nothing about His nature or qualities.

Another difference is that, whereas al-Kindi believed that divine revelation trumped rational reasoning where the two conflicted, such as with the issue of the resurrection of the body on Judgement Day, al-Farābi held that rational philosophical reasoning was more powerful than the symbolic expressions of revealed truths in religion; this despite the fact that he lived in a time when the backlash against philosophers had already begun and with the rationalist Mu'tazilite ideology in retreat and widely viewed with hostility.

Still, while al-Farābi was to extend his predecessor's ideas and has certainly been quoted more widely by later philosophers, partly due to the survival of more of his work, in my view he is not quite as worthy of greatness. For al-Farābi was no polymath, nor was he particularly interested in empirical science. Like many of the Greek philosophers before him, he was less concerned with physics than with metaphysics. In contrast, al-Kindi was the true Renaissance man of Islam.

The philosophical baton would eventually pass from al-Farābi to two men who achieved far greater prominence in Europe than either al-Kindi or al-Farābi and would greatly influence many Renaissance thinkers. They were Ibn Sīna and Ibn Rushd, both of whom being more familiar in the West by their Latinized names: Avicenna and Averroës. But these men achieved what they did only because of the ground laid by al-Kindi. His work in synthesizing Aristotle's teachings with Islamic theology should be viewed as a vital link in an unbroken chain connecting the philosophy of ancient Greece with modern Western philosophy developed by such men as Thomas Aquinas and Descartes. It is a shame that his name is not often mentioned in modern accounts of the history of philosophy.

And so we finally leave behind the time of al-Ma'mūn. Many of the scholars he recruited outlived him to continue the pursuit of his dream. Thanks to al-Ma'mūn, the seed had been sown, and even the waning of Mu'tazilism could not halt the rapid flowering of science in the empire. This passion to understand the world became more widespread, both in Baghdad and elsewhere. With the death of al-Kindi and al-Khwārizmi a new era would begin. Scientific progress in the Islamic world gathered pace and new heroes emerged. By the end of the ninth century and the beginning of the tenth, Baghdad would be dominated by a man who became unquestionably the greatest physician of the medieval world. He is known in the West as Rhazes.

10

The Medic

The physician must pay attention to the patient's strength, the matter of the disease, and its duration; for if the strength is weak, but the disease-matter plentiful and the duration long, then the patient should be offered from the very beginning something which sustains the strength while not increasing the disease-matter – and there is nothing more appropriate for that than the right amount of chicken broth.

Ya'qūb ibn Ishāq,[1] *Treatise on the Errors of the Damascene Physicians*

'Jiddū', as we used to call him, died when I was just 6 years old. I still remember his bristly beard and his stethoscope, and his kind gentle eyes – and the books, so many books. Jiddū was my paternal grandfather in Najaf. Our family trips down from Baghdad to visit my grandparents were the only occasions when my mother had to wear an *abāya*, the black full-body form of *hijab* worn by women in the Middle East. This was necessary in the holy cities of Najaf and Kerbala, even for Europeans like my mother.

Thinking back about Jiddū, he so naturally fits the mould of those grand Abbāsid scholars one thousand years earlier. Most of the images one can find today of the great scientists of Islam tend to be stylized artistic depictions by nineteenth-century Europeans, and all entirely fictitious. The only criteria seem to be that the characters need a turban, a beard (of various shades and lengths) and a flowing gown, and be seated on a rug with a book. That is precisely how I remember my grandfather. And not only did he look the part, he was every bit the scholar himself. He was highly intelligent, wise and well-read. He was first and foremost a writer and poet of some distinction in Iraq. But he was also the local 'wise man' and apothecary in his district of Najaf – hence the stethoscope. I remember his library in an upstairs room of the house, which was kept unchanged after he died. Over the years I often spent time in there looking through his books. To be honest, I never found anything as much worth reading as whatever I had on the go at the time, whether it was *Just William* or *The Famous Five*, or the latest *Shoot* football magazine sent over from England by my maternal grandparents.

Sadly, the library was destroyed. Jiddū's house was in the centre of Najaf, just two minutes' walk from the fabulous golden-domed Imam Ali Mosque. In an intriguing parallel (for me, personally – albeit on a smaller scale) to the fate of the Baghdad House of Wisdom library at the hands of the Mongols in 1258, Saddam Hussein was responsible for the destruction of the 'House of Jiddū' library in the early 1990s when the whole neighbourhood was razed to the ground by the Republican Guards' bulldozers after the Shi'a uprising of March 1991.

Was my grandfather typical of the sort of physician produced in the Islamic world? What real medical training did he have anyway? And if we project medical knowledge back one thousand years into the past, we might rightly ask just what sort of medicine was being practised in the Abbāsid world. Here, again, we find the standard Western view of the state of medical knowledge in early Islam to be very wide of the mark. The mistake has been to confuse the medical knowledge developed and practised during the golden age of Islam with something referred to as 'Islamic medicine'. The latter has a quite specific meaning and refers to a tradition of medicine, still practised today, that fuses the teachings of the Qur'an and *Hadīth* together with Aristotelian philosophy, ancient herbal remedies and dietary advice, all mixed in together with generous dollops of common sense and hocus-pocus. It therefore fits more comfortably into what we would now call complementary holistic medicine rather than medical science proper.

What I hope to convince you of is that, while these factors certainly played a major part in the medical practices of ninth-, tenth- and eleventh-century Baghdad and elsewhere, many Islamic physicians tried to tackle medicine in a more careful, quantitative and objective way – and none more so than Abū Bakr Muhammad ibn Zakariyya al-Rāzi, who was the greatest physician and clinician of Islam and indeed of the whole Middle Ages. He pioneered so many areas of medical science, from paediatrics to psychiatry, that I could fill a page just listing them. So, like al-Khwārizmi and algebra a generation before him, we should first understand what medical knowledge al-Rāzi inherited.

We begin, as we must when digging into the origins of medicine, with ancient Egypt. Despite all the wonders and achievements of the Egyptians, their civilization differed from those of Greece and Babylon in the complete absence of any theoretical or metaphysical concepts associated with its science. For the Egyptians, science was merely a practical tool, and even medicine fell into this category. This is why Plato writes in his *Republic* of the Greeks' love of learning and the Egyptians' love of riches. The Egyptians possessed exceptional embalming skills, but had surprisingly little knowledge of human anatomy. Like other ancient civilizations in India and China with medical traditions stretching back to prehistory, much of Egyptian medicine seems crude and silly to us today. For instance, their remedy for migraine was to rub the side of the patient's head with a poultice made from the skull of a catfish so that the pain could pass through to the animal. But I cannot stress often enough that we should not be too harsh in our judgement of such quaint notions. For they are no sillier than many popular therapies still practised around the world today, including in the so-called 'enlightened' West.

In any case, the ancient Egyptians did develop many sensible procedures, such as the use of lint, the suturing of wounds, supporting fractures with wooden splints, and the heating of a lancet to cut out tumours. Much of Egyptian medicine was later to pass to the Greeks, who would turn it into a proper scientific discipline, culminating in the great works of Galen.

Further east, the Vedic tradition in India has a long history going back to origins in magic, religion and mythology and is still practised in some parts of the world today as a form of complementary medicine. It holds that each of the five elementary substances that make up the universe – earth, water, fire, wind and space – corresponds to a constituent in the human body: tissue, humour, bile, breath and cavities. As with all ancient medicine, and indeed most ancient science, this is mainly a mixture of superstition interwoven with science, but there is always much of practical use and importance.[2]

The Greeks of course excelled in the field of medicine – like almost everything else – and boast the two greatest physicians of antiquity: Hippocrates (*fl.* 420s BCE) and Galen (*c.* 130–216 CE), two men separated by a remarkable half a millennium. I say 'remarkable' here only because, while we often mention these two men in the same breath when talking about Greek medicine, this is somewhat equivalent in timescale to saying that the two giants of modern European cosmology are Copernicus and Stephen Hawking. Hippocrates' legacy to medicine can be compared with that of Pythagoras to mathematics. Like the earlier mathematician, his life and achievements are somewhat shrouded in mystery. Both founded schools of thought that were to become more important than their founders. And like the Pythagorean mathematicians, Hippocratic physicians made an astonishing and lasting contribution to the field of medicine. They understood that the human organism is a complex whole and that true wisdom came from understanding, aiding and stimulating its natural activities. They were the first not to separate body and soul, but to consider man as an integral part of his physical and sociological environment.

Galen is an even more important figure in the history of medicine – many might argue the most important in history. His work and ideas influenced all medical knowledge in the world for more than a thousand years. He was born in Pergamum in *c.* 130 CE, a city famous at the time for its many physicians. After studying in Alexandria he returned to Pergamum to become physician to the College of Gladiators (clearly bringing him much work in surgery and dietetics). In his early thirties he went to Rome, where he gained fame for his public lectures. Following further travel in the Middle East he returned to become personal physician to the emperor. He was a prolific publisher of books on all aspects of medicine.

Medical knowledge in medieval times built extensively on the foundations laid by the ancient Greeks. The most highly prized, and among the first to be translated into Arabic, were several of Galen's medical books. Galen believed that the human body's health depended on a balance between different types of fluids called humours, which circulated through the body, each of which if out of balance would cause illness and a change of temperament. They were (and here I am simplifying the description): yellow bile, which in excess would make the patient bilious or bad-tempered and nauseous; blood, too much of which would make the patient sanguine and flushed; black bile, which in excess would make the patient lethargic and melancholic; and phlegm, which could make the patient 'phlegmatic' or apathetic and emotionally detached. Galen argued that illnesses occur when there is an excess of one of the humours and the cure lies in somehow draining some of it from the body. To do this he recommended techniques like cutting to induce bleeding or the use of emetics to induce vomiting.

Not all of Galen's ideas were so absurd, however. His account of medical anatomy was based on what he learnt from the dissection of monkeys, as human dissection was not permitted, but his work remained unsurpassed in its detail until Andreas Vesalius published his famous illustrated book on human anatomy *De humani corporis fabrica* in 1543. Galen's account of the activities of the heart, arteries and veins endured for more than a thousand years, until Ibn al-Nafīs described the process of pulmonary transit in the thirteenth century and, much later, William Harvey established in the seventeenth century that the blood circulates with the heart acting as a pump. Galen also developed many nerve-ligation experiments that supported Plato's idea that the brain is the command centre of the body controlling all the muscles (rather than the heart, as had been thought by Aristotle). Even as late as the nineteenth century, medical students would still refer to some of Galen's ideas; such was his enduring influence on medicine.

But the physicians of the Islamic Empire were acutely aware that Greek medicine was only one source of medical knowledge. For a start, Islam places a premium on cleanliness and personal hygiene, and it is a requirement of every Muslim to carry out the *wudhū'* (the ritual washing of hands, feet and face before prayer). At a time when the Christian West was obsessed with magic, viewing illness either as divine punishment for sins or, worse, as possession by evil spirits, medics in the Muslim world were following the Greek tradition of trying to understand disease and illness scientifically and finding ways to treat them rationally. What is more, maintaining a healthy body and caring for the sick was now seen as a religious duty. Of course, one has to be careful not to make too strong a contrast between thinking in the East and West, for notions involving magic and demons also existed in the Islamic world.

Into this world came al-Rāzi. We encountered him earlier as a chemist, the man who would take the classification of chemicals further than anyone before him had done, thereby improving on the Greek theory of the four elements by classifying substances according to their chemical properties deduced from laboratory-based experimentation. Like al-Kindi a generation earlier, al-Rāzi was a polymath who also excelled as a philosopher and a musician. But his achievements in a wide range of disciplines pale into insignificance when held up alongside his work in medicine. Here, his fame and impact are as great as those of Galen, and his accomplishments even greater than those of the most famous scholar of Islam, Ibn Sīna, a century later.

Al-Rāzi was born in Rayy in *c.* 854. Today very little remains of this ancient city and the modern Rayy is no more than a densely populated suburb of the vast metropolis of modern Tehran. In his youth, al-Rāzi studied all the subjects one might expect a bright young man to be grounded in at that time, including literature, philosophy, mathematics, astronomy and music. He wrote on a wide range of these subjects, but most of these writings have unfortunately been lost. Luckily, however, many of his most important medical texts have survived, in both Arabic and Latin, and were used extensively alongside those of Galen across Europe in the Middle Ages.

He was an obsessive scholar who devoured all the books he could lay his hands on. Tragically, he slowly went blind later in life, due, according to some accounts, to cataracts; others claim that it was from the long-term damage caused by fumes from the toxic chemicals he worked with early in life as a chemist. However, a quite different reason for his blindness reaches us from the account that appears in Ibn al-Nadīm's *Fihrist*. It is from an unnamed source, who describes his regular visits to al-Rāzi in Rayy: 'I never went in to him without finding him reading or transcribing, whether to make a rough draft or a revised text. He had wet eyes because of all the beans he would always eat, and he became blind due to this at the end of his life.'[3]

It is said that al-Rāzi took up the study of medicine after his first visit to Baghdad, when he was around 30 years old. While there, he studied under the well-known physician Ali ibn Sahl (a Jewish convert to Islam, whose father produced the first Arabic translation of the *Almagest*). Al-Rāzi soon surpassed all his teachers and his reputation grew as the most respected medic in the world. He would combine his vast knowledge of Galenic texts, Hippocratic wisdom and ethical values with an empathic and compassionate nature as a skilled clinician and teacher.

In the Islamic world, al-Rāzi's name will always be associated with some of the earliest hospitals. In Abbāsid times, these were not known by their current Arabic name of *mustashfa*, but rather by the Persian word *bīmāristān* (from Pahlavi *vīmār* or *vemār*, meaning 'sick' and *-stan*, the suffix for 'place'). These institutions were initially modelled on Nestorian Christian establishments, particularly when it came to their administration and reliance on charitable funding. Indeed, one finds that most physicians of ninth- and tenth-century Baghdad were Christian or Jewish.

Charitable endowments within Islamic law, called *waqf*, began to be set up around this time and some of the funds from these trusts went into building hospitals.[4] These multiplied throughout the empire with large cities such as Cairo and Córdoba also boasting dozens of hospitals.

Soon after the turn of the tenth century, al-Rāzi was called upon by the Caliph al-Muktafi to help in selecting the site of a new hospital. He had pieces of fresh meat hung up in various districts of Baghdad. A few days later, he checked the pieces, and he selected the area where the least rotten one was found, stating that the 'air' was cleaner and healthier there. Following the death of the caliph in 907, al-Rāzi returned to his home town of Rayy and took charge of the hospital there.

Later, under the Caliph al-Muqtadir (r. 908–32) several more new hospitals were built in Baghdad.[5] The largest of these, al-Bīmāristān al-Muqtadirī, was built by the vizier Ali ibn Īsa in a part of Baghdad known as *Sūq Yehya* on the east bank of the Tigris. Al-Rāzi, still head of the hospital in Rayy at this time, was recruited again to take over as director of this new establishment.

The renowned Arab traveller Ibn Jubayr describes visiting Baghdad and the then two-hundred-year-old al-Muqtadirī hospital:

> This great establishment is a beautiful structure stretching along the banks of the Tigris. Its physicians make their rounds every Monday and Thursday to examine patients and prescribe for their needs. At the physicians' disposal are attendants who fill drug prescriptions and prepare food. The hospital is split up into various wards, each containing a number of rooms, giving the impression that the place is as a royal palace in which every convenience is provided.[6]

Among the features in medieval Muslim hospitals that distinguished them from their contemporaries elsewhere were their higher standards of medical ethics. Physicians there treated patients of all religions or ethnicities. They were expected to have obligations towards their patients, regardless of their wealth or background. These ethical standards were first laid down in the ninth century by Ishāq bin Ali al-Rahawi, who wrote *The Conduct of a Physician* (*Adab al-Tabīb*), the earliest known Arabic treatise dedicated to medical ethics.

Much of the medical work in Baghdad during the time of al-Rāzi was overseen by Sinān ibn Thābit, the son of the great mathematician and translator Thābit ibn Qurra. Sinan was the equivalent of chief physician and was famously ordered by the Caliph al-Muqtadir to ensure that all physicians sat an examination in order to qualify to practise. They even adopted and adapted to Islamic thought the famous Hippocratic oath.

Al-Rāzi introduced many practical and progressive medical and psychological ideas. He ran the psychiatric ward in the Baghdad hospital at a time when, in the Christian world, the mentally ill were regarded as being possessed by the devil. In fact, he is acknowledged as the father of the fields of psychology and psychotherapy. He also attacked those without medical training who roamed the cities and countryside selling their nostrums and 'cures', and criticized them in his book *Why People Prefer Quacks and Charlatans to Skilled Physicians*, showing his frustration with the way they achieved the fame and fortune that was often denied those with proper medical training. And he wrote of the pity he felt towards those good physicians whose patients would not follow their advice on diet or treatment but then blamed them when they did not recover.

He also made a distinction between curable and incurable diseases, and commented that in the case of advanced cases of cancer and leprosy the physician should not be blamed when he could not cure them. He warned that even highly skilled physicians did not have all the answers, and wrote the aptly titled monograph *Even the Most Skilful Physicians Cannot Heal All Diseases*.

To maximize their chances of successful diagnosis, he advised all medical practitioners to keep up to date with the latest knowledge by constantly studying medical texts and exposing themselves to new information. On medical ethics and medical training, he borrowed much from the writing of both Hippocrates and Galen, which influenced greatly the medical training manuals he wrote.

As Galen had done before him, and as Ibn Sīna would do a century later, al-Rāzi synthesized all known medicine by sorting and categorizing it into different areas, from eye diseases to gastro-intestinal complaints, from dietary advice to case studies. So comprehensive were his working files that they were assembled posthumously into one of the greatest medical texts ever written, *al-Kitab al-Hāwi*. It is still the largest Arabic medical textbook, filling twenty-three volumes in a modern printing. It now survives only in Latin, as *Liber continens*, but it became one of the most highly respected and frequently used medical textbooks in Europe for several centuries. In fact, it was one of just nine texts that composed the entire library of the medical faculty of the University of Paris in 1395. It is to this book that the origins of disciplines like gynaecology, obstetrics and ophthalmic surgery can be traced. His *magnum opus*, the *Great Medical Compendium* (*Kitab al-Jāmi' al-Kabīr*), is often confused with the posthumously published corpus of his notes. What is probably his best-known text, a monograph on smallpox and measles called *Kitab al-Judari wal-Hasba*, which also survives in Latin, is the oldest reliable account of these two illnesses. It is widely regarded as the ultimate masterpiece of Muslim medicine.

It is immediately obvious from reading the *Liber continens* that this is much more than a medical textbook. Scattered throughout is evidence that al-Rāzi was a practising clinician with many personal experiences and case notes. Often, these notes were meant to be studied alongside the Greek treatises on those subjects. For instance, Hippocrates had written in his *Epidemics* on tuberculosis ('pthisis' or 'consumption') as a widespread and almost always fatal disease involving a fever and the coughing up of blood. Al-Rāzi supplements Hippocrates' notes with a case study on the possible dangers of trying to suppress the coughing with medicine:

> A consumptive [i.e. suffering from tuberculosis] elder came to us. He had been repeatedly coughing up much blood over a long period of time. Then it became much more distressing for him, so he took hazelnut and water, which stopped the cough. He felt relief each time he took this, and [apparently] recovered completely. Then he died . . . Consequently, one should avoid remedies that suppress expectoration, except in cases where the matter flows down from the head.[7]

One of the most fascinating insights into al-Rāzi's work as a practising clinician was recounted to me by a friend of mine, Peter Pormann, a leading expert on the history of medicine. He tells of al-Rāzi carrying out the earliest known example of a clinical trial employing a control group.[8] Al-Rāzi begins by selecting two sets of patients, all of whom are showing early symptoms of meningitis: a dull pain in the neck and head lasting for several days, insomnia, exhaustion and an aversion to bright light. He then treats one group with bloodletting, but not the second. He writes that 'by doing this, I wished to reach a conclusion [on the effectiveness of bloodletting]; and indeed all those of the second group contracted meningitis.'[9] Bloodletting, one of the oldest medical practices in the world, dating back to the ancient Egyptians, Babylonians and Greeks, is today known to be harmful to patients and, in the case of meningitis, certainly has no proven benefits. But, in defence of al-Rāzi, we should remember that both Galen and Hippocrates used it, and that physicians would continue to do so until the late nineteenth century. Indeed, the first American President, George Washington, died after being drained of five pints of blood from excessive bloodletting as a treatment for pneumonia. And bloodletting is still used as part of many holistic therapies around the world today, including some in the Islamic world, where it is part of the procedure of 'cupping', or *hijamah*; this despite all the advances in modern medicine that demonstrate its utter ineffectiveness.

The point of this story is to demonstrate the notion of a control group in a trial, and it emphasizes al-Rāzi's commitment to empirical medical science. He even took on the great Galen in his excellent *al-Shukūk ala Jālīnūs (Doubts About Galen)*, in which he criticizes the Greek notion of the four humours. Unfortunately, his work was not followed up and the theory of the humours was later brought back into the medical mainstream by Ibn Sīna. It is disappointing to note that these notions are still adhered to by millions of educated secular Westerners as part of alternative medicine. If only al-Rāzi were around today; with the medical knowledge we have, he would be dumbfounded by the prevalence of such ideas, given his passionate condemnation of medical quackery and its dangers. Just because such practices and beliefs go back thousands of years to ancient Greece, or India, or China, does not make them right. Al-Rāzi knew this and had the courage to say so when he discovered that a particular practice did not work. For instance, in his notes he records that he does not agree with Galen's descriptions of the course of a fever. He rejects the idea, central to the Greek theory of humours, that the body's temperature is raised or lowered when the patient drinks warm or cold liquids; al-Rāzi realized that a warm drink may raise the temperature of the body higher than the temperature of the liquid itself, suggesting that this rise must be triggering a more complicated physiological response in the patient than the simple transfer of warmth. Nevertheless, al-Rāzi was often reluctant to criticize Galen, since other physicians would often accuse him of arrogance for daring to doubt the great man.

In another case study, we get a glimpse of the sort of natural remedies that were around during the time of al-Rāzi. In his treatise on smallpox and measles he is particularly concerned with protecting the eye, for corneal damage from smallpox was a major cause of blindness in the Middle East up until relatively modern times:

As soon as the symptoms of smallpox appear, drop rose water into the eyes from time to time, and wash the face with cold water. For if the disease be favourable and the pustules few in number, you find that this mode of treatment prevents their breaking out in the eyes. But when you see the ebullition is vehement and the pustules numerous in the beginning of the eruption, with itching of the eyelids and redness of the whites of the eyes, in this case pustules will certainly break out there unless very strong measures are adopted; and therefore you should immediately drop into the eyes several times in the day rose water in which sumach [a red lemony spice] has been macerated ... Drop into the eyes some of the juice of the pulp of the acid pomegranate, first chewed, or squeezed in a cloth. Then cleanse the eyelids with the col-lyrium [eye wash] composed of the red horn poppy, the juice of unripe grapes, rusot, aloa and acacia, of each one part, and a tenth part of saffron; and if you also drop some of this collyrium into the eyes, it will be useful at this time.[10]

Returning briefly to his book on alchemy, *The Book of Secrets* (*Kitab al-Asrār*), we see little trace of alchemical mysticism and sym-bolism, despite the evocative title.[11] For al-Rāzi, despite living during the times he did, was not impressed by anything that could not be proven experimentally and have its validity tested. Like the two other great Muslim scientists to follow him in the next century, Ibn al-Haytham and al-Bīrūni, he was meticulous about recording details of his apparatus, methods, experimental conditions and the results of his careful measurements. This was not a text on alchemical magic but rather a real chemical laboratory manual.

On philosophy, al-Rāzi was probably the most free-thinking scholar in the whole of Islam. He believed – as did the Greeks – that a competent physician should also be a philosopher, well versed in the fundamental questions regarding existence. He disagreed with al-Kindi, for example, on the issue of infinity. For him, God did not create the universe from nothing but arranged it out of existing principles. He argued that time exists as absolute and infinite. It does not need motion (and thus matter in space) in order to exist. This is very close to the view of the nature of time reached by Newton (itself overthrown by Einstein).

Finally, what many find most surprising about al-Rāzi is his atti-tude towards religion. Here is a famous quotation from him:

If the people of religion are asked about proof for the soundness of their religion, they flare up, get angry and spill the blood of whoever confronts them with this question. They forbid rational speculation, and strive to kill their adversaries. This is why truth became thoroughly silenced and concealed.[12]

He was particularly harsh in his criticism of all prophetically revealed religions. He says: 'How can anyone think philosophically while committed to those old wives' tales, founded on contradictions, obdurate ignorance, and dogmatism?'[13] This was clearly a dangerous and radical view for someone to adopt at that time and al-Rāzi was branded as a heretic. And yet he was such an important figure in science that any anti-religious views he held are to some extent forgiven. Today, Iran still celebrates 'Rāzi Day' (or 'Pharmacy Day') every year on 27 August.

Before we leave al-Rāzi, here is one final quotation from the man himself that appears in Ibn al-Nadīm's *Fihrist*:

A man from China came to seek me and dwelt with me for about a year. In five months of this time he learned Arabic, both spoken and written, becoming proficient in style, as well as expert and rapid in reading. When he desired to return to his country, he said to me a month in advance, 'I am about to set forth and wish that you would dictate to me the sixteen books of Galen, so that I can write them down.' I said, 'Your time is short and the length of your stay is sufficient for you to copy only a small part of it.' Then the young man said, 'I ask you to devote yourself to me for the length of my stay and to dictate to me as fast as you can. I will keep up with you in writing.'[14]

Ibn al-Nadīm does not record whether al-Rāzi agreed to this.

So far, I may have given the impression that the seat of power of the caliphate in Baghdad is where all the action took place and I have said little about what was going on in other parts of the Islamic world. By the time of al-Rāzi, the Abbāsid dynasty was already weakened and beginning to fragment – partly, one should say, owing to the practical difficulties of governing such a vast empire.

As early as the reign of al-Ma'mūn, various Persian factions had begun to flex their military muscle and to exercise independent authority in the East. A number of autonomous dynasties, such as the Samanids and Saffarids, soon gained power over much of Persia.

These dynasties took on the characteristics of de facto states, with hereditary sultans and princes, armies and revenues. All nominally recognized the sovereignty of the caliphate in Baghdad but knew that it no longer held real power within their borders. By the mid-tenth century, even the pretence of Baghdad's autonomy had disappeared with the rise of the Buyid and Ghaznavid empires. These were then followed by the Turkish Seljuks, marking the end of Abbāsid political dominion over the region.

Al-Rāzi's Baghdad was a vast city and the centre of the civilized world. But by the tenth century, and as a hub of scientific scholarship, it already had rivals elsewhere within the empire. Three cities in particular, separated by thousands of miles, had grown to be centres of scientific activity and flourishing scholarship, with vast libraries, generous patronage and famous sons. They were Bukhara, capital of the Samanid dynasty in Central Asia, the new city of Cairo, where a second House of Wisdom would be established, and, to the far west of the empire in Muslim Spain, Córdoba, for a while the most glorious city in Europe.

So it is now that we leave Baghdad to explore the riches and scientific legacy elsewhere. At the end of the tenth and the beginning of the eleventh centuries we see the zenith (another Arabic word by the way[15]) of scientific achievement. For this is the age of three of the greatest minds in history, probably the only three men portrayed here worthy of the greatness reserved for such as Aristotle, Leonardo da Vinci, Newton and Einstein.

I I

The Physicist

The seeker after truth is not one who studies the writings of the ancients and, following his natural disposition, puts his trust in them, but rather the one who suspects his faith in them and questions what he gathers from them, the one who submits to argument and demonstration and not the sayings of human beings whose nature is fraught with all kinds of imperfection and deficiency. Thus the duty of the man who investigates the writings of scientists, if learning the truth is his goal, is to make himself an enemy of all that he reads, and, applying his mind to the core and margins of its content, attack it from every side. He should also suspect himself as he performs his critical examination of it, so that he may avoid falling into either prejudice or leniency.

Ibn al-Haytham

By the end of the tenth century the translation movement was coming to an end, the Abbāsid Empire was crumbling, less-enlightened caliphs were cracking down on freedom of speech and rationalist enquiry, and the great names associated with the House of Wisdom were already a distant memory. But to infer from this that the golden age of Arabic science was on the wane would be utterly wrong, for the best was yet to come. Despite appearances, this was a period of competitive patronage of the sciences among dynastic rulers across the Islamic world, with enticements offered from many of the courts around the Middle East and Central Asia to attract the very best scholars.

It was during the second half of the tenth century that we see the three most outstanding thinkers in the history of Islam arriving on the scene. The first of these was a man after my own heart: a physicist; in fact, the greatest physicist since Archimedes and the like of whom would not be seen until Isaac Newton seven hundred years later. And acknowledging someone as being the greatest physicist in a span of nearly two thousand years is not done lightly.[1]

The Arab polymath Abū Ali al-Hassan ibn al-Haytham was born in Basra in southern Iraq in *c*. 965. He is often said to be Egyptian, because he spent his later, most productive years there. In fact, I would no more think of him as Egyptian than I would think of Einstein as an American rather than a German. Even more tenuously, it has been argued that he was a Persian rather than an Arab, on the basis that his city of birth, Basra, was under the rule of the Persian Buyid dynasty at the time. Al-Haytham was his grandfather's name, so he is in fact ibn ibn al-Haytham. His Latinized name, Alhazen (or Alhacen) comes from his first name, al-Hassan, but he is known nowadays simply as Ibn al-Haytham.[2]

What I find disappointing – as is often the case with this subject – are the inaccuracies and errors one reads about Ibn al-Haytham's life and achievements. For instance, it is widely stated that he invented the pinhole camera to explain the workings of the eye, and that he beat the Europeans to the law of refraction by six hundred years. Both of these claims are wrong, and my desire to correct these mistakes is not an issue of pedantry but because such trivialities detract from his real legacy, as we shall see.

Ibn al-Haytham was a wonderful experimental scientist and a very colourful character about whom we have a considerable amount of evidence, not all of it reliable, however. Many details about his life have been lost over the years, but thanks to his fame and status there is no shortage of commentaries on his life, some in direct contradiction with each other.

As a young man, he received an excellent education, which suggests that his family were financially secure and moved in the right political and social circles. He showed early promise as a mathematical and scientific prodigy and built up a scientific reputation that quickly spread far and wide. He was given a government post in Basra but, according to an account by a thirteenth-century scholar in Cairo by the name of Qaysar al-Hanafi, he became quickly bored and frustrated by his administrative duties, which took him away from his intellectual pursuits and research. It is unclear what happened at this point but it is said that he was dismissed from his post because of mental illness. What cannot be verified is whether this illness was genuine or whether Ibn al-Haytham deliberately feigned madness to get himself out of an awkward situation – an extreme measure to take for someone dissatisfied with his job.

Around the beginning of the new millennium he wrote an interesting treatise on an enormously ambitious potential civil engineering project. Ibn al-Haytham knew of the importance of the Nile for the prosperity of the people of Egypt and claimed that he could build a dam across the great river that would control its flow and alleviate the twin problems of droughts and floods. He wrote that the Nile's autumn floodwaters could be held by a system of dikes and canals, preserving its waters in reservoirs until the summer drought, when they were needed. News of this work soon reached the ambitious young ruler of Egypt, the Fātimid Caliph al-Hākim.

The Fātimids were a Shi'a dynasty who claimed to be directly descended from the Prophet Muhammad through his daughter Fātima and her husband, Imam Ali. The Fātimids came to power in 909 and ruled over an expanding empire stretching across North Africa. They built their new capital, Cairo, in 969, which, like Baghdad two centuries earlier, rapidly grew in size and importance and would eventually rival Baghdad as a centre of scholarship. The Fātimids regarded themselves as being in direct opposition to the Abbāsids to the east and referred to their own rulers as imams or caliphs. Al-Hākim bi'amr Illāh (985–1021) was the most famous of these. He was known as the Mad Caliph – an unfair title for someone who was really no madder than many other rulers in the medieval world.

While it is true that al-Hākim was regarded as eccentric and somewhat whimsical in his policies – he once famously ordered the killing of all the dogs in Cairo because their barking annoyed him – he also showed his compassionate side when, during a famine, he made a number of sensible laws to ensure the distribution of food to his people.

He had become caliph in 996 at the tender age of 11 and assumed full power at 14. In his early years of rule, there are accounts of his religious persecution of Sunni Muslims, Christians and Jews. But these were not the wilful and randomly violent actions of a mad tyrant but the actions of a ruler desperately trying to hold his struggling empire together. And certainly by the middle of the first decade of the eleventh century he had stabilized his borders and we see in his actions a more tolerant approach. He was most famously a great patron of science and built a library to rival that of Baghdad. It became known as *Dar al-Hikma*, which also translates as the House of Wisdom, but the word *dar* here refers to a larger, grander residence than a mere *bayt*, implying that he was aiming at something not only to rival the Baghdad *Bayt al-Hikma*, but to exceed it in glory.[3] Like al-Ma'mūn in Baghdad, he was keen to attract the big names from around the empire to his new House of Wisdom, the most famous of whom was the great astronomer Ibn Yūnus.

It is not clear whether al-Hākim, impressed with Ibn al-Haytham's reputation as a mathematician, headhunted him, or whether Ibn al-Haytham himself, seeing a chance to move to a prosperous and exciting city, with a brand-new library and generous patron, wrote to the caliph with his idea for the dam. In any case, the Fātimid caliph came to be aware of Ibn al-Haytham's proposal and invited him to Cairo around 1010. Eager to begin, Ibn al-Haytham travelled south to near the location of the modern-day Aswan dam. But he quickly realized that the sheer size of the engineering undertaking was beyond him. While this story, and what happened next, is by no means established, it has become part of Arab folklore. According to the most widely accepted account, as soon as Ibn al-Haytham realized he had bitten off more than he could chew he again feigned madness. For this was the only way he knew to escape the wrath of the caliph. Instead, the caliph consigned him to a mental asylum and there he remained until 1021 when the caliph died. Or, more correctly, when he mysteriously vanished one night while taking a walk. In any case, Ibn al-Haytham was released and he took up lodging in a small apartment near the al-Azhar Mosque in the centre of Cairo.

In common with all scholars throughout history, Ibn al-Haytham badly needed the time and isolation to focus on writing his treatises. His many years in the asylum certainly granted him the seclusion to think and to write. But after his release he began to produce work at a prolific rate. He earned his living through tuition and as a scribe but at the same time worked feverishly on his experiments in optics. It is not clear how much of his greatest work, the *Book of Optics* (*Kitab al-Manāthir*), he had already written by then but the complete text comes to us in seven volumes and has been hugely influential in the history of the field. It would be no exaggeration to say that it ranks alongside Newton's *Principia Mathematica* as one of the most important books in the history of physics.

To most people in the West, and indeed in the Muslim world, Isaac Newton is the undisputed father of modern optics; at least, that is what we are told at school, where our textbooks abound with his famous experiments with lenses and prisms, his study of the nature of light and its reflection, refraction and decomposition into the colours of the rainbow. Even historians of science who acknowledge that work on optics predates Newton often do not go back any earlier than other notables from the European scientific revolution of the seventeenth century such as René Descartes, Willebrord Snell and Johannes Kepler. But studies of the properties of light, particularly catoptrics (reflection of light by mirrors) and dioptrics (refraction of light through lenses) go back all the way to the Greeks.

An interest in optics began in antiquity, with the Babylonians, Egyptians and Assyrians all making use of polished quartz to make rudimentary lenses. The basic principles of geometric optics were laid down by Plato and Euclid and included ideas such as the propagation of light in straight lines and the simple laws of reflection from plane mirrors, while the earliest serious contribution to the field in the Islamic world came from al-Kindi.

Far less well known than these men was a scholar who flourished in Baghdad in the late tenth century, a few years before Ibn al-Haytham, who would advance the subject of optics in a way that has until recently been almost completely ignored. His name was Ibn Sahl and he wrote a treatise around 984 called *On the Burning Instruments* (by which is meant lenses and mirrors that can be used to focus sunlight to create a hot spot). Although such burning methods had been known in antiquity – there is a story that Archimedes used concave bronze mirrors to focus sunlight on Roman warships and set them on fire –

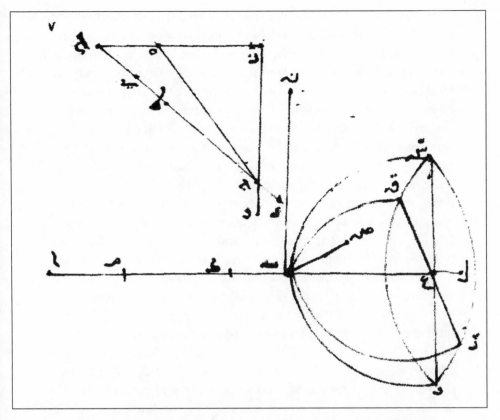

Ibn Sahl's diagram showing the law of refraction of light (through a plano-convex lens) for the very first time. Of interest are the two embedded right-angled triangles in the top left of the diagram. He writes his law in terms of ratios of sides of the two triangles made up from the original path of a light beam and its refracted path as it passes through the lens.

the work of Ibn Sahl is regarded as the first serious mathematical study of lenses for focusing light.[4] The manuscript's pages were recently discovered in two different locations, one part in Damascus and the other in Tehran. The historian Roshdi Rashed was able to fit the two pieces together and reconstruct the full original text, earning himself worldwide acclaim in the early 1990s. The most incredible insight in this work is something that everyone learns about at school: what we call Snell's law of refraction.

To appreciate what Ibn Sahl did, we must again return to the Greeks and the writings of Ptolemy, who had described the refraction of light in his *Optics*. He presented tables of angles of incidence and refraction from different materials, and is credited with proposing an approximate version of the law of refraction by suggesting that the ratio of the angles made by a beam of light on either side of a surface boundary, as it travels between two transparent media, is a constant. We know today that the constancy of this ratio of angles only holds when the rays of light travel between the two media at almost right angles to their surface boundary. This is because what is really constant is not the ratio of the angles themselves but that of their trigonometric sines, and this correct ratio only approximates to that of the angles when they are small: when the rays enter almost vertically. This correct trigonometric ratio was stated by Snell and confirmed independently by Descartes. It is these two men who are therefore usually credited with the law of refraction. However, the now incontrovertible fact is that Ibn Sahl arrived at the same result 650 years earlier. He correctly stated the law geometrically, as the ratio of the sides of triangles of light rays, which is exactly equivalent to the ratio of the sines.[5] Thus, while Europeans have argued over whether it should be referred to as Snell's law or Descartes' law, there is no doubt that the real credit should go to Ibn Sahl. And while much of the work on refraction that was used by the Europeans in the seventeenth century came from Ibn al-Haytham's *Optics*, it is to Ibn Sahl that equal debt is owed.

Despite this, Ibn Sahl was not a scientist in the way that Ibn al-Haytham was. Unlike Ibn al-Haytham, he did not carry out experiments or attempt to understand the physical cause of refraction as a slowing down of light when it enters a denser medium. Ibn Sahl was only interested in understanding enough to construct lenses for the purpose of burning. Nevertheless, his work was hugely influential on Ibn al-Haytham, as were the Arabic translations of a number of Greek texts.

The revolution brought about by Ibn al-Haytham's *Book of Optics* can be understood at many levels. First and foremost, it was a real science textbook, with detailed descriptions of experiments, including the apparatus and the way it was set up, the measurements taken and the results. These were then used to justify his theories, which he developed using mathematical (geometrical) models. The work can be roughly divided into two parts: Books I, II and III are devoted to the theory of vision and the associated physiology of the eye and the psychology of perception, while Books IV to VII cover traditional physical optics. It became a far more important text than Ptolemy's *Optics* and certainly the most influential work in the field until Kepler.

The first Latin translation of Ibn al-Haytham's *Book of Optics* was made during the late twelfth or early thirteenth century as *De aspectibus*.[6] In England, it was to have a great influence on Roger Bacon (*c.* 1214–*c.* 1292), who wrote a summary of it, as well as on his Polish contemporary Witelo (b. *c.* 1230), and it was soon being widely cited across Europe – and would continue to be for several hundred years, far more so than any of the books on optics by Greeks like Euclid, Aristotle and Ptolemy.[7] Equally importantly, later Islamic scholars would make great use of his work and extend it further, such as the Persians al-Shirāzi and al-Fārisi in the thirteenth century, the latter using it for the very first correct mathematical explanation of the rainbow (at the same time as, but independently of, the German Theodoric of Freiberg).

The only Latin printed edition of the *Book of Optics* was published by Friedrich Risner in 1572 under the name *Opticae Thesaurus*, which contained, along with Ibn al-Haytham's *Optics*, Witelo's *Perspectiva* and the work of a lesser-known scholar by the name of Ibn Mu'ādh, which had been translated into Latin even before any of Ibn al-Haytham's work, as *Liber de crepusculis*.[8] This short treatise on the nature of dawn and twilight is fascinating, and for years it was wrongly attributed to Ibn al-Haytham.

When it comes to vision, you might have thought that the way we see things is straightforward. I do not mean by this how the light entering our eyes forms an image on the retina, which is then sent as an electric signal through the optic nerve to the brain to interpret. I mean the far more basic idea that we see things because light from them enters our eyes. Surely this is obvious and always has been. It is remarkable therefore that, until Ibn al-Haytham, scholars' understanding of how vision works was a confused mess. The Greeks had several theories of vision. Euclid and Ptolemy believed in what is called the emission theory, in which we see objects because rays of light are emitted from our eyes to illuminate them; the rays of light leave the eye in straight lines emanating like a cone. An opposing, more sensible view was held by Aristotle, who argued for an intromission theory of vision whereby light enters our eyes from the object we are looking at. However, he did not follow Euclid's geometrical model of rays of light simply reversed in direction; for Aristotle, the space itself between the object and the eye lights up so that the image of the object enters the eye *instantaneously*.

This is how Euclid would have defended his emission theory: we have difficulty seeing a small object like a needle even if it is in front of our eyes; we would have to look directly at it. This experience would be hard to understand if the needle is sending rays to the eye all the time; we should be able to see it if our eyes are open regardless of where we 'look'. The only sensible solution, he claimed, is that the eye must be actively sending rays at the needle in order to see, rather than just waiting passively for the needle to send its rays.[9]

To confuse matters further, Plato and Galen had a combined emission/intromission theory, whereby the eye sends out rays of light to the object being looked at and this then reflects the light back into the eye. This idea was favoured by Islamic scholars such as al-Kindi and Hunayn ibn Ishāq. Ibn al-Haytham changed all this and resolved an issue that so many great minds could not sort out. He begins his *Book of Optics* thus: 'We find that when the eye looks into exceedingly bright lights, it suffers greatly because of them and is injured. For when an observer looks at the body of the sun, he cannot see it well, since his eye suffers pain because of the light.'[10] This implies that it must be the sun's action on the eye that inflicts the injury rather than anything to do with the eye emitting rays. He also uses arguments associated with the phenomenon of afterimage (when we look for a long time at a bright object then look away). He also reiterates an argument of Aristotle's as to the ludicrous notion that we see the stars in the night sky by sending rays out to reach them. Ibn al-Haytham concludes that 'all these things indicate that light produces some effect in the eye'.[11]

He next uses faultless logic to show the absurdity of the emission theory. He argues that if we see because rays are emitted from the eye onto an object, then either the object sends back some sort of signal to the eye or it does not. If it does not, then how can the eye perceive what its rays have fallen on? Therefore there must be light coming back to the eye and this is how we see. But if so, what use is there for the original rays emitted by the eye? The light could come directly from the object if it is luminous, or be reflected from it if it is not. Thus, the rays from the eye are an unnecessary complication and should be dropped. In this way, he used a form of Occam's Razor, the dictum that a phenomenon should be explained using as few assumptions as necessary, attributed to the fourteenth-century English philosopher William of Occam.

But Ibn al-Haytham went further than philosophical arguments, for he did something quite astounding. He used Euclid's geometrical model of the emission theory and applied it to the intromission theory. Now, it is rays emanating from the object that spread out radially in straight lines. In this way, he 'mathematized' his theory of vision.

Interestingly, what he did not do, despite giving the first optical description of the camera obscura,[12] was to connect this to the way the eye works (by projecting an inverted image of the objects we see onto the retina). Thus, while making huge advances on everything that had come before, even to the extent of understanding that vision works via refraction of light through the eye's lens, when it came to how the rays entered the eye, he did not make that final step of explaining how the real image of the object being perceived forms on the retina. Instead, he switched from physics to psychology as soon as the light entered the eye in order to explain how we 'perceive'. This was partly due to the incomplete understanding of the workings of the eye that he had learnt from Galen. It would not be until the turn of the seventeenth century that Kepler would provide the correct explanation by describing the eye as like a camera.

A famous optical effect that Ibn al-Haytham helped clarify is known today as the moon illusion. But until he explained it, no one had realized it was an illusion at all. It is the phenomenon in which the moon appears larger near the horizon than it does when higher up in the sky – and the same occurs with the sun and the star constellations. The earliest recorded mention of the moon illusion goes back to the seventh century BCE and a clay tablet found in the Assyrian King Ashurbanipal's great library of Nineveh. A popular belief among the ancient Greeks, and described by Ptolemy, held that the moon appears larger near the horizon due to a real magnification effect caused by refraction of light by the earth's atmosphere. But on the contrary, we now know that atmospheric refraction actually causes the moon to appear about 1.5 per cent smaller when it is near the horizon than when it is high in the sky. In fact, if we ignore this small effect, it can be shown by direct measurement that the angle the full moon subtends at an observer's eye remains constant as it rises or sinks in the sky. Photographs of the moon at different elevations also show that its size remains the same. A simple way of demonstrating that the effect is an illusion is to hold up a small coin at arm's length with one eye closed, positioning it next to the moon when it is at different positions in the sky, revealing that there is no change in size.

Ibn al-Haytham was the first person to explain this phenomenon as a psychological rather than a physical effect. The first three volumes of his *Book of Optics* contain ideas on the psychology of perception, and it is here that he dismisses the Greeks' idea that the moon appears larger when it is low in the sky because of the refraction of its light through the atmosphere. He shows that this is due to the subjective nature of perspective and is nothing more than an optical illusion. When the moon is high in the sky, there is no other reference body nearby to compare its size to and therefore no way of mentally determining how far away it is. But when it is just above the horizon, it appears closer to us and so we imagine it to be larger. This explanation became accepted throughout Europe after Ibn al-Haytham's translated work, *De aspectibus*, was studied by Roger Bacon and Witelo in the thirteenth century.

After dealing with the nature of vision, Ibn al-Haytham went on to tackle and extend the geometrical optics of Ptolemy and Ibn Sahl – although he never stated the law of refraction in its correct form as Ibn Sahl did, but rather followed the approximate version of Ptolemy. The difference between the two approaches can best be described in the following way. It is the difference between measuring the distance between two points on the perimeter of a circle as being the length of the arc (Ptolemy and Ibn al-Haytham: wrong) and the length of the straight-line chord between them (Ibn Sahl: correct). It is only when the points are close together that the two versions roughly agree, for this is when there is so little curvature that the arc approximates to a straight line.

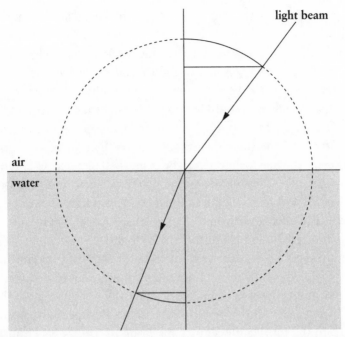

The difference between the Greeks' version of the law of refraction and the correct one described by Ibn Sahl. If you consider a beam of light entering water from above, its path will be bent towards the vertical once it enters the water. According to Ptolemy, it is the ratio of the lengths of the two arcs of the circle (shown as solid curves) that is constant. Ibn Sahl corrected this by stating that it is in fact the ratio of the two straight-line chords just inside the arcs that is constant. This is today described as the ratio of trigonometric sines of the angles made by the path of the light beam in the air and the water.

Where Ibn al-Haytham did go further than Ibn Sahl was in trying to understand the underlying physics of refraction by making use of the idea of resolving vectors describing separately the vertical and horizontal components of velocities, and he understood the notion of light travelling at different speeds in different media. Like Ibn Sahl, he carried out all his work geometrically rather than algebraically, and did not use trigonometric relations, even though others before him, such as the Syrian astronomer al-Battāni, had written extensively on trigonometry. On the whole, although Ibn al-Haytham added much to the science of refraction which he inherited from the Greeks, it is probably fair to say that his contribution to this field was more pre-servative than creative.[13]

One of the new ideas he did introduce was in the study of atmos-pheric refraction (the bending of light received on the surface of the earth from celestial bodies). In common with other contemporaries of his, such as Ibn Sīna, Ibn al-Haytham believed that the speed of light was finite. Where they differed was in their notions about the under-lying nature of light. Ibn al-Haytham believed light to be a continuous ray, whereas Ibn Sīna believed it to be composed of particles (a remark-able insight, given that Newton much later also attributed just such a 'corpuscular' nature to light and Einstein proved it in his work on the photoelectric effect that won him the Nobel Prize in 1921 – nine hun-dred years after Ibn Sīna and Ibn al-Haytham).[14]

Ibn al-Haytham also carried out some of the first experiments on the dispersion of light into its constituent colours and studied shadows, rainbows and eclipses, and his work decisively influenced the theory of perspective that developed in Renaissance Europe, in both science and art. In the fourteenth century his *Book of Optics* was translated from Latin into common Italian, making it accessible to a much wider number of people, including several Renaissance artists, such as the Italians Leon Battista Alberti and Lorenzo Ghiberti, and, indirectly, the Dutchman Jan Vermeer. All made use of his discussions on per-spective to create the illusion of three-dimensional depth on canvas and in carvings.[15]

As a brief aside, I mentioned earlier Ibn Mu'ādh's eleventh-century work on twilight, translated into Latin as *Liber de crepusculis*, which has been wrongly attributed to Ibn al-Haytham.[16] The reason this is of interest is because, in it, Ibn Mu'ādh gives a pretty good estimate of the height of the atmosphere. He recognized that the twilight follow-ing a sunset must be due to illuminated water vapour high in the upper reaches of the atmosphere reflecting sunlight long after the sun has set. He gave a value for the angle of the sun below the horizon at the end of the evening twilight of 19 degrees. This, he argued, is the lowest elevation at which the sun's rays can still meet the upper ves-tiges of the atmosphere. Through the use of simple geometric ideas and a value for the size of the earth provided by al-Ma'mūn's astron-omers, Ibn Mu'ādh calculated the height of the atmosphere to be

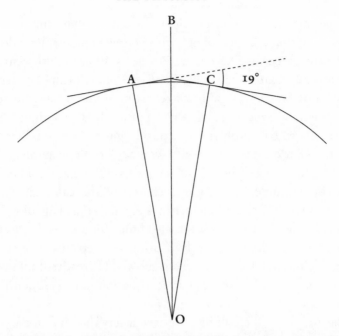

Ibn Mu'ādh's method for calculating the height of the atmosphere. If an observer at A catches the last glimpse of twilight on the horizon along his line of sight, at point B, this means there should be matter at B that is still illuminated by the sun. This is when the sun is 19 degrees below the horizon with its rays coming in along the tangent CB. A little Euclidean geometry tells us that the angle AOC must also be 19 degrees, or that AOB is 9.5 degrees. It is then easy to establish using trigonometry and a knowledge of the size of the earth that the height of B above the surface (Ibn Mu'ādh's edge of the atmosphere) is 52 miles.

around 52 miles. His work found wide interest in the Latin Middle Ages and in the Renaissance. His method and understanding of atmospheric optics was improved upon only when the Danish astronomer Tycho Brahe raised the issue of atmospheric refraction at the end of the sixteenth century and the subsequent optical work of the great Johannes Kepler was published in 1604. But Ibn Mu'ādh's value for the height of the atmosphere is still pretty good. Indeed, the boundary between the earth's atmosphere and outer space, known as the Kármán line, is at an altitude of 62 miles.

In mathematics, Ibn al-Haytham's name is probably best known in association with a famous problem in geometry that came about from his study of the reflection of light from curved mirrors. First described by Ptolemy, it became known in Europe as Alhazen's Problem since it was discussed extensively in his *Book of Optics*. It can be stated as the problem of finding the point of reflection on a concave mirror of a light source in order to reach a given point. It is also often described as the billiard-ball problem: by considering a circular billiard table, find the point on the cushion that you need to bounce the ball off in order for it to hit another. Of course, we are familiar with finding the angles on a traditional 'straight' cushion, and this can easily be solved to make sure the angle of incidence is equal to the angle of reflection. While the same law of reflection also holds for a curved reflector, the problem can no longer be solved using geometry (with a ruler and compass). Instead, Ibn al-Haytham showed his readers that one must use and solve a difficult algebraic equation called a 'quartic' (i.e. involving x^4).

The problem is difficult because even a very tiny shift in the position that the billiard ball or light ray strikes the reflecting surface would lead to it bouncing off at a different angle altogether. Ibn al-Haytham provided the first (partial) solution to the problem using the technique of conic sections described by Apollonius of Perga (*c.* 262–190 BCE). Apollonius' *Conics* is regarded as one of the most important books on mathematics ever written. In it he showed how different types of mathematical curves (circles, ellipses, parabolas, hyperbolas) can be produced when a cone is sliced through at different angles. Ibn al-Haytham knew this work well and even devoted a substantial effort to reconstructing the lost eighth book of the *Conics*.[17] He solved the quartic equation by splitting it into equations for two intersecting curves, a circle and a hyperbola. The points of intersection are the solutions of the problem, but his solution was long and complicated. Amazingly, an exact algebraic solution had to wait until 1997, when Oxford mathematician Peter Neumann showed that the problem could be solved using a theory developed by the French mathematical prodigy Évariste Galois (1811–32).[18]

In astronomy, it is only now that historians of science are beginning to see Ibn al-Haytham's true contribution. In the past, this has been confined to acknowledging that he was one of the first scholars

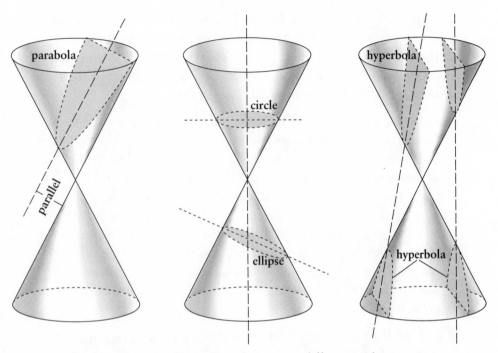

Conic sections. By slicing through a cone at different angles, a variety
of different geometric curves are found, which can be used to solve
certain types of algebraic problems.

seriously to challenge Ptolemy. His challenge, however, was not to the
geocentric idea itself, but rather to Ptolemy's mathematical models.
Those historians of science prepared to dig a little deeper into the subject have found some hidden gems in Ibn al-Haytham's texts. He
wrote twenty-five works on astronomy, which is twice as many as he
wrote on optics.[19] These include treatises on cosmology, astronomical
observation and calculation, and technical applications such as the
determination of meridians, the direction of Mecca and the design of
sundials. But it is his work on what might be called astronomical theory that is most important. For it is on this subject that we find his
criticisms of Ptolemy and many corrections to the *Almagest*. All this
body of work was written during the last decade of his life, when he
was almost exclusively engaged in astronomy.

Just as al-Rāzi took it upon himself to highlight the deficiencies
and errors in the medical writings of Galen, so Ibn al-Haytham did

the same with Ptolemy. Both men pioneered the spirit of *shukūk* ('doubts'), which is so crucial in science. Here is a wonderful example of Ibn al-Haytham's damning response to an anonymous scholar who disapproved of his disparaging remarks about the *Almagest* in his *Doubts on Ptolemy* (*al-Shukūk ala Batlamyūs*):

> From the statements made by the noble Sheikh, it is clear that he believes in Ptolemy's words in everything he says, without relying on a demonstration or calling on a proof, but by pure imitation; that is how experts in the prophetic tradition have faith in Prophets, may the blessing of God be upon them. But it is not the way that mathematicians have faith in specialists in the demonstrative sciences. And I have taken note that it gives him [i.e. the Sheikh] pain that I have contradicted Ptolemy, and that he finds it distasteful; his statements suggest that error is foreign to Ptolemy. Now there are many errors in Ptolemy, in many passages of his books ... If he wishes me to specify them and point them out, I shall do so.[20]

Ibn al-Haytham then really lets the noble Sheikh have it with both barrels, for he does indeed go on to list the errors and mistakes in several of Ptolemy's works: the *Almagest*, the *Book of Optics* and the *Book of Hypotheses*.

Not all scholars agreed with or even understood Ibn al-Haytham's approach. Philosophers in particular resisted his mathematical theories of astronomy. An Andalusian scholar by the name of Ibn Bājja (Avempace) a century after Ibn al-Haytham even argued that he was not 'one of the true experts of his science' and that his criticisms of Ptolemy were based on only a superficial understanding of the Greek's works, having read them only 'in the most simple of ways'.[21]

It is always easier to find mistakes in the work of others than to come up with original ideas of one's own. But Ibn al-Haytham's work in astronomy is still remarkable. For instance, one of his texts, *The Model of Motions of Each of the Seven Planets*, came in three books and outlined a new theory of planetary motion far in advance of anything Ptolemy had written. Modern historians of science now regard it as a monumental achievement and at the cutting edge of science at the time. We must not forget that Ibn al-Haytham still believed in a geocentric model of the universe, but what he wanted above all was to 'mathematize' astronomy as he had done with optics. He wanted to be able to describe the observed motion of the planets in terms of pure geometry and was not particularly interested in the physical mechanism or reason behind their motion. Nor was he interested in the way the planets move in an absolute sense, but only as they are seen to move from the vantage point of the observer on earth. This 'phenomenological' approach is therefore independent of any notion of the earth going round the sun or the sun going round the earth; it was a theory of planetary dynamics from the earth's frame of reference. To help with this, he introduced a new concept – what he called 'required time': the time needed for a planet to trace an arc in the sky. But he treated time in a way that a modern theoretical physicist would recognize, as a parameter in his mathematics; in fact, as a purely geometrical quantity.

A good scientist should never be so arrogant as to be *certain* about anything. Never, that is, apart from on one point: that what we refer to as the modern scientific method is *non-negotiable* in its all-encompassing importance as a world-view. Many would argue it is the *only* world-view that a rational, thinking person can have in explaining how and why the world is the way it is.

I shall expand briefly here on what I mean by the scientific method. While it is true that there are no certainties in science, when scientists say they 'believe' a particular theory to be correct, they mean that it is in all probability a correct description of some aspect of nature. For instance, our current best picture of the subatomic world comes from the predictions of quantum theory developed in the early twentieth century. I believe quantum theory gives us a correct and true description of atoms. However, my belief is not based on the blind faith of religion but is instead based on the way that the theory's incredible predictive power has been tested time and time again over the past century. Similarly, I believe that Darwin's theory of natural selection is the true description of the way that life on earth has evolved. This does not mean that my mind is closed to the possibility of something better coming along in the future to replace it; it is just that I think it highly unlikely that natural selection is wrong given the overwhelming evidence in its favour, both logical and empirical.

As commonly defined, the scientific method is the approach to investigating phenomena, acquiring new knowledge, or correcting and integrating previous knowledge, based on the gathering of data through observation and measurement, followed by the formulation and testing of hypotheses to explain the data. It is often still claimed that the modern scientific method was not established until the Renaissance by Francis Bacon in his work *Novum Organum* (1620) and by Descartes in his treatise *Discours de la Méthode* (1637). But there is no doubt that Ibn al-Haytham, along with al-Rāzi and al-Bīrūni, whom we shall meet in the next chapter, arrived there much earlier.

For Ibn al-Haytham, the supremacy of the scientific method, valuing meticulous and painstaking experimentation and the careful recording of results, became central to his research. It is for this reason that a number of historians have referred to him as the first real scientist. Ibn al-Haytham makes his views clear in the following extract:

> We should distinguish the properties of particulars, and gather by induction what pertains to the eye and what is found in the manner of sensation to be uniform, unchanging, manifest and not subject to doubt. After which we should ascend in our enquiry and reasoning, gradually and orderly, criticizing premises and exercising caution in regard to conclusions – our aim in all that we make subject to inspection and review being to employ justice, not to follow prejudice, and to take care in all that we judge and criticize that we seek the truth and not be swayed by opinion.[22]

In unpicking Ibn al-Haytham's contributions to science we find that his greatness is thus not so much a consequence of any single revolutionary discovery, such as Newton's inverse square law of gravity or Einstein's theory of relativity, or even al-Khwārizmi's algebra. Rather, it is the way he taught us how to 'do' science. I would therefore argue that he has a stronger claim to the title of 'father of the scientific method' than either Francis Bacon or Descartes. Ultimately what Ibn al-Haytham did was to turn experimentation from a general practice of investigation into the standard means of proof of scientific theories.

We have no evidence to suggest that Ibn al-Haytham was not a devout Muslim, but his rational mind meant that he would accept nothing about the world that could not be verified experimentally. He always trusted and relied upon his observational skills and powers of deduction, for he believed that through logic and induction one can reduce all phenomena in nature to mathematical axioms and laws. In this way, he is every bit a modern physicist.

Unlike his two equally famous Persian contemporaries Ibn Sīna and al-Bīrūni, Ibn al-Haytham was not particularly philosophically minded; he was more of an Archimedes than an Aristotle. Like al-Rāzi before him, Ibn al-Haytham embodied the spirit of the experimental method in science. In many ways, even the cynic who refuses to acknowledge that medieval Islam made any great paradigm-shifting discoveries such as those seen in Europe by Copernicus, Galileo, Kepler or Newton must nevertheless acknowledge the great debt we owe to these tenth- and eleventh-century scientists. Robert Briffault, in his book *The Making of Humanity*, puts it thus:

> The Greeks systematised, generalised and theorised, but the patient ways of investigation, the accumulation of positive knowledge, the minute methods of science, detailed and prolonged observation and experimental enquiry, were altogether alien to the Greeks' temperament . . . What we call science arose in Europe as a result of a new spirit of inquiry . . . of the methods of experiment, observation and measurement, of the development of mathematics in a form unknown to the Greeks. That spirit and those methods were introduced into the European world by the Arabs.[23]

12

The Prince and the Pauper

The stubborn critic would say: 'What is the benefit of these sciences?' He does not know the virtue that distinguishes mankind from all the animals: it is knowledge, in general, which is pursued solely by man, and which is pursued for the sake of knowledge itself, because its acquisition is truly delightful, and is unlike the pleasures desirable from other pursuits. For the good cannot be brought forth, and evil cannot be avoided, except by knowledge. What benefit then is more vivid? What use is more abundant?

Al-Bīrūnī

In a famous correspondence around the year 1000 CE, two Persian geniuses argued about the nature of reality in a way that would not sound out of place in any modern university physics department. Of all the great thinkers and polymaths of the Islamic golden age, these two men were giants, for they were in every way the equals of the very best that the golden age of Greece had produced. The younger of the two had been a privileged child prodigy who grew up to become the brash superstar of his age, a celebrity polymath whose philosophy would influence the world's greatest minds, and whose *Canon of Medicine (al-Qānūn fi al-Tibb)* would become the world's most important medical textbook for over half a millennium. His name was Ibn Sīna, better known in the West as Avicenna. The other man, seven years older, quieter, less flamboyant, from a family of modest means, but with an encyclopedic mind and razor-sharp intellect, is less well known today. In fact, remarkably, and unlike many of the great scholars of Islam, there does not exist a Latinized version of his name: Abū Rayhān al-Bīrūni.

Where did these two men come from? Where and when did they meet? And what were the sorts of issues they debated? It is not clear exactly when their famous correspondence took place but it was certainly early on in their careers, when both men were still in their twenties and may have even both been working under the same roof in the royal courts of Gurgānj, the capital of Khwārizm in Central Asia. Al-Bīrūni rightly regarded himself as the superior intellect in matters of mathematics, physics and astronomy, but was genuinely interested in what the younger Ibn Sīna, the more able philosopher, had to say on more abstract metaphysical matters, and so posed for him a list of eighteen questions. Here are just a few of the more philosophical ones:

1. What was the justification for insisting that the heavenly bodies had neither levity nor gravity and that their orbits were perfectly circular around the earth? In other words, why do they not fall towards the earth or float away from it?
2. Why did he (Ibn Sīna) support Aristotle's rejection of the theory of atomism,[1] since the notion of continuous and infinitely divisible matter that Aristotle and Ibn Sīna subscribed to was equally speculative?
3. Do the sun's rays have material substance? If not, how do they transmit its warmth to us?
4. How would he defend the Aristotelian view that rejected the possibility of the existence of parallel universes?[2]

I shall mention here Ibn Sīna's response to just one of these questions: the issue of how the sun's heat reaches us. For here it was not a case of al-Bīrūni challenging Ibn Sīna's philosophical views but an honest desire to see if he could provide a satisfactory answer. Ibn Sīna gives the following explanation:

> You must also know that the heat of the sun does not come to us by descending down from the sun for the following reasons: firstly, heat does not move by itself; secondly, there is no hot body that descends from above and heats what is down below; third, the sun is not even hot because heat that is being created here is not descending from

above for the three reasons already mentioned. Rather, heat occurs here from the reflection of light and air is heated by this process, as can be observed in the experiment of burning mirrors. And you must know that the rays are not bodies – for if they were bodies there would be two bodies in one place: the air and the rays.[3]

Of course, we know now that the sun is indeed very hot and this heat is radiated to us as electromagnetic waves in the same way that its light reaches us, but it would be nearly nine hundred years before James Clerk Maxwell would explain this correctly.

Ibn Sīna dealt with each of al-Bīrūni's eighteen questions carefully, strongly defending his (and Aristotle's) views. But many of his clever, slippery and often evasive answers were unsatisfactory to al-Bīrūni, who challenged them with his own impeccable logic. It would appear that the tone of the correspondence from both men grew increasingly confrontational, even acrimonious. Al-Bīrūni sounds as though he is throwing down the gauntlet to his younger adversary, while Ibn Sīna's famous arrogance is clearly in evidence.

And the questions were not all of such an abstract nature, for it seems that al-Bīrūni was also keen to see if he could get some long-standing mysteries solved, such as why ice floats on water (Ibn Sīna thought this was due to tiny air pockets trapped inside the ice making it lighter than water – of course we know now that ice floats because it is less dense than liquid water).

Eventually, Ibn Sīna left the correspondence to his most able student, al-Ma'sūmi, an act that must have been a painful snub to al-Bīrūni; in particular, al-Ma'sūmi's tone is somewhat impatient, as though he is exasperated by al-Bīrūni's rejection of earlier answers from his master, whom he refers to as 'the Wise One'. The following is an example of al-Ma'sūmi's correspondence: 'As for your response to the Wise One . . . I do not think it was correct, and it would have been better had you worded your comment more appropriately. Further, had you perceived what the Wise One meant by his noble words on this issue, you would not have allowed yourself to make this objection.'

Just as fascinating as the ideas being discussed by these two men is the world they inhabited. Both were born in the land of Khwārizm (modern Uzbekistan) that had already produced the father of algebra, al-Khwārizmi, two centuries earlier. But they came from contrasting backgrounds.

That Abū Rayhan Muhammad al-Bīrūni (973–1048) ranks as one of the greatest scientists of all time makes it all the more puzzling that his name is so little known in the West. He was a polymath with a free-ranging and formidable intellect; not only did he make significant breakthroughs as a brilliant mathematician and astronomer, he also left his mark as a philosopher, theologian, encyclopedist, linguist, historian, geographer, geologist, anthropologist, pharmacist and physician. He was also, alongside al-Rāzi and Ibn al-Haytham, one of the earliest and leading exponents of the modern scientific method of experimentation and observation.

Little is known about his early life, as he left no autobiographical details. We know that he was born near the city of Kath in Khwārizm in a family of modest means that, while Persian in every way, had originally come from Tajikistan to the east. His distinctive name is thought to come from the Persian word for 'outsider' and could refer either to his family's Tajik origins or to the fact that he came to Kath as a boy from an outlying suburb, or it may have been a name given him later in life. What is unusual is that the name is not given to any other scholars of the period, many of whom would have travelled far and wide. So it could simply be that he was born in a place called Bīrūn, near Kath.

As a young man, he worked in the courts of the Banū Irāq princes of Kath, who ruled over that region of Khwārizm on behalf of the Samanid dynasty. But peace was shattered when a rival dynasty from across the river Oxus[4] overran the city in 995, and al-Bīrūni had to flee. He travelled first to the Samanid capital, Bukhara, where he came under the protection of the Samanid ruler, Prince Nūh ibn Mansūr, and befriended another deposed ruler, Prince Qābūs of Gorgan (a city in northern Persia near the Caspian Sea). But making influential friends was not enough for al-Bīrūni; he needed to go where he could continue his research, particularly in astronomy. He considered going west to Baghdad, but decided against it as it was too far to travel, and so made his way instead to Rayy, where he spent a miserable few years living in poverty, unable to gain royal patronage to support his work.

His luck turned a few years later when, in 999, he received an invitation from the newly restored Prince Qābūs in Gorgan and gladly left Rayy behind. To Qābūs he would dedicate his great historical text *The Chronology of Ancient Nations*, a book still regarded today as one of the greatest sources of medieval history ever written.

By the early years of the new millennium, with his reputation secure as one of the leading thinkers of his generation, he was lured back to a more peaceful Khwārizm and its capital Gurgānj (known today as Old Urganch, or Kunya Urgench, in Turkmenistan) where the ruling Mamūnid sultans, whose power struggle with the Banū Irāq princes had caused him to flee Kath a few years earlier, were now more welcoming. Crucially, they had renewed their patronage of scholarship and were keen to attract the top scholars to work in their courts. Al-Bīrūni would spend many productive years within a circle of brilliant young minds, including the precocious Ibn Sīna, in an intellectual environment not seen since the glory days of the House of Wisdom in Baghdad nearly two centuries earlier.

Better known by his Latinized name of Avicenna, Abū Ali al-Hussein ibn Abdullah ibn Sīna (980–1037) is the best-known scholar of Islam. Just as the work of Aristotle can be regarded as the climax of ancient Greek philosophical thought, so Ibn Sīna's work stands as the pinnacle of medieval philosophy. Born near Bukhara, and in contrast with al-Bīrūni, Ibn Sīna enjoyed a privileged upbringing as the son of politically influential parents who were part of the ruling Samanid elite. By an early age, he had memorized the entire Qur'an and much of Persian poetry. One man who played an important role in his early life was his tutor, Abū Abdullah al-Nātili, about whom Ibn Sīna later wrote in typically arrogant style: 'Al-Nātili was extremely amazed at me; whatever problem he posed for me I conceptualized better than he, so he advised my father against my taking up any profession other than learning.'[5] Ibn Sīna also describes how as a teenager he mastered medicine and found it not to be intellectually challenging enough, and so turned to philosophy. He continued to practise medicine, however, and was already treating patients at the tender age of 16. After successfully treating Prince Nūh ibn Mansūr himself he was given as a reward free access to the royal library in Bukhara. It was there that he would complete his education, covering every area of human knowledge. He wrote his first work, dedicated to Prince Nūh, called *A Treatise on the Soul in the Manner of a Summary*, which is extant in both Arabic and Latin. While more of a student essay than a mature scholarly work, it would nevertheless lay the foundations for much of his philosophical writing later in life.

Thus, around the time al-Bīrūnī was struggling miserably to establish himself in Rayy, Ibn Sīna was happily devouring the great texts on medicine and philosophy in Bukhara. But it was not long before their fortunes would be reversed, for, coinciding with al-Bīrūnī's luck suddenly taking a turn for the better when he left for Gorgan, Ibn Sīna was compelled to leave his home city for good. The heightening tensions between the Samanid dynasty and the Ghaznavids to the south forced him to flee north to the relative safety of Gurgānj,⁶ where he would be joined a few years later by the returning al-Bīrūnī. But despite this setback Ibn Sīna's career soon flourished, and he became a huge celebrity during his lifetime. He never married, and is said to have been a man of striking good looks who enjoyed the company of women and more than the odd glass of wine. He was also arrogant to the point of being scornful of the 'lesser mortals' around him.

In contrast, al-Bīrūnī, while every bit as self-assured, even arrogant, as Ibn Sīna, had a very different personality. Like Ibn Sīna, he never married or had a family, but he did not seek power or wealth and was single-mindedly devoted to his research. It is said that when, later in life, he dedicated his great work on astronomy and geometry, *The Mas'ūdi Canon*, to the sultan of the Ghaznavid state, al-Mas'ūd, the sultan rewarded him with an elephant loaded with silver coins. But al-Bīrūnī would not accept the gift and sent it back, saying that he had no need for such wealth. This example is not an indication of al-Bīrūnī's humility, but rather of his lack of interest in worldly possessions.

Around the year 1012, with the threat of invasion from the Ghaznavid Empire in the south growing ever greater, Ibn Sīna decided it was time to leave Gurgānj. He set off to seek greater fame and fortune in the royal courts of Persia, evading Ghaznavid capture while searching for a safe haven and the all-important patronage that would enable him to continue his studies. He spent time in Gorgan, where he began writing his great *Canon of Medicine* and first met his lifelong

disciple and biographer, al-Juzjānī; and then in Rayy, where he practised medicine in the royal court and refined many of his philosophical
thoughts. Still nervous of the advancing shadow of the Ghaznavids,
he moved on, first to Qazwīn, and finally settled in Hamadan in 1015.
There he befriended the Buyid Amir Shams al-Dowla, whom he cured
of colic, and was soon appointed as his new vizier. Apart from a shaky
start in the job when he was briefly imprisoned to appease insurgent
soldiers unhappy with his appointment, Ibn Sīna lived life to the full
in Hamadan, fulfilling his administrative duties during the day, teaching and writing in the evening and partying through the night.

Ibn Sīna became increasingly outspoken on philosophical matters
and his writing betrayed his uncompromising rationalist views and
commitment to the supremacy of logic. Although he was a very spiritual man – and much of his philosophy was theological in flavour – he
was nevertheless labelled a heretic by the conservative orthodoxy.
It did not help that he lived a lifestyle some regarded as hedonistic.
However, he refused to moderate his rationalist views and also
argued that he preferred a rich and broad yet short life to a narrow,
long one.

Al-Bīrūni meanwhile had chosen to sit it out in Gurgānj. But in
1017 the Ghaznavids finally invaded Khwārizm. Their ruler, Sultan
Mahmūd, took al-Bīrūni and several other scholars back with him to
his capital, Ghazna in modern Afghanistan. Whether al-Bīrūni was
taken as a prisoner or went willingly is not clear, but this move did not
stop his scholarly output and he soon began one of his most famous
works, *The Determination of the Coordinates of Cities* (*Kitab Tahdīd
Nihāyāt al-Amākin li-Tashīh Masāfāt al-Masākin*), which he completed in the summer of 1025 and which is essentially a textbook on
spherical geometry.

By 1031 he had completed his *magnum opus, The Mas'ūdi Canon,*
which he dedicated to the Ghaznavid Sultan Mas'ūd. Then, after years
of travel around India, he completed his last great work, *The History
of India* (*Ta'rīkh al-Hind*), which is to this day an important source of
information for modern Indologists.[7] For instance, his analysis of the
relationship between Islam and Hinduism is a wonderful early study
of comparative religions.

Ibn Sīna had to uproot yet again in 1023, this time for political reasons, leaving Hamadan in a hurry for Isfahan, where he would spend the last fifteen years of his life working under the patronage of Sultan Ala' al-Dowla. At the time, Isfahan was one of the power-houses of Persian scholarship. A famous saying about this still beautiful city that exemplifies its status and importance a thousand years ago was '*Isfahān nesf-e jahān*' ('Isfahan is half the world').

What of the scientific legacy of these two great men? In the case of the other scientists we have encountered it has been quite clear-cut what their main contributions have been, despite all of them being poly-maths: Jābir the chemist, al-Khwārizmi the algebraist, al-Kindi the philosopher, al-Rāzi the clinician, Ibn al-Haytham the physicist; but when describing the achievements of Ibn Sīna and al-Bīrūni, the best I can do is pluck out a few highlights.

As a physician, Ibn Sīna's fame today is due to his *Canon of Medicine*, which became the standard medical textbook in both the Islamic world and Europe (where it was even more widely known and used than al-Rāzi's *Liber continens*) for the next six hundred years – an extraordinary shelf life for an academic text, particularly as it also supplanted the writings of Galen and Hippocrates, the two giants of Greek medicine. It is remarkable because it synthesized all Greek, Persian and Indian medical knowledge as well as Ibn Sīna's own work, such as his discovery and explanation of contagious diseases and a detailed description of the anatomy of the human eye.

One of the volumes of the *Canon* contains a section on bone frac-tures, and has aspects of a modern medical textbook in the way it describes causes, types and forms of all kinds of fractures, along with methods of treatment. Ibn Sīna was the first physician, for instance, to advocate what we now know as the theory of delayed splintage, by suggesting that fractures should not be splinted immediately but only after several days. This is still a respected idea in medicine today. He also discussed how to deal with a fracture to the first metacarpal bone in the thumb, which modern textbooks describe as the 'Bennett's frac-ture' after the man who supposedly 'discovered' it in 1882, nearly nine centuries after Ibn Sīna's description.

However, while the *Canon* (a name that derives from the Arabic word *Qānūn*, meaning 'law' – which itself comes from the Greek *kanōn*) is Ibn Sīna's most famous work, it is not his greatest contribution to science. That accolade without doubt goes to his *Kitab al-Shifā'*, which is commonly translated as the *Book of Healing*. But unlike the *Canon* this was no medical text; the word *shifā'* actually means 'cure', in the sense that the book was written as a general compendium of knowledge in the hope of curing the world of the disease of ignorance.

In all, *al-Shifā'* contained nine volumes on logic and eight on the natural sciences. Other volumes covered arithmetic, geometry, astronomy, music and, of course, metaphysics. It is in a section on psychology, for instance, that we encounter one of Ibn Sīna's most famous arguments: the 'floating man' thought-experiment. With it, Ibn Sīna refutes the moralist belief of earlier Muslim theologians that our physical bodies are all that exists. He does this by describing a scenario that he believed proves the immateriality of the human soul:

> Suppose that a man is created all at once, fully developed and perfectly formed but with his vision shrouded from perceiving all external objects – created floating in the air or in space, not buffeted by any perceptible currents of the air that supports him, his limbs separated and kept out of contact from one another, so that they do not feel each other. Then let the subject consider whether he would affirm the existence of his self. There is no doubt that he would affirm his own existence, although not affirming the reality of any of his limbs or inner organs.
>
> Hence the one who affirms has a means to be alerted to the existence of his soul as something other than the body and to his being directly acquainted with this existence and aware of it.[8]

The extent to which this idea was to influence later thinkers, such as the seventeenth-century early modern philosopher René Descartes, remains a matter of speculation. However, Descartes's immortal words, *Cogito, ergo sum* ('I think, therefore I am'), on the issue of mind/body dualism, run remarkably close to Ibn Sīna's arguments; and it is well known that others, such as David Hume, built their arguments on the floating man.

More generally, Ibn Sīna attempted to construct an all-encompassing metaphysical model of reality that would allow him to prove the existence of God using logic. Although he studied the work of Aristotle and Plato, he was without doubt the most original philosopher of the medieval world. Modern historians in fact like to divide medieval philosophy into two eras: pre-Ibn Sīna, in which the greatest Islamic philosophers such as al-Kindi, al-Rāzi and al-Farābi essentially modified, extended and criticized Aristotelianism, and post-Ibn Sīna, in which philosophers such as al-Ghazāli and Ibn Rushd modified, extended and criticized what is referred to as Avicennism (the philosophy of Ibn Sīna). I would argue that just as Ibn al-Haytham should be regarded as the world's greatest physicist in the time span between Archimedes and Newton, so Ibn Sīna was the colossus of philosophy between Aristotle and Descartes. His synthesis of philosophy and Islamic theology would influence later Jewish and Christian scholars such as Maimonides in the twelfth century and Roger Bacon and Thomas Aquinas in the thirteenth.

Ibn Sīna's harshest critic was the theologian al-Ghazāli (1058–1111), who famously wrote *The Incoherence of the Philosophers* (*Tahāfut al-Falāsifa*) as a direct attack on the Aristotelian approach of Ibn Sīna as being anti-Islamic. But this work would not be the last word on the subject, for the Andalusian philosopher Ibn Rushd would write a brilliant defence of Ibn Sīna and Aristotelianism in his stinging rebuttal to al-Ghazāli, which he called *The Incoherence of 'The Incoherence'* (*Tahāfut al-Tahāfut*).

It is not surprising that Ibn Sīna is a national icon in Iran today, and one can find countless schools and hospitals named after him in many countries around the world. Indeed, his legacy stretches even further, for there is an 'Avicenna' crater on the moon, and in 1980 every member country of Unesco celebrated the thousand-year anniversary of Ibn Sīna's birth. As a philosopher he is referred to as the Aristotle of Islam; as a physician he is known as the Galen of Islam.

Yet al-Bīrūni was the better natural scientist. He adopted a critical stance on Aristotle, arguing that the Greek's reliance on pure thought and reasoning had often led him to the wrong conclusions. Instead, al-Bīrūni insisted on careful observation and scientific experimentation to test Aristotle's ideas, and it was this careful empirical approach that led to his many impressive discoveries in physics and astronomy. He was also an exceptional mathematician and developed techniques for solving cubic equations and extracting cube, and higher, roots. He also advanced the field of trigonometry beyond the earlier work of the brilliant Persian mathematician Abū al-Wafā' (940–98).

An important application of his mathematics was in solving the *qibla* problem (determining the direction of Mecca), which had to be addressed each time a new mosque was built anywhere in the Islamic Empire. It required knowledge of the accurate coordinates of longitude and latitude of all cities, as well as a mastery of spherical geometry. In these matters, al-Bīrūni was peerless.

In his famous *Mas'ūdi Canon*, completed around 1031, al-Bīrūni employed mathematical techniques that had never been used before, and developed rudimentary methods in calculus for the first time, which he used to describe the motion and acceleration of heavenly bodies, thereby laying the foundations for Newton's laws of motion in the *Principia Mathematica* more than six hundred years later.

Despite having supreme confidence in his own abilities, and his comfortable relationships with the various rulers from whose patronage he benefited, al-Bīrūni was a man who did not like rocking the establishment boat, and he willingly toed the orthodox religious line of his masters. For example, he denounced al-Rāzi for his criticism of religion and even went so far as to claim that the physician's blindness later in life was divine punishment for his heresy. Whether this was the pronouncement of a rational genius hiding behind the cloak of religious conservatism, or whether al-Bīrūni was simply a more devout Muslim than al-Rāzi (which would not have been difficult), we shall probably never know. Nor was al-Bīrūni a willing politician, but the needs of a life of unrest forced him to become involved in the affairs of state. He famously once wrote of how he was required to mediate in disputes between different rulers: 'I was compelled to participate in worldly affairs, which excited the envy of fools, but made the wise pity me.'

Another example is his fascinating position on the issue of heliocentrism versus geocentrism. There is no doubt that, in common with the vast majority of Islamic scholars, al-Bīrūni subscribed wholeheartedly to the geocentric model of the universe. He even went so far as to argue about the ordering of the orbits of the sun and planets around the earth. However, a contemporary of his, the Baghdadi astronomer al-Sijzi (c. 950–c. 1020), had proposed a heliocentric universe.

Al-Bīrūnī was well aware of this work and even collaborated with al-Sijzi, and so, rather than dismiss it out of hand in favour of geocentrism, he was initially neutral on the matter. He famously stated that all astronomical data could be explained just as well by supposing that the earth turns daily on its axis and revolves annually around the sun as by assuming that it was stationary. So, while al-Bīrūnī had philosophical issues with heliocentrism, he was still brilliant enough to appreciate, like Ibn al-Haytham, that one can only accept a scientific theory based on empirical evidence. And since the data could not discriminate between heliocentrism and geocentrism, he was in no position to decide. Indeed, even Copernicus' much later, and correct, heliocentric model was really no more than a guess. For while it would later be seen to have heralded the birth of modern European science, it came before Galileo pointed his telescope at the sky and before Newton derived his inverse-square law of gravitation (the two ingredients needed to *prove* Copernicus was correct).[9]

The position of al-Bīrūnī on cosmology can be compared with another much more recent scientific debate, over the correct interpretation of quantum mechanics, the theory of the subatomic world developed in the early decades of the twentieth century. In that case – and this is an issue that has yet to be satisfactorily resolved – the argument was over the physical reality of certain aspects of the microcosm, such as the apparent ability of subatomic particles to be in two places at once. But here, too, no experiment we care to devise has been able to point us to any one of several possible interpretations of what is going on. The Danish physicist and father of quantum mechanics, Niels Bohr (who for some reason reminds me a lot of al-Bīrūnī transported in space and time to 1920s Copenhagen), argued that, since experiment cannot resolve the issue, it is a purely metaphysical question and just a matter of philosophical taste. Al-Bīrūnī's attitude towards cosmology would seem to me similar to this modern 'positivist' position: if experimental evidence cannot discriminate between two competing theories, they are necessarily equally valid and it is a waste of time worrying about it. In the case of the model of the solar system, the issue would be resolved many centuries after al-Bīrūnī. Quantum mechanics is still waiting for its Copernicus, Galileo or

Newton. I should add that this idea of positivism has also been attributed to Ibn al-Haytham, who states quite clearly in his *Book of Optics* that metaphysical speculation is not true knowledge unless it can be supported by empirical proof.

On theology, al-Bīrūni held a view that is still a point of contention in the world today: he stated that the Qur'an 'does not interfere with the business of science nor does it infringe on the realm of science'. Like the earlier scholars of al-Ma'mūn's Baghdad, al-Bīrūni was, it seems, more than able to separate his rationalist approach to scientific enquiry from his religious beliefs.

Al-Bīrūni's best-known, if not most important, achievement in science was his famous determination of the circumference of the earth from an ingenious measurement of the height of a mountain. (The method had been mooted by al-Ma'mūn's astronomer Sanad two centuries earlier – but we only have al-Bīrūni's account of it.) His experiment was carried out between 1020 and 1025 while on his travels with the Ghaznavid Sultan Mahmūd in north-west India. During his time at a fort in a place called Nandna, in modern Pakistan and about 60 miles south of Islamabad, he observed a high mountain to the west.[10] It was exactly what he had been looking for because it overlooked the flat Punjabi plains that stretched out as far as the eye could see, enabling him to fix the angle of the line of sight to the horizon very accurately when looking out from the top of the mountain.

I shall describe his technique in detail, for it requires no more than elementary geometry, and yet is astonishingly ingenious. In his *Determination of the Coordinates of Cities*, al-Bīrūni begins his description of the method by referring back to the famous measurements carried out first by Eratosthenes and later repeated by al-Ma'mūn's astronomers. Then, with his legendary sharp wit, he writes the immortal lines: 'Here is another method for the determination of the circumference of the Earth. It does not require walking in deserts.'[11] His first step is to determine accurately the height of the mountain while standing on the flat plain near its base. He has a square board of sides one cubit (roughly 20 inches) and ruled with equal divisions along its edges. (If you are not mathematically inclined you may want to skip the next few paragraphs.)

Call the square board ABCD and stand it vertically on edge C as

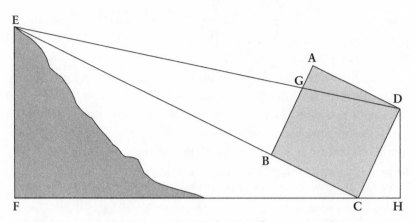

Al-Bīrūni's method for measuring the height of a mountain by geometric means (comparing ratios of sides of similar triangles).

in the diagram. From D, hang a ruler that can swivel freely. First, make sure that the side BC is in line with the peak of the mountain (point E) and then fix the square in this position. Now rotate the ruler so that it is also pointing along a line with the mountain peak and hence cuts the side AB at some point, G. We now have two similar triangles: ADG and CED (because both are right-angled at A and C, and both have equal angles ADG and CED since the lines CE and DA are parallel). So, we can now equate the ratios of sides such that AG:AD = CD:CE. Since three of these sides are known, we can work out the fourth length, CE.

Next, let a small stone drop freely from the corner D and mark where it lands, at H, then measure the distance along the ground, HC, with the now detached ruler. Now we can compare two other right-angled triangles: DCH and CEF, where F is the (inaccessible) point marking the base of the mountain directly below E. We note that since angles DCH and ECF add up to 90 degrees (since DCE is a right angle) then angle DCH must equal angle CEF (as angles ECF and CEF also add up to 90 degrees). So the two triangles DCH and CEF are also similar and we can again compare ratios of sides: CH:CD = EF:EC. Again, we have just one unknown side: EF, the height of the mountain.

In practice, the length AG will be very small because the lines of sight to the mountain peak along CBE and DGE will be almost parallel. But al-Bīrūni assures us that he was able to make this careful measurement.

With the mountain's height now known, he can use this value to work out the size of the radius of the earth. But he must first climb to the top of the mountain, with an astrolabe accurate enough to measure very small angles. In his writing, al-Bīrūni describes two different mathematical ways of determining the radius. I shall explain it here using a third method, which amounts to the same thing.

From the top of the mountain, the angle of dip of the horizon, TAH, from the horizontal AH is measured. (Note that al-Bīrūni determines the horizontal by using a plumb line to find the vertical.) He found this angle to be 34 minutes of arc (just over half a degree). Because the angle ATO is a right angle (since the line AT is a tangent to the circle – a geometrical theorem that Euclid has taught generations of schoolchildren for two millennia), then the angles TAH and TOA are equal. Now all that is needed is some elementary trigonometry. The cosine of the angle TOA is equal to the ratio OT : OA, where OT is the radius of the earth. But OA = OB + BA, where OB = OT = the radius, and BA is the known height of the mountain. Thus, the only unknown quantity involved is the radius of the earth and a little rearranging will give us its value. Al-Bīrūni was very familiar with the use of trigonometric tables. He calculated the radius of the earth to be 12,803,337 cubits, which, when multiplied by twice pi, gives a value for the circumference of the earth that is within 1 per cent of the modern value – just under 25,000 miles.

It is often recorded how remarkably accurate the value arrived at by al-Bīrūni was, closer than anyone had achieved in the past. But the fact is that there are a number of uncertainties, such as an accurate definition of the cubit and the Arabic *mīl*, and the fact that all these calculations assume an exactly spherical earth (whereas we know the circumference to be greater around the bulge of the Equator than it is round the poles). What is remarkable about al-Bīrūni's method, therefore, is not the closeness of his result to the modern value but the ingenuity of the method itself and the care needed to measure the quantities accurately, particularly the very small angles.

I shall not discuss al-Bīrūni's many contributions to other scientific

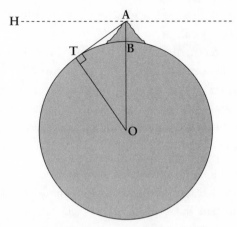

Al-Bīrūnī's method for calculating the circumference of the earth.

disciplines, but feel it is important to mention briefly his work in earth sciences. Travelling widely in India, al-Bīrūnī not only made a detailed study of its geography, history and culture, he also wrote tellingly on its geology. He discovered that the subcontinent was once a sea before it became land,[12] but thought that this was due to the gradual build-up of alluvium rather than the correct and far more dramatic continental drift:

> But if you see the soil of India with your own eyes and meditate on its nature, if you consider the rounded stones found in earth however deeply you dig, stones that are huge near the mountains and where the rivers have a violent current: stones that are of smaller size at a greater distance from the mountains and where the streams flow more slowly: stones that appear pulverized in the shape of sand where the streams begin to stagnate near their mouths and near the sea – if you consider all this you can scarcely help thinking that India was once a sea, which by degrees has been filled up by the alluvium of the streams.[13]

He has also been described as the first anthropologist, having written detailed comparative studies on the religions and cultures of the peoples he encountered over a wide swathe of Asia.

If one were forced to choose between the three giants of medieval science, Ibn al-Haytham, al-Bīrūnī and Ibn Sīna, as to who was the greatest of all then I can do no better than to refer to the historian George Sarton, in his definitive *Introduction to the History of Science*. Given that the three men lived at the same time, he defines the first half of the eleventh century as the 'Age of al-Bīrūni'.

I end this chapter as I began, with another quotation from al-Bīrūni, in which he defends the pursuit of scientific knowledge against anti-scientific attitudes in the societies he encountered – still an issue in many parts of the world to this day:

> The extremist among them would stamp the sciences as atheistic, and would proclaim that they lead people astray in order to make ignoramuses, like him, hate the sciences. For this will help him to conceal his ignorance, and to open the door for the complete destruction of sciences and scientists.[14]

If these sentiments, which so eloquently make the case for rationalism, are the most important legacy of Arabic science, then this underrated and little-known Persian genius was certainly its greatest advocate.

13

Andalusia

*During the most splendid period of Islamic Spain, ignorance
was regarded as so disgraceful that those without education
concealed the fact as far as possible, just as they would have
hidden the commission of a crime.*

S. P. Scott, *History of the Moorish Empire in Europe*

The Strait of Gibraltar that separates the south-west tip of Europe
from the continent of Africa is named after the Rock of Gibraltar, from
the Arabic *Jebel Tāriq* (or 'Tāriq's mountain'), the huge limestone
promontory overlooking the Mediterranean. Tāriq ibn Ziyad was the
Umayyad general who crossed over into Spain in 711 CE, extending
Islamic rule into Europe. On reaching land and confronting the forces
of the Christian Visigoths, he is said to have burned his army's ships in
the harbour to stop his men from fleeing back to Africa. In a speech to
his soldiers, famous right across the Arabic-speaking world to this day,
he is supposed to have said: 'Men, where can you flee? The sea is
behind you, and the enemy in front of you. There is nothing for you,
by God, except for truth and strength of character.' The victory of
Tāriq's army marked the beginning of the Muslim conquest of Spain
and almost eight hundred years of Islamic religious and cultural influence in the lands known as Andalusia.

But this influence was far more than simply that of an occupying
power. At its height, the golden age of the city of Córdoba in central
Spain rivalled that of Baghdad for its riches, culture and size, even its
great library. During the relatively short period of the so-called Andalusian Umayyad caliphate (929–1031), Córdoba became the most

important city in Europe and saw wonderful achievements in science every bit as rich and varied as those under the Islamic dynasties of the East.

Before I discuss some of these scientific achievements and the leading characters responsible, such as the ninth-century inventor Ibn Firnas, the tenth-century surgeon al-Zahrāwi and the twelfth-century philosopher Ibn Rushd, I shall hurry through a brief history of Andalusia. I cannot do it justice in just a few pages, nor will I apologize for neglecting to cover the wonderful art and culture of the period, for mine is still a story about science, and that story is an easier one for me to tell. The reason for this is that the golden age of Arabic science in Spain did not last very long. So concentrated was it in time, in fact, that most of the leading scientists, physicians and philosophers worthy of mention were contemporaries. All were of course products of a somewhat different Islamic culture, far from the Abbāsids of the Middle East and Persia.

Possibly most importantly, in the broader discussion of the scientific achievements of medieval Islam, it was mainly via Spain that we see the transmission of Arabic science into Europe, a process that took longer than the two-century duration of the translation movement which brought Greek science to the Arabs.

The official Umayyad caliphate's rule in the East had been ended by the Abbāsids in a famous battle on the banks of the river Zab near Mosul in Iraq on 25 January 750 CE. To ensure that they did not try to claw back their power, the Abbāsids ordered the massacre of every member of the Umayyad royal family. But they were not as thorough as they had hoped. One young Umayyad prince by the name of Abd al-Rahmān, a grandson of an earlier caliph, managed to escape. Together with his close companion Bedr, this 16-year-old prince evaded the Abbāsid guards by swimming across the Euphrates. With the help of tribes still loyal to the Umayyads, Abd al-Rahmān made his way to Egypt and eventually across North Africa and into Spain. By 756, with courage and intelligence, he had slowly built up a power-base, capturing first the city of Seville, and then Córdoba, defeating the Abbāsid governor there and making it his new capital. He immediately proclaimed himself the first Umayyad *amīr* of Andalusia, Abd al-Rahmān I, refusing to recognize the Abbāsid caliphate in Baghdad.

To begin with, there was open and widespread hostility among the Arabs of Spain towards anything coming from the Abbāsid capital, which was seen as being dominated by degenerate non-Arabs (Persians) and, by extension, not true Muslims.

It was not until the reign of Abd al-Rahmān's great-grandson, Abd al-Rahmān II (r. 822–52), that peace and prosperity, and with them an intellectual awakening, began to take root. Thus, at the same time that al-Ma'mūn was setting up his House of Wisdom in Baghdad, Córdoba was also tentatively seeing the first green shoots of scholarship. Abd al-Rahmān II dedicated himself to attracting the very best scholars his generous patronage could buy in the hope of rivalling Baghdad as a centre of learning. But modernization would come only slowly, and Abd al-Rahmān II had to bring about change cautiously.

Culturally, Córdoba first tried to imitate Baghdad, and its people loved to hear from travellers arriving from the East about the latest stories, fashions and songs. One of the first to join Abd al-Rahmān's court was an Iraqi musician by the name of Ziryāb (Blackbird) – nicknamed from his dark complexion, beautiful singing voice and fine appearance. A jealous music teacher had driven Ziryāb out of Baghdad, so he had made his way to Córdoba in 822 where Abd al-Rahmān hired him at a handsome salary. Ziryāb would take Islamic Spain by storm and quickly became a cultural icon, introducing the Córdobans to the very latest ideas from metropolitan Baghdad, from music and eating customs to hairstyles, perfumes and deodorants – he even oversaw the development of toothpaste, which was to become very popular across Spain. Not only did he become the arbiter of taste in ninth-century Andalusia, a cornerstone of Spanish music and art, he was also a generous patron of the sciences.[1]

By the late ninth century, Andalusians had obtained Arabic copies of several of the translated Greek texts as well as the work of some of the great figures of ninth-century Baghdad, such as al-Khwārizmi and al-Kindi. The philosophy of the Mu'tazilite movement had reached Spain from the East during the reign of Abd al-Rahmān II, but had made very little impact to begin with. However, by the second half of the ninth century, travellers from the East were starting to be noticed, to the extent that they began to be subject to persecution by the still conservative Andalusian establishment.

The true golden age of Andalusia is considered to have begun with the reign of Abd al-Rahmān III in 929.[2] This ruler would not be satisfied with the title of *amīr* and instead elevated himself to full caliph, putting his power and prestige on a par and in direct competition with the caliphate in Baghdad. In the early years of his reign he was preoccupied with putting down the many dynastic wars, uprisings and tribal revolts that had been going on for decades. All were eventually crushed and he was able to unite the whole of Spain. In many ways, Abd al-Rahmān III was a ruler in the mould of the great Harūn al-Rashīd of Baghdad a century earlier. Like Baghdad, Córdoba was now a vast and glorious city: the largest, most prosperous, and certainly the most cultured, in Europe.

It was Abd al-Rahmān's son, al-Hakam (r. 961–76), who would warrant an even stronger comparison with an Abbāsid counterpart, this time with al-Rashīd's son, the great al-Ma'mūn himself. Just like al-Rashīd and al-Ma'mūn, these Andalusian rulers now had the luxury of peace and prosperity, with scholars enjoying their generous patronage. Al-Hakam, mirroring al-Ma'mūn's obsession with books, would use the vast sums of money at his disposal to satisfy his own obsession. He would send men to the East to obtain copies of all the books they could lay their hands on, enabling him to build a great library within the royal palace next to the Great Mosque of Córdoba, which would soon hold almost half a million books – the largest library in Christian Europe at the time had no more than a few hundred manuscripts. Al-Hakam employed many scribes to make copies of all books brought back. The philosopher Ibn Hazm records that the library catalogue alone filled forty-four volumes of fifty folios each.[3] Of course, the difference between Córdoba and Baghdad was that there was little in the way of a translation movement here, for most of the books that al-Hakam acquired were in Arabic already.

The most famous legacy of the rule of this father and son was a palace-city complex built a few miles outside Córdoba, known as *Medinat al-Zahrā'* (the word *medina* meaning 'city'; see Plate 5). It was begun by Abd al-Rahmān III in 936, but the origin of its name is lost in the mists of time. Some say it was to please his mistress, Zahrā', whose statue stood over the main entrance; others, that it was named after the Prophet's daughter, Fātimat al-Zahrā'. This second explanation seems the more likely, for the newly self-declared caliph was keen to show his subjects, and the world, his power and religious credentials. The building of the palace city began at a time when Abd al-Rahmān was beginning to turn his attention to expansion into North Africa, which was at this point under the control of the Shi'a Fātimid dynasty, also named after the Prophet's daughter. Therefore, another possible explanation for the name is the desire of the Sunni Umayyads to antagonize the Fātimids.

Al-Zahrā' has been called the 'forgotten Versailles of the Middle Ages', but it was not the first such palace city to be built in the Islamic world: the Abbāsid Caliph al-Mu'tasim (younger brother of al-Ma'mūn) had founded the city of Sāmarra in 836, 80 miles north of Baghdad, when he had to leave the capital after its populace revolted against his hated Turkish guard. At the time, Sāmarra was referred to as *Surra man Ra'a* ('Delighting Him Who Sees It').[4] The famous spiral cone minaret (*malwiyya*) of the great mosque of Sāmarra remains today one of the most iconic legacies of the medieval world (see Plate 4). The mosque itself was in its day the largest in the world.

The Andalusian city of al-Zahrā would have seemed dazzling and opulent to visitors from the Christian North, who were regularly welcomed there by the caliph. And just like the palace city of Sāmarra a century earlier, al-Zahrā was more than the caliph's summer retreat away from his capital, Córdoba. It became the new centre of government when Abd al-Rahmān relocated his administration there just ten years after he had begun building it. It is sad to think that this glorious city would be utterly destroyed a little over sixty years later, as we shall see, during a bloody civil war that would bring to an end the Umayyad caliphate, if not Muslim rule, in Andalusia.

When al-Hakam died in 976 he was succeeded by his 10-year-old son Hisham, but power was quickly seized by his vizier, Abū Āmir al-Mansūr (*c.* 938–1002), who became the de facto ruler. Better known in the West as Almanzor, his reign marked the peak of Muslim power in Spain. He had arrived in Córdoba to study law and literature but was ruthlessly ambitious and had engineered his way into being appointed manager of the estates of young Prince Hisham. Within a few years he had eliminated his political rivals and, when al-Hakam died, was in a strong position to serve his own interests by securing the succession of the young Hisham to the throne ahead of his brother. Over the following three years he consolidated his power by taking advantage of the youth and inexperience of Hisham to gain absolute control. The young caliph was effectively imprisoned in Medinat al-Zahrā', which al-Mansūr had closed to all outsiders, completely isolating him. Al-Mansūr then built a new palace on the other side of Córdoba to which he moved all administrative affairs. The Umayyad caliphate was thereby reduced to little more than a ceremonial role, mirroring what was happening to the Abbāsid caliphate in Baghdad.

Al-Mansūr disapproved of science; so much so that many books that had been preserved and collected at great expense by al-Hakam were publicly burned; only those on medicine and mathematics were spared. With his death in 1002, interest in subjects such as philosophy was revived, but this optimism was short-lived. Al-Mansūr's son Sanjūl (Sanchuelo) had tried to claim the title of caliph for himself from the weak and ineffective Hisham. This led to an angry and violent uprising among the population of Córdoba still loyal to the Umayyad family. Meanwhile, North African Berbers, whom al-Mansūr had unwisely and increasingly relied upon, were gathering strength. In 1009 they chose to back a descendant of Abd al-Rahmān III as a rival caliph and, after a brief power struggle, matters came to a head when Berber forces laid siege to Córdoba between 1010 and 1013, destroying Medinat al-Zahrā' in the process. Many of the books from al-Hakam's wonderful library that had not been destroyed by al-Mansūr were now either auctioned off to raise funds for the beleaguered city or plundered by the Berber troops. Medinat al-Zahrā' would be quickly forgotten and remained buried for nine hundred years until its ruins were uncovered in 1911.

With Córdoba's demise, the caliphate was finally abolished in 1031 and Andalusia disintegrated into a number of city-states whose rulers were known as *mulūk al-tawā'if* ('the kings of the regions'). In the West, they are commonly referred to as the Taifa kings. These kingdoms were constantly at war with each other, competing for land and resources, but all were militarily weak. When Muslims first arrived in Spain in 711, they had been a powerful fighting force, but over the years had gradually grown soft. By the tenth century, the geographer

Ibn Hawqal had noted that Andalusians no longer had an appetite for warfare.[5] Instead, their armies were made up of European slaves and North African Berbers.

With the increasingly successful raids and conquests from the Christian north and west (Portugal), the Taifa kings eventually asked for the help of the Islamic Berber rulers of the Maghreb. When Toledo was captured in 1085 by Alfonso VI of Castile, the Berbers moved in to secure what remained of Islamic lands. The Almoravids (al-Murābitūn – meaning 'Those Ready for Battle') ruled from 1085 to 1145, and they were followed by another dynasty, the Almohads (al-Muwahhidūn – 'The Unitarians'), who ruled until 1238. Both were powerful dynasties that at their height ruled over much of north-west Africa, and both were intolerant in their treatment and persecution of the large Jewish communities within the cities, creating a widespread anti-intellectual atmosphere. Meanwhile the Christian *Reconquista* continued unabated, squeezing the land under Muslim rule ever tighter. By the mid-thirteenth century, only the Kingdom of Granada remained under Berber control. The final defeat came at the hands of Ferdinand of Aragon and Isabella of Castile, when the Alhambra fortress palace fell in 1492, signalling the end of Islamic rule in Spain and nearly eight hundred years of Arab culture, the traces of which can still be seen throughout the southern half of the country today.

Before the arrival of Islam, Christian Spain had had very little by way of a scientific tradition. So the Arabs who arrived there in the early eighth century were greeted with a situation very different from that of the early Abbāsids of Baghdad, who were able to draw upon the rich culture of the Persians and, to a lesser extent, the Greek philosophy and medical knowledge available to the Nestorian Christians, who had previously been under Byzantine rule. The early Muslims in Spain were frontiersmen in a province a long way from home, and a long way from the centre of the action. As such, they lagged far behind the Abbāsids, and when scholarship and cultural activity did finally get going it tended to be very derivative, copying what was going on in Baghdad. Added to this was the fact that there was no stimulus to scholarship brought about by a translation movement such as took place in Baghdad, and so we find that original science grew slowly in Andalusia.

But grow and blossom it eventually did. At its peak, Andalusian science was dominated by medicine and philosophy rather than the exact sciences of mathematics and astronomy. As in the East, the early physicians in Muslim Spain were mostly Christians. But now, rather than studying the texts of Galen, they had access to the best that the Islamic East could offer, such as the translations of Hunayn ibn Ishāq. A merchant from the city of Jaen to the east of Córdoba, who had travelled to Baghdad, was one of the early facilitators of this trade. While in Baghdad, he met with the great al-Rāzi around the year 920 and brought back to Spain copies of some of his books.

The very first of the great Andalusian scientists is also probably the best known. In fact, he was the only medieval scientist I had heard of, as a boy growing up in Iraq. His name was Abbās ibn Firnās (810–87), the legendary inventor and the Leonardo da Vinci of Islamic Spain. He is also regarded as the world's first aviator. He is honoured on Arabic postage stamps and has airports named after him, as well as a crater on the moon. But I always associate him with the excitement of my summer holidays. For his statue, with his famous flying contraption, stands majestically in the central reservation of the Baghdad International Airport road. I always knew we had arrived at the airport for another exciting trip to England, when we passed Ibn Firnās. A most colourful character, and a remarkable polymath and inventor, he lived during the reign of Abd al-Rahmān II. He had come to Córdoba to teach mathematics and music, after travelling to study in Baghdad.

Ibn Firnās had an insatiable curiosity and foolhardy courage. He made his famous attempt at controlled flight when, at the age of 65, he built a rudimentary hang-glider and launched himself from the steep side of a mountain in Rusafa (known in Spanish as Arruzafa), a few miles north-west of Córdoba. Some accounts claim he remained airborne for several minutes before landing badly, hurting his back. Although he was able to alter his altitude and direction in order to reach his target landing spot, he had not taken into account the importance of birds' tails in flight and later said that the landing could have been improved by providing a tail apparatus. Much of this story comes from unconfirmed reports and it is unclear whether he had the original idea watching another stuntman by the name of Armen Firman or whether this was just the Latinized name of Ibn Firnās himself.

It was in medicine that Andalusia was to display an early bloom. Many of its scholars travelled to Baghdad during the mid-tenth century to learn from top physicians like al-Rāzi and to study the Arabic translations of the texts of Galen. Among these physicians was the most famous surgeon of the medieval world, Abū al-Qāsim al-Zahrāwi (c. 936–c. 1013) (Abulcasis), who practised in al-Zahrā', whence his name is derived, as court physician to the Caliph al-Hakam. His list of contributions to medicine is truly remarkable: he invented more than a hundred new surgical instruments, many of which are still in use today (such as the forceps used in childbirth), and he was the first to use catgut for internal stitching, the surgical hook, spoon, rod, speculum and bone-saw, the surgical needle, the syringe and the lithotomy scalpel. He pioneered the use of inhalant anaesthesia with sponges soaked in a concoction of narcotics including cannabis and opium. He also made advances in dentistry and perfected the performance of tracheotomies.

Al-Zahrāwi's work was to have a huge impact on Europe and the teaching of medicine during the Renaissance. Indeed, his legacy in the field can be compared with that of al-Rāzi and Ibn Sīna. His most famous text was a huge encyclopedia on medicine and surgery known as *Kitab al-Tasrīf* (*The Method of Medicine*). Its glorious full title translates as *The Arrangement of Medical Knowledge for One Who is Not Able to Compile a Book for Himself*. Written around the year 1000 CE, this thirty-volume work includes anatomical descriptions and classifications of diseases as well as sections on orthopaedics, ophthalmology, pharmacology, nutrition and, most importantly, surgery. For perhaps five centuries during the European Middle Ages, the *Tasrīf* was one of the primary sources for European medical knowledge, along with al-Rāzi's *al-Hāwi* and Ibn Sīna's *Canon*, and served as a reference for all doctors and surgeons. Some of the treatises that make up the *Tasrīf* were quickly translated into Latin and eventually printed in the fifteenth and sixteenth centuries.[6]

The volumes on surgery are divided into three sections: on cauterization, on operations and on the treatment of fractures and dislocations.

Throughout his work we find many illustrations of surgical instruments originally drawn by al-Zahrāwi himself (see Plate 10). Here, for instance, is his description of the syringe, regarded as being the very earliest accurate account of the instrument in the history of medicine:

> When there occurs an ulcer in the bladder, or there is a clot of blood or a deposit of pus in it, and you wish to instil into it lotions and medicaments, this is done with the help of an instrument called a syringe. It is made of silver or ivory, hollow, with a long fine tube, fine as a probe . . . The hollow part containing the plunger is exactly of a size to be closed by it, so that any liquid is drawn up with it when you pull it up; and when you press it down it is driven in a jet.[7]

The other famous Andalusian physician was Ibn Zuhr (Avenzoar), who was born in Seville around 1091 and became another of Islam's great medical clinicians, second only to al-Rāzi in the whole of Islam. His writing, like that of al-Zahrāwi, was to have a big influence on medical practice in Christian Europe.

In the eleventh and twelfth centuries, astronomers in Andalusia took up the challenge earlier posed by Ibn al-Haytham, namely to question Ptolemy's methods and to correct his errors. An anonymous eleventh-century astronomer is known to have written a book called *Recapitulation Regarding Ptolemy (al-Istidrāk ala Batlamyūs)* that has yet to be recovered. It was said to include a list of objections to Ptolemy's astronomy, and the work is famous because it led to a movement known as the 'Andalusian Revolt' that included not just astronomers but the very best of the Andalusian philosophers, such as Ibn Tufayl and Ibn Rushd.

In the late eleventh century, al-Zarqāli (Arzachel) built the first universal astrolabe that, unlike its predecessors, which had been designed to work at a particular latitude, could be used anywhere in the world. The device became known in Europe as a *saphaea* (from the Arabic *safīha*). Al-Zarqāli made a number of important measurements and even deduced that the orbit of Mercury is not circular but oval-shaped. Some writers have naively and wrongly claimed that he was somehow pre-empting Kepler's elliptical orbits with this discovery. However, he still had Mercury orbiting the earth. Nevertheless, al-Zarqāli was one

of just two Islamic astronomers to be mentioned in Copernicus'
De revolutionibus (along with al-Battāni).

Another Andalusian scholar, Ibn Bājja (Avempace) (d. 1139), whom
we met earlier as the man who attacked Ibn al-Haytham's criticism of
Ptolemy, famously proposed that the Milky Way was made up of very
many individual stars and only appears to have a continuous misty
glow from the effect of refraction in the earth's atmosphere (although
it has been claimed that al-Bīrūni knew this more than a century
earlier).

There also seems to have been a group of Arab and Jewish astronomers who carried out observations in Toledo around 1060. This
group produced a *zīj* based on those of al-Khwārizmi and the Syrian
astronomer al-Battāni. It would seem that these 'Toledan Tables' were
far from the best or most accurate examples of Islamic astronomical
measurements, but they had the advantage of being produced in
Toledo, the single most important city for the transmission of Arabic
science to the West. As such, the Toledan Tables were quoted by many
later influential European astronomers, including Copernicus. They
even make it into Chaucer's *Franklin's Tale*, proving that which parts
of Arabic science are best known today is often down to serendipity
rather than quality.

Many of the Andalusian philosophers were inspired by the works
of al-Kindi, al-Farābi and al-Rāzi, which had reached Spain early on.
Among them are several men who deserve more than a cursory mention. The first of these is Ibn Hazm (994–1064), a contemporary of
the three great scholars of the East that we encountered in the last two
chapters: Ibn al-Haytham, Ibn Sīna and al-Bīrūni. Inevitably, he has to
some extent been overshadowed by them and has therefore probably
not received the recognition he deserves, but many historians regard
him as being just as great a thinker, if not a scientist as such, as they
were.[8] He was a philosopher, theologian and historian and one of the
most original thinkers in Muslim Spain. Probably best known for his
work in jurisprudence and theology, he became a controversial writer
and political activist for his continued support of the collapsing
Umayyad dynasty in the first decades of the eleventh century.

Without doubt, the most famous of the Andalusian philosophers
was Abū al-Walīd Muhammad ibn Ahmed ibn Rushd (Averroës)

(1126–98), who is considered by many to be the father of secular thought in Europe and one of the most important philosophers of all time. He is famous for extending the work of the previous Islamic philosophers (the *'ulamā'*) such as al-Kindi, al-Rāzi, al-Farābi and Ibn Sīna in integrating Aristotle's philosophy with Islamic theology. Being the last in this line of Islamic thinkers and the one on Europe's 'doorstep', his work was to become well known across the continent. Show the average educated European the long list of medieval Islamic philosophers and the only two names they are likely to have even heard of will be Avicenna and Averroës. Indeed, if you look carefully at Raphael's wonderful painting in the Vatican *The School of Athens* (1510), depicting the world's greatest philosophers, the only Muslim you will find is Ibn Rushd. Of course, for Raphael – as indeed for any European – the two central characters in the painting are, unsurprisingly, Plato and Aristotle. But no other Muslim philosopher makes it, not because they are not worthy enough but because Raphael would not have known of them. Thomas Aquinas believed Ibn Rushd to be so important that he referred to him as 'the Commentator' to contrast with the other great master, Aristotle, who was known simply as 'the Philosopher'.

Ibn Rushd trained as a judge (*qāthī*) and worked first in Seville, which was the capital of Andalusia at that time, and then in Córdoba. Biographical reports from the period refer to him as a jurist rather than a philosopher, but it was his philosophical ideas that would so hugely influence European scholars. His interpretation of Aristotelian philosophy, known as Averroism, developed into a school of thought that had a lasting effect on Christian theologians keen to explore whether Aristotle's philosophy could be merged or reconciled with Christianity in the same way it had with Islam.

During the golden age of Andalusia, there were large and prosperous Jewish communities that for the most part coexisted peacefully alongside Muslims and flourished in the major cities. But with the slow decline of the golden age came a worsening of relations between the two communities that led to several pogroms in the eleventh century and horrific massacres of the Jews, particularly at the hands of the Berber dynasties. Many Jews fled from their homes in Córdoba, Toledo and Granada for more tolerant parts of the Islamic and

Christian worlds. Among them was the famous Jewish scholar Mūsa ibn Maymūn, better known today as Moses Maimonides, who excelled as a great philosopher and physician.

Born in Córdoba in 1135, Maimonides had to flee with his family in 1148 when the city was captured by the Almohads and, after many years on the move, they finally settled in Egypt. His most famous philosophical work was *The Guide for the Perplexed*, which laid the foundations for much of subsequent Jewish philosophical thought. He was a big admirer of Andalusian Muslim philosophers such as Ibn Bājja and Ibn Rushd, but was also well versed in earlier philosophers from the East such as al-Farābi and Ibn Sīna.[9] While the three mono-theistic religions differ on a wide range of issues, they all tackle the same big questions, such as the meaning of good and evil, the exist-ence of free will and the nature of the afterlife. And all medieval philosophers wrestled with the conflicting notions of revelation and reason. In this sense, what Maimonides took from the Islamic phi-losophers and applied to Jewish theology was no different from what Thomas Aquinas did for Christian theology.

And so we finally come to the most important legacy of Andalusia. For it is through Spain that so much of Arabic science reached Europe. While there were other avenues of transmission and translation, such as through Sicily and along the trade routes with city-states like Venice, as well as through the efforts of Christian travellers in the East such as the Englishman Adelard of Bath (1080–1152), it was nevertheless first and foremost the recapture of Islamic Spain by the Christians that would give Europe access to the wealth of knowledge produced in the Islamic world. Just as Baghdad had been the centre of the thriving translation movement from Greek into Arabic, so cities like Toledo became the centres of translation of the great Arabic texts into Latin.

The very first translations took place as early as the tenth century, and consisted of a collection of treatises on the astrolabe discovered at the monastery of Ripoll in Catalonia.[10] This Benedictine monastery in northern Spain was founded by the, presumably aptly named, Count Wilfred the Hairy (Guifré el Pilós, in Catalan) in 879, who used it as a centre to repopulate a region that sat as the buffer zone between the Islamic Empire to the south and the Christian Franks to the north. The monastery eventually became a great centre of learning and boasted an impressive library.[11]

One of the first scholars to study these early translations was Gerbert d'Aurillac (c. 945–1003), a French monk who developed a deep love for Arab culture and science and who had heard about their many wonderful achievements in mathematics and astronomy, including the work on the Hindu-Arabic numerals. He was introduced to the work of the great Islamic scholars by a bishop from Barcelona by the name of Atto, who had travelled to Córdoba to meet with al-Hakam and had returned smitten by Andalusian culture. Gerbert would later be the first Christian scholar to carry Arabic science across the Pyrenees into Europe.[12] What makes this story so fascinating is that he eventually rose through the ranks of the Catholic Church to become Pope Sylvester II. It seems fitting that Christian Europe was first introduced to the science of the Islamic Empire by a pope!

Probably the most prolific translator of Arabic science into Latin was the Italian scholar Gerard of Cremona (1114–87), every bit as important in the story of the transmission of science as his Baghdadi Christian counterpart Hunayn ibn Ishāq three centuries earlier. He had travelled to Toledo in order to study Arabic and was famously the first to translate Ptolemy's *Almagest* into Latin. He also edited for Latin readers the Toledan Tables, which despite their shortcomings were still the most accurate compilation of astronomical data in Europe at the time. Gerard translated many books, covering most areas of science, including the work of some of the biggest names, such as al-Khwārizmi, al-Kindi, al-Rāzi, Ibn al-Haytham, Thābit ibn Qurra, Hunayn ibn Ishāq and the Banū Mūsa brothers. He also translated al-Zahrāwi's medical encyclopedia, meticulously copying his surgical illustrations. It is thanks to Gerard that al-Zahrāwi was for a long time held in higher regard in Europe, as the great Abulcasis,[13] than he was in his native lands.

I still feel as though I have not done Andalusian scholarship justice in this brief chapter, for I have said nothing about the travel writer Ibn Jubayr (1145–1217) or the historian and philosopher Ibn al-Khatīb (1313–74). I will, however, say a little about the geographer al-Idrīsi (c. 1100–66). Educated in Córdoba, he travelled widely and would finally settle in Sicily, where he was employed by the Norman King

Roger II to produce a new world atlas. It was completed in 1154 as *The Book of Roger (al-Kitab al-Rujāri)* and better known as the *Tabula Rogeriana*. It is regarded as the most elaborate and complete description of the world made in medieval times and was used extensively by travellers for several centuries, for it contained detailed descriptions of the Christian north as well as the Islamic world, Africa and the Far East (see Plate 14). The atlas describes the earth as a sphere with a circumference of 23,000 miles, and maps it in seventy rectangular sections. The historian S. P. Scott wrote a century ago that

> the compilation of al-Idrīsi marks an era in the history of science. Not only is its historical information most interesting and valuable, but its descriptions of many parts of the Earth are still authoritative. For three centuries geographers copied his maps without alteration. The relative position of the lakes which form the Nile, as delineated in his work, does not differ greatly from that established by Baker and Stanley more than seven hundred years afterwards, and their number is the same.[14]

An interesting feature of al-Idrīsi's map, as with all medieval Arabic maps, is that it is drawn upside down, with the north at the bottom.

In the next chapter, I want to focus on astronomy and trace its development during medieval times. For, more than any other discipline, this story highlights the way scientific progress is a continuum. While progress may speed up and slow down, see highs and lows as civilizations rise and fall, and get passed on like a baton in a relay race of discovery, one story exemplifies more than any other the debt owed by European scholars to the giants of the Islamic world. Throughout this book I have highlighted the achievements of the astronomers of the Islamic Empire in the period between Ptolemy and Copernicus. But how important were they really? After all, they believed almost to a man that the sun revolves around the earth, and they had no telescopes that would persuade them otherwise. So, prepare to meet some new characters, without whom the father of modern astronomy, the man who finally delivered the heliocentric model of our solar system, Copernicus, might as well have followed his own father into the copper trade from which he derived his name.

14

The Marāgha Revolution

Accordingly, since nothing prevents the earth from moving, I
suggest that we should now consider also whether several
motions suit it, so that it can be regarded as one of the planets.
For, it is not the centre of all the revolutions.

Nicolaus Copernicus

By this stage in our journey the reader should no longer be in any doubt
that the scientific revolution in sixteenth- and seventeenth-century
Europe could not have taken place had it not been for the many advances
made in the medieval Islamic world in philosophy, medicine, mathematics, chemistry and physics. But one discipline in particular deserves
rather more careful consideration and analysis. As I write these words in
2009, the scientific community is celebrating an important anniversary
that may have passed the wider world by. Amid all the publicity over
Charles Darwin – the year 2009 being the two-hundredth anniversary
of that great man's birth and 150 years since the publication of his *Ori-*
gin of Species – it has gone somewhat unnoticed that it is also designated
as International Year of Astronomy. For 2009 marks the four-hundredth
anniversary of an event that, more than any other, signalled the birth of
modern astronomy. It was during the summer of 1609 that Galileo first
pointed his new telescope into the sky to reveal the wonders of the
cosmos (just as Robert Hooke would half a century later use the microscope to reveal the wonders of the world of the very small).

But Galileo's telescope did so much more than simply bring the distant heavenly bodies closer to us; it banished millennia of confusion and
guesswork about our place in the universe. The traditional historical

narrative, however, is that it was not Galileo who deserves the mantle of founder of modern astronomy but the earlier Polish astronomer Nicolaus Copernicus (1473–1543).

It is a fact of life that oversimplified accounts of the development of science are often necessary in its teaching. Most scientific progress is a messy, complex and slow process; only with the hindsight of an overall understanding of a phenomenon can a story be told pedagogically rather than chronologically. This necessitates the distilling of certain events and personalities from the mêlée: those who are deemed to have made the most important contributions. It is inevitable therefore that the many smaller or less important advances scattered randomly across hundreds of years of scientific history tend to be swept up like autumn leaves into neat piles, on top of which sit larger-than-life personalities credited with taking a discipline forward in a single jump. Sometimes this is perfectly valid, and one cannot deny the genius of an Aristotle, a Newton, a Darwin or an Einstein. But it often leaves behind forgotten geniuses and unsung heroes.

In astronomy, this 'coarse-graining' appears, superficially, to be particularly tempting. For Ptolemy's *Almagest* was so influential as the culmination of Greek astronomical thought that it is not regarded as having been truly replaced until Copernicus wrote his *De revolutionibus* thirteen hundred years later. That work was to signal a true paradigm shift, one of the most dramatic in the history of human thought. For that is the moment when mankind ceased to occupy the centre of the universe as described by Ptolemy's geocentric cosmology. Copernicus would show that it is in fact the earth that revolves around the sun rather than the other way round.

But you are perhaps wondering whether you are really now expected to abandon even this most established of narratives. Is even the great Copernican revolution about to be relegated to the ignominy of a hidden debt to earlier Arabic astronomers who arrived there first? The history of astronomy that leads up to Copernicus is rich and subtle and deserves to be unpicked carefully. I shall tell it, as I have tried to do throughout this book, as objectively and clearly as I can, leaving you to make up your own mind at the end about the issue of – yes – that inevitable hidden debt.

*

Let us first review just why astronomy was so important in Islam. There are two distinct ways in which religion played a role in medieval Islamic astronomy. The first is the obvious one. Astronomy was from the start seen as a science 'in the service of Islam'. Careful astronomical measurements could provide the faithful with tables, charts and techniques that were crucial in determining the times of prayer, the beginning and end of Ramadan (the month of fasting), as well as the all-important *qibla* (the direction towards Mecca for prayer). This relationship turned out to be mutually beneficial, for it is clear that Islam provided social legitimacy to astronomy and even gave astronomers the excuse and opportunity to tackle interesting scientific problems that were not necessarily part of this 'service'.[1]

The second way that Islam played an important role was in its insistence on a clear distinction being made between astronomy as an exact science and the superstitions associated with astrology, which was seen as a direct challenge to Islamic doctrine by giving powers to the stars that should be reserved only for God. It therefore encouraged astronomy to become 'metaphysically neutral'.[2] Thus, we find that astrology, where it continued, was seen as part of natural philosophy rather than the exact science of astronomy. Despite this split, there were nevertheless the inevitable attacks on astronomy and astronomers from the religious orthodox who still associated it with the 'ancient sciences' of the Greeks and, as such, deemed it un-Islamic.

And yet astronomy flourished. It did much more than repeat and check the measurements found in Greek texts like the *Almagest*. Initially, this was certainly its whole extent, with al-Ma'mūn's astronomers producing new and improved star charts and tables. These men were followed by a long line of wonderful astronomers who would carry out meticulous measurements far more accurate that anything the Greeks could have managed. Among the greatest of these were the Syrian astronomer al-Battāni (Albatenius) (*c.* 858–929) and the Egyptian Ibn Yūnus (*c.* 950–1009); both are widely regarded as the greatest observational astronomers of Islam.

Among the many improvements and corrections to Ptolemy's astronomical measurements were those to his values for the length of the year, the obliquity of the ecliptic (the angle of tilt of the earth's axis of rotation relative to the plane of its orbit), the precession of the fixed stars (now known to be due to the gradual shift in orientation of the earth's axis of rotation) and the solar apogee (the furthest distance of the sun from the earth).[3] So extensive and important were these new measurements that I am tempted to describe them more fully, but I will do no more than record that Copernicus himself was well aware of the work of al-Battāni in particular in this regard and indeed quoted him regularly in his *De revolutionibus*.

I wish, however, to return to Ptolemy and the cosmological model that the Muslim astronomers inherited from him. For without understanding its successes and faults we cannot hope to navigate our way through the centuries of Islamic astronomy that led to Copernicus. To begin with, as already mentioned, the most important distinction one can make between Ptolemy and Copernicus is the monumental switch from a geocentric to heliocentric model of the universe. Yet Copernicus was not the first to suggest that the earth went round the sun.

The very first known astronomer to propose a heliocentric model was the Greek Aristarchus of Samos (*c.* 310–230 BCE), who stated correctly that the earth rotated around its own axis, and in turn revolved around the sun. Like his contemporary, Eratosthenes, Aristarchus had calculated the size of the earth, and estimated the size and distance of the moon and sun. From these, he concluded that the sun was six to seven times wider than the earth and thus hundreds of times larger in volume. Some have suggested that his calculation of the relative size of the earth and sun led Aristarchus to conclude that it made more sense for the earth to be moving around the much larger sun than the other way round. His writings on the heliocentric system are lost, but some information is known from surviving descriptions and critical commentary by his contemporaries, such as Archimedes. In a famous passage in *The Sand Reckoner*, Archimedes writes:

> You know that most astronomers designate by the word cosmos the sphere whose centre coincides with the centre of the Earth ... But Aristarchus, the Samian, published in writing certain hypotheses in which it follows from the suppositions that the cosmos must be many times greater than the one mentioned before. He assumes namely that the fixed stars and the Sun remain stationary, while the Earth moves round the Sun through the circumference of a circle.[4]

Little did Archimedes know that Aristarchus' description was spot on. Aristarchus also believed the stars to be very far away, and saw this as the reason why there was no visible parallax.

The only other astronomer known to have been a supporter and follower of Aristarchus' heliocentric theory was a Babylonian by the name of Seleucus (c. 190 BCE). In fact, Aristarchus and Seleucus were probably the only astronomers in antiquity to embrace the notion that the earth revolves around the sun.[5] According to the Greek biographer Plutarch, Seleucus was the first to prove the heliocentric system through logical reasoning, but it is not known what arguments he used, and even this interpretation of Plutarch's writing is itself disputed[6] since Seleucus' 'proof' of the heliocentric theory may have amounted to no more than computing a table of numbers based on the theory.

The heliocentric model was quickly rejected, however, by some of the greatest minds in ancient Greece in favour of a geocentric one. Indeed, the best observational astronomer of antiquity, Hipparchus (fl. c. 162–127 BCE), dismissed the heliocentric model of Aristarchus completely. Hipparchus carried out his work on the island of Rhodes, but had close contact with other astronomers in Alexandria and Babylon. His emphasis on careful measurement, his willingness to revise his own beliefs in the light of new evidence and his renowned unforgiving criticisms of sloppy reasoning of other scholars such as Eratosthenes place him, almost uniquely among the Greeks, as an early adherent of the scientific method. Indeed, he would not have looked out of place among great Islamic astronomers such al-Battāni, Ibn al-Haytham and al-Bīrūni. Hipparchus' most important astronomical work concerned the orbits of the sun and moon (within a geocentric model) and their distances from the earth. He famously worked out that the moon's mean distance from the earth is sixty-three times the earth's radius, just a few percentage points larger than the correct value. He also discovered the precession of the equinoxes (the path traced by the earth's axis of rotation, like the wobble of a spinning top).

But the man who had the greatest influence on astronomy in ancient times was none other than Aristotle himself, almost a century before Aristarchus. And Aristotle has a lot to answer for. It is his model of the cosmos, as described in his great work *On the Heavens*, which would colour and shape humanity's notions about the nature of the universe for almost two thousand years. But he was barking up the wrong cosmic tree; it is Aristotle, rather than Ptolemy, to whom humanity owes its long and mistaken fixation with the geocentric universe. In fact, of all the fallacies, muddles, wrong turns and dead ends in the history of science, the Aristotelian universe was the most dramatically wrong.

Aristotle's basic idea was that the earth occupies the privileged centre of what was known as the celestial spheres, or orbs, with all other heavenly bodies (moon, sun, Mercury, Venus, Mars, Jupiter, Saturn – only five planets were known – and the 'fixed' stars) moving in perfect circular orbits around it. His cosmological model comprised a very complex system of fifty-five spheres, which did rather well at predicting the observed motion of all these bodies across the sky. One can even go so far as to say that this was almost a proper scientific theory.[7] It seems to have been accepted universally soon after its inception, even though new observational data from Hipparchus and others necessitated certain modifications to it.

One of the most serious anomalies was to do with the motion of the planets, particularly Mars. It was known that planets moved across the sky from east to west at a faster rate than the fixed stars. But this rate was not constant. In fact, relative to the stars, they would slow down, speed up, and sometimes even double back on themselves. This 'retrograde' motion could not be accommodated in Aristotle's model and a fix was devised by Hipparchus and later perfected by Ptolemy.

By the time Ptolemy published his *Mathematical Treatise*, around 150 CE, later to be known of course by its Arabic title of *Almagest*, Aristotle's model had been extended, tweaked and modified in order to match the observed motion of the heavens. But it had strayed from the ideal of perfect concentric spheres that Aristotle had proposed. Even the simplest of motions, that of the sun, was not straightforward. One way of modelling its 'orbit' around the earth was for it to move around a circle, known as the 'eccentric', the centre of which is shifted away from the earth. In this way, the Greeks could model what we now know to be the earth's elliptical path around the sun. Another model, equivalent to the 'eccentric' idea, was for the sun to move around a small circle called an epicycle, whose centre itself moves around a circle centred on the earth. Both models, epicycles and eccentrics, were shown by Ptolemy to be equivalent (see Plate 14).

Ptolemy's greatest achievement was his theory of planetary motion. There does not appear to have been any satisfactory theoretical model to explain the rather complicated motions of the other five known planets before the *Almagest*. What he did was to combine together the two alternative methods for describing the motion of the sun. The path of a planet therefore consisted of circular motion on an epicycle with the centre of this epicycle moving round a circle, the centre of which was itself offset from the earth. Even this did not quite work, however, and Ptolemy's innovation was to take a further step by introducing the concept of the *equant*, which deserves a brief explanation.

The equant is an imaginary point in space that is the mirror of the earth, displaced equally on the other side of the centre of the deferent about which a planet's epicycle rotates. Crucially, it is the point about which the centre of the epicycle moves at *uniform angular velocity*. According to Ptolemy, the equant is the point in space at which the planet's epicycle centre is 'seen' to move round at a constant angular rate, even though it is not located at the centre of this orbit. So from the vantage point of the true centre of the deferment, the epicycle centre would be moving round in a circle, but speeding up and slowing down. And there you have it. Simple really!

When it came to modelling the motion of the moon, and the variation of the positions of the eclipses, things became really messy, and I shall not try to go into them here. Ptolemy ended up with even more circles moving around circles. The whole thing became convoluted and unwieldy. And yet, it worked.

Things fared little better in Indian astronomy in the period between Ptolemy and the birth of Islam. Early Indian astronomers had also proposed a heliocentric model. But the two giants of medieval Indian science, Āryabhata and Brahmagupta, seem to have considered and abandoned it in favour of a geocentric model, although they had correctly proposed a spherical earth that rotated on its axis. On the whole, Indian astronomy developed out of pre-Ptolemaic Greek ideas,[8] most probably from the much earlier contact with Greek

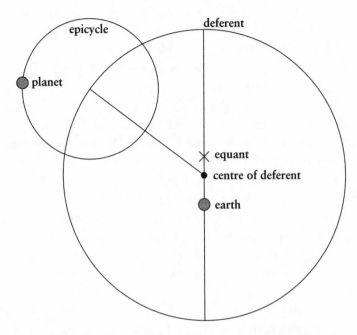

The Ptolemaic model of planetary motion around the earth.

knowledge at the time of Alexander the Great and the Indo-Greek kingdom that followed. Both Āryabhata and Brahmagupta were to have a huge influence on astronomy in early Islam but, ultimately, it was Ptolemy more than anyone else who was to lay the foundations of medieval astronomy.

And so we fast-forward to the eleventh century. We have seen how Ibn al-Haytham had set the *shukūk* ball rolling by casting doubts on Ptolemy's astronomy, separating observational astronomy from cosmology – in a sense, doing what Newton was to do more famously in separating physics from philosophy more than six hundred years later. But Ibn al-Haytham's *shukūk* movement, while inspiring many scholars, from Central Asia to Spain, to really question the mathematical models of the Greeks, had a major flaw: it was still utterly wedded to the geocentric model. While they laboured to get rid of messy equants and epicycles, they did so solely in order to return to the Aristotelian ideal of perfect concentric spheres, with the earth at the very centre of all rotations.

Ibn al-Haytham argued that Ptolemy's cosmology was just not physically possible: one cannot have a sphere that rotates about an axis that does not pass through the sphere's centre – this would cause a 'wobbling' motion that would surely need explaining. Of course, Ibn al-Haytham had no knowledge of the law of gravity or the concept of the centre of mass, yet he was intuitively on the right track in insisting that a mathematical model should reflect physical reality. The whole basis of the *shukūk* movement that he started in astronomy can be summarized by saying that he could not accept a cosmological model that was physically impossible.

A few lone voices could be heard feebly arguing for a real revolution in astronomy, for the heliocentric model had not disappeared entirely. One interesting character I have not mentioned thus far is Abū Ma'shar al-Balkhi (Albumasar) (*c.* 787–886), a Persian scholar who studied the texts of Ptolemy and Aristotle. He is notable for two reasons. First, many of his works were translated into Latin in the first half of the twelfth century, before much of Europe had been introduced to Aristotelian cosmology. Al-Balkhi was thus their first encounter with many of Aristotle's philosophical ideas. Secondly, al-Balkhi had cleverly proposed a 'halfway house' cosmological model, with all the planets orbiting around the sun, apart from the earth, which still sat in its special position at the very centre of the universe with the sun revolving around it. Al-Balkhi's work was known to al-Bīrūni, who, it seems, took it quite seriously, but only as a philosophical problem rather than a scientific one. It is amusing to note that what drove al-Balkhi was his obsession not with astronomy but with astrology. This is the main reason why his work was of such interest to medieval European scholars: for them, it was still the fascination with astrology that drove astronomy.

We should not forget another astronomer, al-Sijzi, who, like his more illustrious contemporary, al-Bīrūni, was influenced by al-Balkhi's work. Al-Sijzi also seems to have proposed a heliocentric model, but there are few details about his work other than that (according to al-Bīrūni) he built a heliocentric astrolabe.

The important distinction to make here is that all these pre-Copernican heliocentric models were more metaphysical than mathematical. The real advances were being made in theoretical astronomy, particularly in the mathematical models of celestial mechanics pushed forward by Ibn al-Haytham. We therefore need to take a closer look at some of these advances, for the little-known yet huge debt owed by Copernicus to Muslim astronomers cannot be merely that he was not the first to propose a heliocentric model.

By any measure, the golden age of Islam and its wonderful scientific achievements were beginning to wane by the eleventh and twelfth centuries. It might be argued that this had more to do with the anticlimax of no longer finding anyone to match the brilliance of Ibn al-Haytham, Ibn Sīna and al-Bīrūni. But this is somewhat unfair, for one could equally claim that Greek science ended with Aristotle in the fourth century BCE. To admit to a scientific decline in the Islamic Empire is one thing, but we must not forget that this was a slow process from the heady heights of the early eleventh century – and it was a long way down. In astronomy, by contrast, the best was yet to come. Despite the Mongol conquests of the Muslim East in the mid-thirteenth century, another two unlikely giants of astronomy emerged: a thirteenth-century Persian polymath who became a member of a religious sect known as the Assassins, and a fourteenth-century timekeeper in a Damascus mosque. More than any others, these two men would progress Ibn al-Haytham's programme.

Nasr al-Dīn al-Tūsi was born in 1201 in the city of Tūs (as his name suggests) in Khurasan in eastern Persia. The city was at the time one of the largest and most important in the whole of Persia and was the place of birth of other notables such as Jābir ibn Hayyān and the poet al-Firdawsi. Even by the standards of some of the more colourful characters we have encountered on our journey, al-Tūsi was a fascinating individual. He studied theology with his father, a prominent Shi'a cleric, but also learnt logic, philosophy and mathematics from his uncle. He completed his education in the city of Nishapūr and quickly gained a reputation as an outstanding scholar. But these were troubled times in Khurasan, for the Mongols were advancing from the east and al-Tūsi could not settle into academic life with this looming shadow. So he accepted the invitation to join a secretive religious sect known as the *Hashashīn* in the relative security of their mountain stronghold.

The Hashashīn were an offshoot of Isma'īli Shi'ism that had split from the Fātimid dynasty and initially gained widespread support east of the Fātimid capital Cairo, in what is now northern Syria, Iraq and Iran. However, they had quickly found themselves isolated and marginalized. In 1090, under their charismatic leader Hassan-i-Sabbāh, they retreated to the Alborz mountains of northern Iran, gained control of a number of strategically important fortresses and set up their headquarters in the mountaintop castle of Alamūt ('Eagle's Nest').

It was at Alamūt that al-Tūsi settled, some even say was imprisoned, for it is not clear whether he would have been able to leave if he had wished. The Hashashīn most probably derived their name from the Arabic/Persian word *hashīsh*, meaning 'grass', because of their cultivation of a wide variety of herbs on the lush farmlands around their forts (and not, as one story goes, because they would come down from the mountains to fight their enemies high on marijuana – hence the term 'hashish'). Because they did not have a conventional army to fight those in the Abbāsid caliphate who opposed them, they would carry out covert raids and assassinations, spreading terror among the population. Indeed, the modern word 'assassin' comes directly from *hashashīn*, for even after their political power was lost, they continued to be used by the Mamlūk dynasty as hired killers for a fixed fee.

Al-Tūsi was a lucky man. He was to escape, not once but twice, the fate of so many countless hundreds of thousands who were killed by the Mongols. The cities of Tūs and Nishapūr were completely destroyed around 1220 by the Mongol army, under Hūlāgū Khan (c. 1217–65), grandson of Genghis Khan. In Alamūt, al-Tūsi was able to pursue his studies in relative peace for almost thirty years. He built an observatory and a library and was even able to attract other scholars to work with him. But this tranquillity was shattered in 1256 when Hūlāgū's army finally arrived at the foothills of Alamūt. Visiting the ruins of the fort today, it is hard to imagine how any army could have breached its walls, which sit isolated and inaccessible atop craggy rocks. But breach them the Mongols did and the Hashashīn were defeated. Al-Tūsi of course had other plans and quickly convinced the Mongol leader that he was worth sparing. Depending on which side of the story one believes, he was either abducted by or rescued by the Mongols. Some even accuse him of selling out to them and betraying his Isma'ili faith too readily.

Whatever his motives, the world should be grateful to al-Tūsi for his survival instincts. He convinced Hūlāgū to employ him as his scientific adviser and that he could predict his astrological chart for him. However, in order to do this he would need the resources to build a new observatory where he could make a range of astronomical measurements. Construction began on the observatory at Marāgha to the east of Tehran in 1259 and it quickly became the world's greatest centre for astronomy. Its centrepiece – instead of today's giant telescopes – was an enormous brick construct on which was laid a metal arc, aligned with the meridian, known as a mural sextant (or Fakhri sextant), many feet high, and on which were marked degrees, minutes and even seconds of arc. Astronomers would line up the celestial object under study using a sighting arm, or dioptra, called the alidade (from the Arabic al-'idada, meaning 'marked ruler') and then make a reading from the markings on the arc, giving the definitive, accurate position of the object in the sky. A system of counter-weights and pulleys was used to allow the observer to manipulate the huge alidade.⁹

Al-Tūsi gathered around him a large group of talented astronomers. His reputation by this time had spread far and wide and he attracted scholars from as far away as China to work with him. The completed zīj, known as the 'Ilkhānī Tables', was a masterpiece. But then so was so much of al-Tūsi's work. For example, his book The Transversal Figure (Shakl al-Qitā') completed and extended Islamic mathematicians' work on trigonometry and is regarded as the very first book devoted to trigonometry as an independent branch of mathematics, as opposed to specific 'techniques' in the service of astronomy. In it, he extended for the first time a well-known theorem called the 'sine rule' from plane triangles to spherical triangles, and extended the work of mathematicians such as Omar Khayyām on number theory. He also wrote extensively on philosophy and logic, and was instrumental in keeping alive the spirit of scientific enquiry in the Islamic world following the Mongol destruction of so many great centres of learning, including the great libraries of Baghdad.

Marāgha under al-Tūsi became much more than just an observatory, for it would also play a major role in the revival of many of the sciences. Most importantly, it lends its name to what historians today refer to as the Marāgha Revolution, a school of thought that took on the challenge first laid down by Ibn al-Haytham to overhaul Ptolemaic astronomy.

Al-Tūsi's most influential book was his *Memoir on Astronomy* (*al-Tathkira fi 'Ilm al-Hay'a*), which is widely regarded as the most important and original book on astronomy to be written in the medieval world. In it, al-Tūsi describes a geometric construction, now known as a Tūsi-couple,[10] which involves a small circle revolving around the inner rim of a larger circle twice its diameter. The clever feature is that a point on the circumference of the smaller circle will be seen to oscillate back and forth in linear motion along a diameter of the larger circle. By means of this construction, al-Tūsi succeeded in reforming the Ptolemaic planetary models, by doing away entirely with the awkward equants.

There is nothing much left to see at the ruins of the Marāgha complex today other than the base of the enormous armillary arm that was its centrepiece. But there had been offices, libraries, even a mosque, in what was the equivalent of a complete research institution such as one might see today. Alongside al-Tūsi were a number of other notable astronomers who also began to tackle the mathematical models of Ptolemaic astronomy, such as al-'Urdi and al-Shirāzi. But when we refer today to the astronomers of the Marāgha School we do not restrict ourselves to those who worked at the observatory, which brings me to the second personality I must introduce before I can return to Copernicus.

By the twelfth and thirteenth centuries an interesting reorientation was taking place in the way astronomy was perceived and funded by Islamic rulers, who were increasingly suspicious of its links to astrology. Thus, unlike the case of al-Tūsi and Hūlāgū, in which funding for the new observatory was secured only on the pretext of producing astrological charts, many Islamic astronomers became increasingly reliant on religious patronage for work solely in the service of religion. In a way, this freed them from the pressure of indulging their political patrons with unscientific and superstitious pursuits (al-Bīrūni in particular was known to be unhappy about having to work on astrology to supplement his income). And so we find that, outside Marāgha, most astronomical work was carried out by *muwaqqits* (the timekeepers of the mosques), whose job it was to determine the precise time for prayer from astronomical measurements and sundial readings.

The most famous of all these *muwaqqits* worked in the great Umayyad mosque in the centre of Damascus. His name was Ibn al-Shātir (1304–75) and he is regarded as the world's greatest astronomer of the fourteenth century. In popular culture, he was famous for building the most accurate and sophisticated sundial ever seen at the time. When it was completed, its ceremonial erection on an outside ledge near the top of one of the mosque's minarets was said to be an event marked by grand celebrations among the people of Damascus. In this way, Ibn al-Shātir could take his measurements and then signal to the *mu'azzin* at the top of the minaret at the precise time for him to begin his call for prayer. The original sundial, now kept at the National Museum of Damascus, was damaged when a nineteenth-century *muwaqqit* by the name of al-Tantāwi tried to move it, wrongly claiming that it was not aligned correctly. He then replaced it with an inferior replica that survives to this day (see Plate 17).

But Ibn al-Shātir's true legacy to astronomy was in his use of al-Tūsi's mathematical trick of overhauling Ptolemy's clunky models by replacing them with new solar and lunar theories that were far more advanced. In this sense, Ibn al-Shātir is regarded as the last great Islamic astronomer of the Marāgha School.

By the time of Copernicus, European scholars had already mastered Ptolemaic astronomy. Two in particular, the Austrian Georg Peurbach (1423–61) and the German Regiomontanus (1436–76), wrote several texts that served as the main sources of Copernicus' education. In particular, their co-authored *Epitome of the Almagest* is regarded as the finest textbook on Ptolemaic astronomy ever written[11] and was studied very carefully by Copernicus together with his copy of a Latin translation of the *Almagest* (a 1515 Venice printing of Gerard of Cremona's translation). However, it was more than just Greek astronomy that interested Copernicus. He learnt from the *Epitome* about the work of early Arabic astronomers such as Thābit ibn Qurra and al-Battāni as well as studying the Toledan Tables, and would later refer to some of this work in his *De revolutionibus*.

None of this is particularly surprising. Far more telling is a cursory

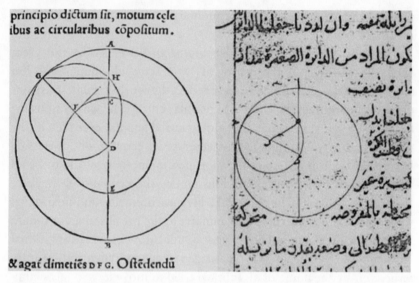

The famous comparison between the Tūsi-couple diagrams of al-Tūsi in his
work of 1261 (on the right) and that of Copernicus in 1543. It is not the
similarity of the shapes that is remarkable but the identity of the letters
labelling the points. Where al-Tūsi has an *alif* Copernicus has an *A*, where
there is a *bā* he has a *B*, *jīm* becomes *G*, *dāl* becomes *D*, and so on
following the order of the letters of the Arabic alphabet.

comparison of the geometric diagrams of planetary models showing
the Tūsi-couple in the *De revolutionibus* and al-Tūsi's *Memoir on
Astronomy*, which are extraordinarily similar, even to the extent of
agreement in the labelling of the different points on the circles:
al-Tūsi's Arabic letter denoting each point having been replaced by its
Latin counterpart.[12] Most dramatically of all, Copernicus' lunar and
solar models, and the model for the motion of Mercury, are exactly
those developed by Ibn al-Shātir and al-Tūsi.

How can this be? Surely the whole point of Copernicus' great
advance was that his heliocentric model *broke away* from the 'fixes'
to the Ptolemaic model, however mathematically clever they may
have been. None of the Marāgha astronomers, including Ibn al-Shātir,
had taken that revolutionary step away from geocentrism (although,
in the case of Ibn al-Shātir's lunar model, the distinction between
heliocentricity and geocentricity is irrelevant since the moon does

indeed orbit the earth). The point here is a subtle one, for what is crucial is not only that Copernicus was using the mathematical tricks developed by the Marāgha School, but that without them he would simply not have been able to arrive at his final heliocentric model. Like the Marāgha astronomers, Copernicus was initially far more concerned with the lack of uniform motion in the Ptolemaic system, with its reliance on equants and deferents. Indeed, so close was Copernicus' approach to those of the Marāgha astronomers that he is now often regarded by historians as the last and most notable champion of the Marāgha School, rather than the first of the modern era. The Marāgha School is thus the link between Ptolemy and Copernicus, without which it is hard to understand how the Copernican revolution could have taken place.

Most historians now believe that the planetary models developed by al-Tūsi and Ibn al-Shātir found their way to Europe (perhaps via Constantinople) and provided Copernicus with the inspiration for his astronomical models. The idea of the Tūsi-couple may have arrived in Europe without the translation of any Arabic text into Latin, and an exact chain of transmission has not yet been identified. Certainly, several manuscripts containing the Tūsi-couple are still extant in Italy, where Copernicus studied between 1496 and 1503 and where he could have encountered the Marāgha theories.

But is all this fair? Are we somehow belittling Copernicus' great achievement by tagging him onto the end of a long line of 'geocentrics'? Certainly, his reintroduction of the heliocentric hypothesis was an act of great intellectual daring. In the preface of the *De revolutionibus*, Copernicus tells Pope Paul III, to whom he dedicates the book, of his great reluctance to publish his theory of the motion of the earth around the sun for fear of ridicule. He goes on to say that he was almost driven to give up on the work altogether and it was only the persistent entreaties of his close friends that convinced him to go ahead.[13]

As far as the idea of heliocentricity is concerned, it is now clear that sixteenth- and seventeenth-century Europeans, including Copernicus himself, were well aware of Aristarchus and his early heliocentric model, and that Copernicus was somewhat disappointed that the Greek had got there first. He even withheld Aristarchus' name in his writing, apart from a footnote in an early version of his *De revolutionibus* which he later deleted.[14]

So not only was the mathematics that Copernicus used in developing his planetary model borrowed from the Islamic world, the heliocentric system to which he applied it had been known (but largely ignored) for nearly two millennia also. Despite all this, I quote from one of the world's leading authorities on Islamic astronomy, George Saliba, who puts it thus:

> There is no question of doubting the originality or genius of Copernicus by implying that he was less brilliant because he used fundamental theorems already discovered and used in Arabic astronomy some two or three centuries earlier. Nor is there any doubt that anyone else could lay claim to the theory of heliocentricity with which Copernicus has become so firmly associated. In fact, if the Copernican revolution is understood to mean the abandonment of geocentricity and the adoption of heliocentricity, which was the masterpiece of Copernicus' work, then it is clear that he remains the unchallenged master of that revolution, and there is no precedent within Arabic astronomy that is in any way similar to heliocentricity.[15]

There is a nice comparison to make here with Einstein's development of his Special Theory of Relativity at the beginning of the twentieth century. I shall therefore make a brief detour to describe his ideas in order to shed light on the analogy I wish to make.

The theory of relativity states that different observers moving relative to each other would disagree about distances and time intervals between two events. But since no one can claim to be in a privileged frame of reference, the notion of absolute lengths and times disappears. This could only be understood by unifying the concepts of space and time, which are intertwined mathematically through a set of equations known as Lorentz transformations (after the Dutchman Hendrik Lorentz, who first wrote them down a year before Einstein published his work). Indeed, much of the groundwork for relativity theory had already been carried out before Einstein, and an early form of the equations had been independently proposed by Lorentz and the Irish physicist George Fitzgerald in the 1890s to explain a famous experiment on the propagation of light.

The trouble was that Lorentz and Fitzgerald had the right equations, and got the right answer, but for the wrong reason. They misinterpreted what was going on by sticking to the widespread notion of the all-pervading 'aether' that was believed to carry light waves through space. Einstein's great achievement was to propose a simple postulate with which he was able to give the correct interpretation of the physics. The notion that light needs some kind of medium to carry it along – in the same way that a water wave needs water – was shown by Einstein to be unnecessary. Everything slotted into place when he made the bold suggestion not only that a beam of light can travel through empty space but that it would be measured by us to have the same speed, no matter how fast we are moving relative to it.

This crucial concept and the ideas that followed, in which space and time are unified, give us a far deeper understanding of our world. While Lorentz and Fitzgerald's equations turned out to be correct mathematically, it was Einstein who gave them the correct interpretation. We see that the value of a good interpretation of a scientific theory brings us closer to the truth, for without a valid interpretation we would still be groping in the dark, no matter how well our theory agreed with experiment.

The same can be said of Copernicus. The Marāgha astronomers may have devised the correct mathematics, but it was Copernicus who applied it with the right interpretation. Those before him had either proposed the right heliocentric cosmology without the underpinning mathematical theory, or they had come up with the mathematical theory applied to the wrong physical system. With a combination of insight and courage, Copernicus brought the two together. In a nutshell, he turned the philosophical idea of heliocentrism into a fully predictive mathematical theory.

There is one final parting comment to make before we leave this story. Copernicus did not of course give us a proper scientific theory. His was a mathematical model based on a hypothetical picture of the physical universe, for he had no knowledge of the law of gravitation. In fact, while he improved on Ptolemy's cosmology by removing the earth from the centre of the universe and replacing it with the sun, we now know that even this was not quite right. To Copernicus, the outer sphere of the fixed and distant stars was also centred on the sun. But we have learnt that our sun sits on an outer arm of an average spiral galaxy in a nondescript part of the universe, and certainly not at the universe's centre. How could poor Copernicus know this before the invention of the telescope? Indeed, modern cosmology based on Einstein's theory and centuries of ever more comprehensive and accurate astronomical data have convinced us that the universe has no centre at all, much as the *surface* of the earth has no centre. What Copernicus described correctly (apart from the elliptical orbits that had to await the work of Kepler) was only our sun-centred solar system. So despite his undoubted genius, I stand by my belief that Copernicus was the last astronomer of the Marāgha School. As for the father of modern astronomy, that title should go to Galileo, for the real revolution only took place with his use of the telescope that was finally to prove Copernicus, and Aristarchus, right.

15

Decline and Renaissance

The history of science, like the history of all civilization, has gone through cycles.

Abdus Salam, Nobel Laureate

Several parallels immediately strike us when we compare the first great translation movement from Greek to Arabic with the second one from Arabic to Latin, jumping three hundred years from ninth-century Islamic Baghdad to twelfth-century Toledo in Christian Spain. Just as classics of Greek science such as Euclid's *Elements* and Ptolemy's *Almagest* were translated and refined several times by different people, so too were Arabic classics like Al-Khwārizmi's *al-Jebr* and Ibn al-Haytham's *Optics*. One can even reel off the list of the most prominent members of this second translation movement who carried out much of the work. The Englishmen Adelard of Bath and Robert of Chester and the Italian Gerard of Cremona are probably the best known; all three worked on translating al-Khwārizmi's texts on mathematics. Other prominent names include Daniel of Morley, John of Seville, Herman the Dalmatian and Plato of Tivoli. The activity reached its peak around the middle of the twelfth century when a translation centre was set up by a bishop named Raymond of Toledo. Some of the translators, like their earlier counterparts in Baghdad, were very able scientists in their own right, although it is fair to say that there were no truly original thinkers among them of the stature of al-Khwārizmi, al-Kindi, Hunayn ibn Ishāq or Thābit ibn Qurra; nor was the Toledo school anywhere near as prolific as the House of Wisdom in Baghdad.

Among the most important Arabic texts to be studied early on was al-Khwārizmi's *al-Jebr*, which was first translated into Latin in 1145 by Robert of Chester (a few years before Gerard of Cremona's version).[1] Robert was thus the first person to introduce the word 'algebra' into Europe. He also gave us the word 'sine', for the trigono-metric quantity defined as the ratio of two sides of a right-angled triangle.[2] But the way we arrived at this word from its Hindu origins also deserves mention, not least because most historians have got it slightly wrong.

Etymologically, we must begin with the Sanskrit word *jya-ardha*, which means 'half the bowstring' (or, geometrically, half the chord of a circle – see diagram opposite). The word *jya-ardha* was abbreviated by Hindu mathematicians to *jiva*, and this was transliterated in Arabic as *jiba* (since there is no 'v'-sounding letter in the Arabic alphabet). This was in turn written with just the two letters *j* (*jīm*) and *b* (*bā'*). It is not clear to me whether this was a deliberate abbreviation or because the two vowels in the word were short sounds, and are there-fore not written in Arabic. When Robert of Chester came to translate this word, he misread it as *jayb*, which in Arabic means 'pocket' (and not, as so many scholars have claimed 'fold', 'bosom', 'bundle' or 'bay'). So he simply used the Latin word for pocket: *sinus*. Finally, English usage converted this word to 'sine'. The first published use of the abbreviation 'sin', along with 'cos', and 'tan', was by the sixteenth-century French mathematician Albert Girard. Interestingly, in Arabic today the word for sine is in fact pronounced *jayb*.

So Arabic science began its osmosis into Europe. While, in compari-son with the Islamic Empire, Western Europe was well and truly mired in its Dark Ages, we do occasionally find more-enlightened rulers encouraging a limited form of scholarship. For instance, the Viking King Cnut (Canute) of England, Norway and Denmark (r. 1016–35) attracted a number of scholars from northern France over to England. Later, the Norman King William (the Conqueror) also encouraged learning, and we witness the arrival in England of a mathematician, Robert of Lorraine, and an astronomer, Walcher of Malvern, towards the end of the eleventh century. Walcher is regarded as the very first English astronomer and is noted for using an astrolabe to measure the time of several solar and lunar eclipses and computing a set of tables

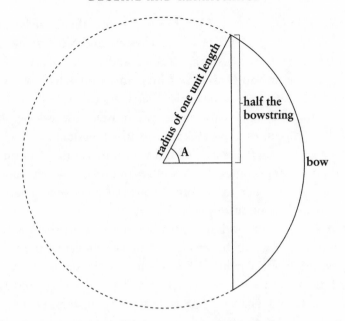

The origin of the trigonometric sine of an angle as described by Hindu mathematicians.

giving the time of the new moons. He was also the very first English scholar of Arabic and one of the first translators of Arabic treatises into Latin.

We have seen how the very earliest transmission of Arabic science into Europe was thanks to men like Gerbert d'Aurillac in the tenth century. The process very gradually picked up pace over the next few centuries as the *Reconquista* brought more of the Andalusian centres under Christian control. But Spain was not the only avenue of transmission. Two other vital cities were Venice, which traded with many of the dynasties in the Muslim world, and Palermo, the capital of Sicily.

In 1061 a Norman mercenary by the name of Roger Guiscard arrived at the shores of Sicily with his army. Over a period of thirty years, he gradually wrested control of the island from its Muslim rulers. He reigned under the title of Grand Count Roger I and was pragmatic enough to make use of much of the Arabs' machinery of government. In fact, like the Muslim rulers before them, the Normans were initially very tolerant of other religions and Sicily remained a land of religious freedom, with Muslims and Jews living peacefully alongside Catholic and Orthodox Christians, while Hebrew, Arabic, Latin and Greek were recognized as official languages. His son, Roger II, reigned for forty-two years (1112–54), mostly now as king; under his rule Sicily became a powerful and wealthy kingdom that included the whole of the southern half of Italy, with its capital, Palermo, as one of the most important cultural centres of Europe. We encountered him earlier as the ruler for whom the great Andalusian geographer al-Idrīsi wrote his famous *Book of Roger*.

But to what extent did Europe really remain in the shadow of the Islamic Empire? It would be wrong to dismiss completely any form of original scientific scholarship in Europe during the Islamic golden age, for there are always isolated pockets of intellectual activity and excellence wherever and whenever one looks in world history. Two notable lights and original thinkers who shone in the medieval darkness were the Italian Thomas Aquinas (*c.* 1225–74), and the Englishman William of Occam (*c.* 1288–1347). However, there were very few other Christian scholars whose achievements could rival their Muslim counterparts until the end of the fifteenth century and the arrival of Renaissance geniuses such as Leonardo da Vinci. By that time, European universities would have contained the Latin translations of the works of all the giants of Islam, such as Ibn Sīna, Ibn al-Haytham, Ibn Rushd, al-Rāzi, al-Khwārizmi and many others. In medicine in particular, translations of Arabic books continued to be studied and printed well into the eighteenth century.

Among the European scholars influenced by their Islamic counterparts before them were Roger Bacon, whose work on lenses relied heavily on his study of Ibn al-Haytham's *Optics*, and Leonardo of Pisa (Fibonacci), who introduced algebra and the Arabic numeral characters after being strongly influenced by the work of al-Khwārizmi. Some historians have even argued that the great German astronomer Johannes Kepler may have been inspired to develop his groundbreaking work on elliptical orbits after studying the work of the twelfth-century Andalusian astronomer al-Bitrūji (Alpetragius), who had tried and failed to modify the Ptolemaic model. While far from the most important of Islamic astronomers, al-Bitrūji's *Principles of Astronomy* (*Kitab al-Hay'a*) became very popular in Europe.[3]

Of course, the influence of Arabic scientists on the rest of the world, and Western Europe in the Middle Ages in particular, extended far beyond their achievements in the pure sciences. For example, I have not gone into detail about their contribution to what is described as the Islamic agricultural revolution and with it new methods of irrigation, or their creation of whole new chemical industries such as glassmaking and ceramics, or the sugar-refining industry. Their engineering feats in building dams, canals, waterwheels and pumps and their technological advances in clockmaking – all these advances in many ways changed the lives of millions of ordinary people directly and immediately.

Rather than turn this into a dry and lengthy list, I shall mention in passing just one example of a gift from the Arabs that I for one am rather grateful for: coffee – especially as it was originally banned in Europe as a 'Muslim drink'. Its use can be traced back to ninth-century Ethiopia where, according to legend, an Arab goatherd named Khalid observed that his goats became livelier after eating the berries of the coffee plant. Intrigued, he boiled the berries in water to produce the first cup of coffee. From Ethiopia, the drink spread to Egypt and Yemen, but it was in Arabia that coffee beans were first roasted and brewed as is done today. By the fifteenth century coffee had reached the rest of the Middle East, Persia, Turkey and North Africa.

In 1583, Leonhard Rauwolf, a German physician, gave this description of coffee after returning from a ten-year trip to the Near East:

> A beverage as black as ink, useful against numerous illnesses, particularly those of the stomach. Its consumers take it in the morning, quite frankly, in a porcelain cup that is passed around and from which each one drinks a cupful. It is composed of water and the fruit from a bush called bunnu.

From the Muslim world, coffee first spread to Italy via Venice and quickly to the rest of Europe. The first European coffee house opened in Italy in the mid-seventeenth century. The colonial Dutch then began to grow it in Indonesia and, by the early eighteenth century, thanks to the efforts of the British East India Company, coffee finally became popular in England.

The story of coffee finally comes full-circle when, in 2007, an agreement was reached after a high-profile court battle between the government of Ethiopia, the home of coffee, and the coffee giants Starbucks over copyright of trademark names of certain Ethiopian coffee beans.

When it comes to feats of engineering in the Islamic Empire, I can do no better than to mention its most famous engineer, Ibn Isma'il al-Jazari (1136–1206), and describe his best-known invention. Originally from al-Jazīra, a region of northern Mesopotamia, he became one of the greatest clockmakers in history. His six-foot-high water-powered 'Elephant Clock' is one of the engineering wonders of the medieval world; an object of artistic beauty as well as engineering brilliance (see Plates 19 and 20). It used Archimedes' water principles combined with Indian water-timing devices and was made up of a hollow model of an Indian elephant ridden by two Arabian figures, on a Persian carpet, with Chinese dragons and an Egyptian phoenix. The clock is based on what is called a perforated float, which acts as the actuator and timekeeper for all parts of the clock. Inside the belly of the hollow elephant is a tank of water in which is floating a bowl with a tiny hole in its bottom. The hole has been carefully drilled to allow in water at a precise rate, such that the bowl completely fills and sinks in exactly half an hour. A small chain that can only flex up and down keeps the bowl close to the side of the tank thus allowing it to only move vertically.

As the bowl fills, it gradually submerges into the tank and pulls on a string attached to a pulley above the elephant that cause the scribe to slowly rotate, marking out the minutes. Once full, the bowl sinks more rapidly, triggering several mechanisms: a separate compartment within the float forces air through a flute, which gives off a sound suggesting the phoenix at the top of the clock is singing. It also pulls on a channel at the top of the clock that contains a number of metal balls. This channel tilts and releases a ball that rolls down, first onto fan blades that force the phoenix to rotate, then into the mouth of one of the dragons, causing it to tip forward. As it does so, its tail rises and pulls on the float in the belly of the elephant. This action raises the float to the surface while tipping and emptying it to allow the whole half-hour process to be repeated. Meanwhile, the ball falls out of the dragon's mouth onto a plate that moves the elephant driver's arms as well as striking a cymbal hidden inside the elephant. Once the ball is released from the dragon it pivots back up again ready to receive another ball one hour later (since the two dragons alternate their actions with each ball). Of course the ball channel would have to be constantly replenished with balls for the clock to continue working.

If you were to measure scientific output by plotting the number of practising scientists in both Europe and the Islamic Empire along a thousand-year timeline, you would see the curve rising slowly in the Islamic world around 700 CE, more rapidly during the time of al-Ma'mūn's House of Wisdom in the first half of the ninth century and peaking around 1000 CE, then beginning its long, slow decline over the next five hundred years. In contrast, European scientific activity was negligible until the early fifteenth century, when it suddenly burst into life. It overtook the Islamic world around the mid-fifteenth century and kept on rising – and is still doing so today. So, before I address the issue of the decline of science in the Islamic world, I shall briefly explore how and why it took off so spectacularly in Europe.

The Renaissance was a cultural movement that spanned roughly the fourteenth to the seventeenth century. Beginning in Florence in Italy and later spreading to the rest of Europe, it saw developments in all intellectual pursuits: in literature, philosophy, art, politics, science and religion. But its beginnings are perhaps best known through the contributions of such men as Leonardo da Vinci and Michelangelo.

While nineteenth-century historians were keen to emphasize that the Renaissance represented a clear 'break' from medieval thought and practice – in particular, that the 'scientific revolution' which began in the mid-sixteenth century heralded the beginning of the modern age – it is now more correctly seen as an acceleration of a continuous process stretching back to antiquity. It is certainly wrong – as I have gone to some lengths to argue – to think of the Renaissance as marking the birth of science or the scientific method. Rather, one can consider it as a 'rebirth' of European scholarship that had long been lost, and this was due in no small part to the discovery of Greek and Arabic texts and their translation into Latin, just as Islamic scholars had earlier discovered the Greek works of antiquity that had fallen into obscurity. Most notably, of course, the conquest of Spain meant that Renaissance scientists had access to such riches as the libraries of Toledo, Córdoba and Granada.

It is interesting to consider why the Renaissance began in Florence, and not elsewhere in Europe, or indeed elsewhere in Italy. Some historians have postulated that Florence was the birthplace of the Renaissance simply as a result of luck, because great men like Leonardo, Sandro Botticelli and Michelangelo happened to have been born in Tuscany at around the same time. But these great men were able to rise to prominence only because of the prevailing cultural conditions, just as ninth-century Baghdad allowed the emergence of a scientific movement led by men such as al-Kindi and al-Khwārizmi. Many historians have emphasized the role played by the Medici family in patronizing and stimulating the arts in a way not too dissimilar to the role of early Abbāsid caliphs.

If we recall the influence of al-Ma'mūn in turning the House of Wisdom from a palace library into possibly one of the greatest centres of learning the world has ever seen, we appreciate the crucial role played by the caliph as a patron of scholarship as well as the importance of a sustained period of peace and prosperity that encouraged the best minds to come together with their infectious enthusiasm, passion and drive. Even in ninth-century Baghdad we see that later, weaker, caliphs were less inclined to encourage and finance scientific scholarship, and that this was inevitably accompanied by a drop-off in the rate of scientific advances.

In more recent times, another period of rapid scientific advances took place, in the early decades of the twentieth century. Again, I do not believe it was luck that saw the coming together in Copenhagen, at the newly created Niels Bohr Institute, of such geniuses as Werner Heisenberg, Paul Dirac and Wolfgang Pauli, who all contributed to the development of the new atomic theory. At any point in history, if the opportunities are available and the sociopolitical conditions favourable, there will be those who take on the challenge.

Another parallel to draw between the golden age of Islam and the

European Renaissance is that between the rationalist Mu'tazilites in Baghdad and the Humanist movement in Italy, as exemplified by Niccolò de' Niccoli (1364–1437) and Poggio Bracciolini (1380–1459). Like the Mu'tazilites, the Humanists stressed the extraordinary ability of the human mind to rationalize and understand the world around it. There is also no doubt that the Renaissance saw significant changes in the way the universe was viewed and the methods with which scientists sought to explain natural phenomena. Whereas the Abbāsid period saw an intermingling of science and religion, the early Renaissance saw the overlap of science and art, with men such as Leonardo making observational drawings of anatomy and nature.

But the crucial thesis of this book all along has been that the most widely cited and significant development of the era, the birth of the modern scientific method, did not originate during this time at all. This revolutionary new way of learning about the world, as exemplified by the work of Copernicus and Galileo, focusing on empirical evidence rather than on the Aristotelian 'final cause', was, we now know, already well established in the tenth and eleventh centuries by al-Rāzi, Ibn al-Haytham and al-Bīrūni.

There were many factors in the European Renaissance that undoubtedly influenced the rate of scientific progress, such as the invention of the printing press, which allowed the transmission of new ideas far more rapidly than before, just as the paper mill had done for the Abbāsids. Other, later, inventions such as the telescope and microscope revolutionized astronomy, biology and medicine.

Between the thirteenth and sixteenth centuries we do indeed see a marked drop in the sheer volume of original scientific output across the Islamic world. In comparison with Renaissance Europe, awash with riches from the New World, confident in a new-found self-belief so reminiscent of al-Ma'mūn's Baghdad, the many dynasties of the Islamic world were facing an uphill struggle against fragmentation and religious conservatism, even apathy, towards pure scientific research that was not in the service of religion, military might or economic wealth. Long after the sun had begun to set on Baghdad, new centres such as Fātimid Cairo, Umayyad Córdoba and Ma'mūnid Gurgānj had risen and fallen.

So, what went wrong? What were the reasons for this slow decline in scientific progress and output in the Islamic world? I shall first address the two most commonly cited reasons, both of which provide quite abrupt end-dates to the golden age of Arabic science.

Many in the Western world have argued that the conflict between the Islamic orthodoxy and the rationalist Mu'tazilite movement, which ultimately culminated in the work of the theologian al-Ghazāli (1058–1111), marked the beginning of the end of the scientific age there. Al-Ghazāli's critique of the philosophy of Ibn Sīna and others in his *Incoherence of the Philosophers* attacked their fascination with Aristotle and the assimilation of his ideas into their philosophy. As such, al-Ghazāli marks a clear move towards a more conservative, even mystical, interpretation of Islamic theology.

Al-Ghazāli remains one of the most respected thinkers in Islamic history, and the effect of his ideas upon orthodox mainstream Islam cannot be understated. He even influenced Thomas Aquinas and other Europeans two centuries later. But the innate religious conservatism of the school of thought that grew around his work inflicted lasting damage on the spirit of rationalism and marked a turning point in Islamic philosophy. In fact, many Muslims to this day see him as having won some sort of intellectual argument that has regrettably left a whole chain of wonderful thinkers, spanning al-Kindi, al-Farābi, al-Rāzi, Ibn Sīna and Ibn Rushd, labelled as heretics. This cheapens and debases the wonderfully rich ideas these men gave the world. What is more, this view is somewhat unfair on al-Ghazāli himself who was a highly competent scientist in his own right.

So why is this still held up as one of the main reasons for the decline of rational scientific enquiry? Al-Ghazāli was primarily attacking a theological and metaphysical viewpoint that relied upon Platonic and Aristotelian logic, arguing that such a reliance on Greek philosophical ideas was anti-Islamic. This dispute has been simplified to an out-and-out struggle between irrational religion and rational science, which is both naive and silly. In any case, other disciplines, such as mathematics, astronomy and medicine, should not have been affected by this purely philosophical dispute – and to a large extent, they were not.[4]

The other argument often held up to explain the cessation of original scientific thinking in the Islamic world is an even lazier argument. It is that the golden age came suddenly crashing to an end in 1258 with the Mongols' destruction of Baghdad, during which most of the books in the House of Wisdom were destroyed by the Mongolian army of Hūlāgū. Although accounts differ, many historians estimate that a large fraction of the city's population, which by then could have numbered close to a million people, were massacred by the Mongols within the space of a single week in February of that year. So fierce was the assault, in fact, that Baghdad never recovered, and, after five hundred years, Abbāsid rule was suddenly over.

This tragically abrupt end to the golden age of Islamic science was certainly the version that I dimly remember being taught during my own history lessons back at school in Iraq. Indeed, it is very much the view taken by Baghdadis, who cannot imagine anything of any note going on elsewhere in the empire. But Baghdad was far from being the only centre of scholarship in the Arabic-speaking world by the middle of the thirteenth century. By this stage there were dozens of flourishing centres in science, across North Africa and Spain, and to the east in Persia and Central Asia. After all, scholars like Ibn Sīna and al-Bīrūni probably never even set foot in Baghdad. Thus, while the destruction of the city in 1258 clearly dealt a terrible psychological blow to Islam as a whole, this single event cannot shoulder too much of the blame.

So if we cannot blame al-Ghazāli's conservatism or the Mongols' sacking of Baghdad, where do we turn? Some modern historians within the Muslim world have argued that the main reason for the decline was Western colonialism, while others claim there was hardly any decline at all. I can fully understand why the latter stance is often taken: it at least counters the view that nothing of note took place in that part of the world after the twelfth century – after all, we have seen that in astronomy major work was still going on in places like Marāgha and Damascus well into the fourteenth century. So, if nothing else, the decline was slower and later than usually suggested. As for political factors such as colonialism, the role they played was a subtle one. The colonial masters of many parts of the Islamic world from the eighteenth century onwards would have felt it necessary to belittle and downplay the achievements of the great centres of learning such as Abbāsid Baghdad and Umayyad Córdoba in order to rationalize and justify their imperialist superiority over large parts of Africa and Asia. But no one can claim that in doing so they were stifling any real spirit of rational enquiry or blocking the creative genius of an Ibn al-Haytham or an al-Bīrūni. For the plain truth is that those heady days were long gone.

One significant factor that played a role was the reluctance of the Muslim world, and the Ottoman Empire in particular, to embrace the printing press quickly enough. This is particularly poignant when one considers that the first ever book to be printed in England was the *Dictes and Sayings of the Philosophers*, in 1477,[5] which was an English translation of an Arabic text (via Latin, then French) originally written in the late eleventh or early twelfth century.[6] So, why this lack of enthusiasm to accept the printing press in the Islamic Empire?

Printing in Arabic type presented the early typesetters with far greater problems than Latin because of the cursive nature of Arabic script and the added complication when joining up the letters, due to the different shapes they take according to their position in a word. Thus, the design and casting of the large amount of different type and the composition of the text were more complicated than for other alphabets. Early typesetters of Arabic even tried to mimic the calligraphers by including additional shorter-sounding vowels (not letters in their own right but dashes and squiggles appearing above or below consonants) along with other symbols such as the *shadda*, which changes the stress or emphasis of some letters. Nowadays, none of these appear in printed Arabic, as the pronunciation of the words is either obvious or grammatically implied.

Muslims showed an intense aversion towards printing well into the seventeenth century. In the Islamic world, calligraphy was, and still is, far more than just an art form or an aesthetic style; it was a means of cultural identity. Printing in moveable type meant that the flowing harmony of this beautiful tradition was being reduced to a mechanistic process, and it was strongly resisted.

But early European printers with an eye for business spotted the potential of an untapped market, and one of the very first books to be printed in Arabic, by the Paganinis of Venice in 1537, was the Qur'an itself. A few years ago I had the opportunity to study the sole surviving copy of this ambitious project. It was discovered in the 1980s by the Italian historian Angela Nuovo in the library of the Franciscan Friars of San Michele in Isola, Venice,[7] and it would appear that very few, if any, native Arabic-speakers have had the opportunity to study it. I was very intrigued therefore to have a close look at it, particularly as it has long been surrounded by an aura of mystery.

On scanning through it, I quickly found several typographical errors. For instance, the Arabic word for 'that' is *thālika*. This appears in the text, incorrectly, with an 'a' sounding vowel instead of an 'i': a slanted dashed line above the 'l' rather than below it, changing the pronunciation to *thālaka*, which is meaningless. This seemingly trivial misspelling of a word in the Muslim holy book would have been regarded as sacrilegious, and it is no surprise that the Ottomans, who had been offered several hundred copies by the valiant Venetian printers, rejected them.

This failure of the trading Venetians to convince the Ottomans of the benefits of the printing press prevented it from spreading beyond Istanbul to other parts of the Islamic world. When Arabic printing was finally introduced in Turkey in 1727, only geography, history and language books were printed: all religious books were specifically excluded from this authorization.

But a drop in the volume of scientific output does not imply a drop in the quality of scholarship where it did continue. For this reason, I wish finally to discuss the achievements of three more great figures: a thirteenth-century physician, a fourteenth-century historian and social scientist and a fifteenth-century mathematician. Not only will this highlight that it was more than just Islamic astronomy that continued to flourish in the Middle Ages, I also feel I simply could not leave out any of these three men from my account of Arabic science.

A popular general knowledge quiz question is: 'Who was the first scientist to explain blood circulation?' The traditional, 'correct', answer is that it was the English physician William Harvey in 1616. But as is so often the case with science, the story is not so straight-forward. Evidence uncovered in a Berlin library in 1924 showed conclusively that the groundwork for his discovery was laid by the Syrian physician (and, inevitably, polymath) Ibn al-Nafis (1213–88), who was the first to describe correctly what is called the pulmonary transit, concerning how blood is carried from the right side of the heart to the left, via the lungs. Galen believed that blood passed from the right to the left ventricle in the heart via tiny passages through the thick wall separating the two sides. Ibn al-Nafīs, who was one of the medieval world's most brilliant anatomists, was the first to challenge this notion and provide the correct explanation. In his manuscript *Sharḥ Tashrīḥ al-Qānūn* (*Commentary on Anatomy in Ibn Sīna's Canon*), discovered in Berlin, he states:

> the blood from the right chamber of the heart must arrive at the left chamber, but there is no direct pathway between them. The thick septum of the heart is not perforated and does not have visible pores as some people thought or invisible pores as Galen thought. The blood from the right chamber must flow through the vena arteriosa (pulmonary artery) to the lungs, spread through its substance, be mingled with air, pass through the arteria venosa (pulmonary vein) to reach the left chamber of the heart . . .

Impressive though this advance in medical understanding is, the concept of 'pulmonary transit' is not the same as pulmonary circulation; there is no explanation in Ibn al-Nafīs's work of the circular return of the blood from the left ventricle to the right, and we should be careful therefore not to credit him with the complete discovery of blood circulation.[8] However, there is evidence that his work, translated into Latin, may have been known to sixteenth-century European physicians such as Michael Servetus, Andreas Vesalius and Renaldus Colombo, all of whom would in turn influence Harvey. And it was Harvey who finally, correctly, described blood circulation through the beating of the heart. (Even Harvey did not understand the physiology of the lungs, though, whereby carbon dioxide is dissipated from the blood and replaced by oxygen – something that had to await the work of the chemist Antoine Lavoisier in the eighteenth century.) All this just goes to show, once again, the gradual and cumulative process of scientific progress.

Ibn al-Nafīs was born in Damascus, but spent most of his career in Cairo. He is another example of a polymath who made a number of contributions in many fields long after Baghdad's golden age. He was a notable historian, linguist, astronomer, philosopher, logician and author of fiction. In medicine, he was also the first to develop the concept of the body's metabolism and is regarded by many historians of science as the greatest physiologist of the Middle Ages and one of the greatest anatomists in history.

Of all the great thinkers of the Islamic world, the only one I regard as the equal of my triumvirate of eleventh-century geniuses, Ibn al-Haytham, Ibn Sīna and al-Bīrūni, is the Tunisian polymath Ibn Khaldūn (1332–1406). The reason I have not discussed him earlier is partly because he lived so much later than what is commonly regarded as the golden age, and because his greatest work was in history and the social sciences, rather than the natural sciences. However, he is in every way a match for al-Bīrūni in terms of the sheer number of disciplines he excelled in.

The twentieth-century economist and political scientist Joseph Schumpeter has carefully studied the history of economic theory as far back as Aristotle and argues that Ibn Khaldūn is without doubt the true father of economic science. In fact, it is worth comparing him with the man whom many economists might regard as the father of modern economic theory, Adam Smith. For when one considers the sheer number of original ideas and contributions across so many areas of economic thought that Ibn Khaldūn invented we are left in absolutely no doubt that he is more worthy of the title.[9] Ibn Khaldūn discovered a number of key economic notions several hundred years before their 'official' births, such as the virtues and necessity of a division of labour (before Smith), the principle of labour value (before David Ricardo), a theory of population (before Thomas Malthus) and the role of the state in the economy (before John Maynard Keynes). He then used these concepts to build a coherent dynamic system of economic theory.[10]

Not only was he the forerunner of European economists, such was his intellect that he is also considered to be the undisputed founder and father of the field of sociology. His best-known work is the *Muqaddima*, which literally means 'Introduction' or 'Prologue'. But neither word really does it justice, and it is more correctly translated as *The Prolegomenon*. The book is a treatise on human civilization in which Ibn Khaldūn discusses at length the nature of the state and society. It is essentially the first volume of a larger treatise dedicated to the history of the Arabs and those states and peoples that had played, in Ibn Khaldūn's view, a historically significant role. The historian Arnold Toynbee said of the *Muqaddima* that it is 'undoubtedly the greatest work of its kind that has ever yet been created by any mind in any time or place'.[11]

My final character is a fifteenth-century mathematician who worked at a flourishing scientific centre, which belies the notion that all vestiges of the golden age had disappeared for good. His name is Jamshīd al-Kāshi (*c.* 1380–1429) and he is far and away the greatest mathematician of the fifteenth century. He worked in the city of Samarkand under the great Ulugh Beg, grandson of Tamerlane, the Mongol who founded the Timurid dynasty that ruled over Central Asia (and which would later create the Moghal Empire in India that lasted until the nineteenth century). Ulugh Beg was himself no slouch as a mathematician and astronomer, and was able to attract many great thinkers to the city of Samarkand, at that time one of the few real powerhouses of world scholarship and learning. He built an impressive observatory that became the natural successor to Marāgha, and his astronomers produced a *zīj*, completed in 1437 and known as *Zij-i-Sultani*, that is regarded by many to be even greater than al-Tūsi's Ilkhānī Tables. It contains almost a thousand stars and was the most comprehensive star catalogue to be produced in the period between Ptolemy and Tycho Brahe.

As for al-Kāshi, he arrived in Samarkand around 1417. I have already mentioned in Chapter 7 how his treatise *The Calculators' Key* was the definitive work on decimal fractions. He would also use decimal fractions to write down a value for pi, which he had calculated, accurate to sixteen decimal places. What is impressive about this achievement is that he carefully states in advance how accurate he requires his result to be and therefore the precision to which he has to work at each stage of his lengthy calculation in order to achieve the desired final result. Indeed, he states that he wishes the value to be so precise that, when it is used to calculate the circumference of the universe (according to the then estimated dimensions) the result would agree with the true value to within the thickness of a horse's hair.[12]

Al-Kāshi's best-known contribution to mathematics, however, is the very first derivation of the cosine rule in trigonometry, which allows the calculation of the length of a side of any triangle provided an angle and the other two sides are known. In fact, it is still known in French as the *théorème d'al-Kashi*.

A few years ago, I took part in a light-hearted debate at the Royal Society in London as to whether Isaac Newton or Albert Einstein deserves the accolade of the greatest scientist who ever lived. I was asked to put the case for Einstein. My argument rested on the premise that Einstein had shown how the Newtonian picture of the universe was wrong and needed to be replaced by a grander, more accurate, description of physical reality. Einstein's Special Theory of Relativity of 1905 concerned far more than his well-known equation, $E=mc^2$. He showed that the three dimensions of space must be treated in a unified picture together with the dimension of time, and that there is no such thing as absolute space or absolute time. Ten years later, his General Theory of Relativity showed that Newton's picture of the force of gravity as the invisible glue pulling all bodies in the universe together was also inaccurate. Einstein produced what is still regarded as the most beautiful scientific theory ever developed, which stated that the force of gravity is the result of the curvature of space-time around a body: a geometrical picture of reality. Where Newton went, Einstein went further, and deeper. In this sense, he clearly eclipsed the accomplishments of Newton.

But is this fair? Surely we must judge each man's achievements in the context of what was known at the time? For neither Einstein nor Newton lived in a vacuum, and each of them stood on the shoulders of past giants, allowing them to see further than others had before. Thus, given the circumstances and knowledge available, we cannot deny Newton's remarkable achievements and greatness.

I have already described, in considering the achievements of Copernicus, how Einstein's papers on the Special Theory of Relativity in 1905 heralded a revolution in physics. It was his breakthrough that brought about the paradigm shift in our understanding of reality, and not the preparatory work of those who came before him. But it is also true that there would not have been a theory of relativity without the work of Jules Henri Poincaré and Lorentz, a few years earlier.

Similarly, much is made of the conflict between Newton and his contemporary, the German mathematician Gottfried Leibniz, over who most deserves credit for the invention of calculus. The truth is that they arrived at their discoveries independently. But neither man started from scratch; and indeed much of the groundwork had been laid down half a century earlier by the great French mathematician Fermat, not forgetting the contributions of such men as Thābit ibn Qurra, Ibn al-Haytham and al-Bīrūni, or indeed Greeks such as Archimedes, and Chinese and Indian mathematicians (notably Āryabhata in the sixth century CE). The point is that it is natural and right when apportioning credit for scientific discoveries to probe issues relating to historical contingency, as well as political and social factors. We tend almost always to be too generous to those who made the most recent steps in a scientific discipline, who inevitably reap the rewards of all antecedent discoveries, while not giving enough credit to those who made the first, and least profitable steps, even though those are often the most important ones.

Those who argue that modern science began with the European Renaissance while at the same time claiming that Newton was a greater scientist than Einstein by virtue of what was known at the time cannot have it both ways. For if Newton's contributions to the field of optics, say, in the seventeenth century were remarkable, then what of those of Ibn al-Haytham six hundred years earlier? Ibn al-Haytham may not have placed optics on the same firm mathematical footing as Newton did, but his contribution was no less important, just as Newton's contribution to the understanding of gravity was no less momentous than Einstein's.

16

Science and Islam Today

With well over a billion Muslims and extensive material resources, why is the Islamic world disengaged from science and the process of creating new knowledge? ... Common sense and the principles of logic and reason [are] our only reasonable choice for governance and progress. Being scientists, we understand this easily. The task is to persuade those who do not.

Pervez Hoodbhoy

Having come to the end of our journey, it is appropriate in this final chapter to take a closer look at the state of science and the spirit of rational enquiry in the Islamic world today. Has it recovered from recent centuries of decline, neglect, religious conservatism, stagnation, colonial rule and every other impediment to progress one cares to think of?

Many commentators argue that to look back continually to the past glories of the scientific achievements of the Islamic world can actually impede the progress of Muslim countries today; that such reminiscing neglects the crucial difference between modern science, defined as that which began with the scientific revolution of Renaissance Europe, and the medieval thinking of the Islamic world, which, they claim, was no more than a kind of 'proto-science', crude attempts to make sense of the world blurred with theology and the occult. Surely it would be far more sensible for the Muslim world to adopt a modern, secular rationalism based on twenty-first-century scientific knowledge and modern attitudes to scientific research? So, as a practising scientist and unapologetic atheist myself, why would I be advocating that Muslims can advance scientifically in the modern world only by adopting ways of thinking from a thousand years ago?

I hope I have convinced you by now that the boundary between the medieval science of the Islamic world and modern science is based on outdated notions in which the achievements of Islamic scholars across a range of scientific disciplines are either downplayed or not fully appreciated. While it is true that advances in science throughout history often take place only in fits and starts, with long periods of stagnation in between, this impression is exaggerated when we focus on just one part of the world. The progress and development of scientific ideas show a more continuous process as ideas evolve and spread, with scholars from different cultures and civilizations exchanging ideas and translating and commenting on texts. Often new ideas and breakthroughs remain undiscovered and so are hit upon independently more than once, sometimes simultaneously.

Of course, it is certainly true that the most important scientific advances tend to be down to individual geniuses: men such as Newton and Einstein brought about what are known as paradigm shifts in our understanding of the world. But these were possible only because of the accumulation of many earlier, smaller advances in understanding until a sort of bottleneck was reached, such that existing ideas and theories could no longer be sustained, allowing for a revolutionary way of thinking. But my point is not about the scientific achievements themselves but about the culture that makes such achievements possible, a culture that thirsts for and respects knowledge and learning.

Throughout this book, I have tried hard not to preach but to tell the story of a forgotten part of history, or at least one that is not widely enough known. I recall as a boy in Iraq hearing about al-Kindi, al-Khwārizmi, ibn Sīna and ibn al-Haytham only in history lessons at school rather than science lessons. I also hope, in reminding those in the Muslim world today of their rich scientific and scholarly heritage and how our current understanding of the natural world has been due in no small part to the contributions of Arabic science, that a sense of pride can be instilled and propel the importance of scientific enquiry back to where it belongs: at the very heart of what defines a civilized and enlightened society.

There are well over a billion Muslims in the world today, around a quarter of the world's population, spread over many more than the fifty-seven member states of the OIC (Organization of the Islamic Conference) in which Islam is the official religion. They include some of the world's wealthiest nations, such as Saudi Arabia and Kuwait, as well as some of the poorest, like Somalia and Sudan. The economies of Muslim countries like the Gulf States, Iran, Turkey, Egypt, Morocco, Malaysia, Indonesia and Pakistan have been growing steadily for a number of years. And yet, in comparison with the West, the Islamic world still seems somewhat disengaged from modern science.

The leaders of many of these countries understand very well that their economic growth, military power and national security all rely heavily on technological advances. The rhetoric is therefore often heard that they require a concerted effort in scientific research and rapid scientific development in order to catch up with the rest of the world's knowledge-based societies. Indeed, government funding for science and education has risen sharply in recent years in many of these countries and several have been overhauling and modernizing their national scientific infrastructures. So what do I mean when I say that most are still disengaged from science?

Here are a few statistics that make the point. In a study in the late 1990s[1] it was found that, on average, the Muslim world spent less than half of 1 per cent of their GDP on research and development, compared with five times that percentage in the developed world. Even more emphatically, data from Unesco and the World Bank showed that a group of twenty representative OIC countries spent 0.34 per cent of their overall GDP on scientific research between 1996 and 2003 – just one-seventh of the global average of 2.36 per cent. These studies were backed up by a third report in 2005 by COMSTECH, an OIC ministerial committee established in 1981 to study possible means of strengthening cooperation among the OIC member states. Muslim countries have fewer than 10 scientists, engineers and technicians per 1,000 of the population compared to the world average of 40, and 140 for the developed world. Between them, they contribute only around 1 per cent of the world's published scientific papers. Indeed, the Royal Society's *Atlas of Islamic-World Science and Innovation* reveals that scientists in the Arab world (comprising

17 of the OIC countries) produced a total of 13,444 scientific publications in 2005 – some 2,000 fewer than the 15,455 achieved by Harvard University alone.[2]

But it is the quality of basic scientific research that is of more concern. One way of measuring the international prominence of a nation's published scientific literature is via its relative citation index (RCI): this is the number of cited papers by a nation's scientists as a fraction of all cited papers, divided by its own share of total papers published, with all citations of its own literature excluded to prevent bias. Thus, if a country produced 10 per cent of the world's scientific literature, but received only 5 per cent of all citations in the rest of the world, its index would be 0.5. In a league table compiled in 2006 by the US National Science Board of the world's top forty-five nations ranked by their RCI in physics, only two OIC countries even register – Turkey with 0.344 and Iran with 0.484 – and only the latter shows a marked improvement over the period between 1995 and 2003. Switzerland topped the table with a RCI of 1.304.

A renowned Pakistani physicist, Pervez Hoodbhoy, recently highlighted the current dire problem.[3] He argues that at Quaid-i-Azam University in Islamabad, where he works, the constraints he encounters are typical of those in many Pakistani public-sector institutions. Quaid-i-Azam University, he tells us, has several mosques on its campus, but no bookshop. And yet this is one of the leading research universities in the Muslim world.[4] Contrast this with al-Ma'mūn's obsession with books and the many wonderful libraries in medieval Baghdad, Cairo and Córdoba.

Is this no more than the complaint of one disgruntled individual? Well, far more telling is the story of another Pakistani physicist, indeed the greatest Muslim scientist of the twentieth century. His name is Abdus Salam (1926–96), and in 1979 he shared the Nobel Prize for physics with two Americans (Sheldon Glashow and Steven Weinberg) for his part in developing what is called the electroweak theory, one of the most powerful and beautiful theories in science, which describes how two of the four fundamental forces of nature (the electromagnetic force and the force of radioactive nuclear decay) are connected. There is no doubt in my mind that his work places him as the greatest physicist of the Islamic world for a thousand years. Not since Ibn al-Haytham and al-Bīrūni has there been a more influential figure in the field.

Born in the Punjab in 1926, Abdus Salam has a name which is in fact a Western corruption (which he readily accepted for convenience) of a single first name, Abd al-Salām. As a Muslim, Salam's life was to be for ever clouded by his adherence to a relatively obscure sect called the Ahmadis, of which there are believed to be around ten million members worldwide, almost half of them living in Pakistan. Although Salam was a pious Muslim, because of his non-orthodox religious convictions he was excommunicated by Pakistan in the 1970s. Despite this, he remained loyal to his country and worked tirelessly to promote science. But Salam's dream of a scientific renaissance in the Islamic world was never realized and he left behind the following damning indictment: 'Of all civilizations on this planet, science is weakest in the lands of Islam. The dangers of this weakness cannot be over-emphasized since the honourable survival of a society depends directly on its science and technology in the condition of the present age.'[5]

It would be a gross mistake, however, to single out religious conservatism alone for the lack of scientific progress in the Muslim world. Far more telling are the antiquated administrative and bureaucratic systems many Muslim countries inherited long ago from their colonial masters and that have still not been replaced, along with the lack of political will to reform, tackle corruption and overhaul failing educational systems, institutions and attitudes. Fortunately, things are changing fast.

If the religious conservatism of the Muslim world is to blame for backward attitudes towards science, we should also be wary about the rest of the world, where we find that science is coming under attack from many religions and belief systems. Even in the so-called 'enlightened' developed world we encounter an alarmingly large proportion of the populace that regards science with suspicion, even fear. This is exacerbated by the increasingly important role science plays in our lives, whether in technology, medical advances, tackling climate change and dwindling resources, or in addressing ever more fundamental questions about the universe and our place in it. Nowhere is the backlash against rational science seen more clearly than in the rise of creationism in the United States and parts of Western Europe. The current row between evolutionary biologists and advocates of intelligent design shows how the tensions between science and religion are far from being restricted to the Muslim world.

Many people are afraid of science and even blame it for the world's problems. Leaving aside the genuine rational worries many people have about the global catastrophe of climate change, pandemics or concerns over energy and water supplies – all of which can and will be addressed and solved only by responsible scientific solutions – many other worries, over GM crops producing Frankenstein food, hybrid embryo research producing Frankenstein babies, or nuclear power leaving future generations a legacy of toxic radioactive waste, are more often than not based on unfounded fears arising from a misunderstanding of the science involved. Add to these the rise in belief in the supernatural and paranormal, New Age therapies, horoscopes, UFOs and alien abductions, even conspiracy theorists denying the Apollo moon landings, and one is left with the feeling that the 'reason versus revelation' arguments that took place in early Islam look quite tame, indeed intellectually rigorous, in comparison.

Nevertheless, there are undeniable tensions between science and religion in some parts of the Muslim world that must be addressed. Anti-scientific attitudes are easy to find in Muslim societies and are now flourishing on the Internet, with thousands of elaborately designed Islamic websites purporting to prove that the Qur'an predicts the Big Bang, black holes, quantum mechanics, even the notion of relativistic time dilation. When I discuss this with Muslim colleagues I always tell them of a fascinating encounter I had with two imams at a religious *madrassa* in Isfahan in Iran a few years ago. They both told me the same thing: that the Qur'an is not a textbook on mathematics or physics, or on medicine or astronomy. It is a book that tells a billion Muslims how to live their lives and to seek God's wonders of creation by observing the world around them, by acquiring knowledge through scientific enquiry. This need never conflict with or threaten their spiritual beliefs.

The problem is that many Muslims see modern science as a secular, even atheist, Western construct, and have forgotten the many wonderful contributions made by Muslim scholars a thousand years ago. They are unable to separate science from religion and therefore do not see (modern) science as indifferent or neutral with respect to Islamic teaching. Some prominent Islamic writers have even argued that scientific disciplines such as cosmology actually undermine the Islamic belief system.[6] Science is attacked therefore on the grounds that it 'seeks to explain natural phenomena without recourse to spiritual or metaphysical causes, but rather in terms of natural or material causes alone'. Well, yes, this is entirely what science is about and what it should be about; I can do no better than to refer back to that wonderful comment by al-Bīrūni which I quoted at the top of Chapter 12.

Fortunately, this view is by no means universal. Many Muslims today completely reject the notion that science and religion are incompatible. In fact, given the current climate of tension and polarization between the Islamic world and the West, it is not surprising that many Muslims feel indignant when accused of not being culturally or intellectually equipped to raise their game when it comes to scientific achievements.

To remind both Muslims and non-Muslims of a time when Islam and science were not at odds, albeit in a very different world, is crucial, not only for science to flourish once again in that part of the world, but as one of the many routes towards a future in which Muslims are able to feel not under threat from science, just as they were able to feel a thousand years ago.

As for how this can be achieved, the obvious first step is serious financial investment. Clearly, bigger science budgets encourage greater scientific activity and it has been shown that, among Muslim countries, there is a strong positive correlation between the number of top universities in a country and its GDP. And many Muslim governments, from Malaysia to Nigeria, are currently investing quite astonishing sums of money in new and exciting projects in an attempt to create world-class research institutions. For instance, the rulers of several of the Gulf States are building new universities, with manpower imported from the West for both construction and staffing.

But it is not simply a matter of throwing money at the problem. What is even more important is the political will to reform and to ensure real freedom of thinking. Nader Fergany, director of the Almishkat Centre for Research of Egypt, is the leading author of the *Report on Arab Human Development*. This report has stressed that what is needed above all else is a reform of scientific institutions, a respect for the freedoms of opinion and expression, ensuring high-quality education for all, and an accelerated transition to knowledge-based societies and the information age.[7]

I shall end on a positive note and mention briefly three exciting new projects that have received considerable publicity in the Middle East. The first is a new science park that opened in the spring of 2009 in a sprawling metropolis called Education City on the outskirts of Doha, the capital of Qatar, which is home to a number of branch campuses of some of the world's leading universities. The Qatar Science and Technology Park hopes to become a hub for high-tech companies from around the world that, one imagines, will try to emulate the success of California's Silicon Valley.

Just as ambitious is a brand-new $10 billion research university called KAUST (King Abdullah University of Science and Technology) just completed on the west coast of Saudi Arabia near the city of Jeddah. It is an international research university that opened its doors for the first time in 2009 and has been heralded not only as a 'living testament to the inspirational and transformational power of science and technology that will spread the great and noble virtue of learning' but, more interestingly, as 'the new House of Wisdom that will rekindle the great Arabic heritage of scientific enquiry'.[8] Incredibly, the vast campus of this international research university, complete with state-of-the-art laboratories and a $1.5 billion budget for research facilities over its first five years, was built from scratch in less than three years. In a pioneering move, it is the first fully co-educational institution in Saudi Arabia, allowing women to sit alongside men in lecture halls rather than in separate rooms. It promises to provide researchers the freedom to be creative and to embody the very highest international standards of scholarship, research and education. These will be in four key areas relevant to Saudi Arabia's plans to exploit solar energy and to develop crops that can survive the country's hot, dry terrain. Many of the top universities in Europe and the United States have been clamouring to be associated with it for – one hopes – scholarly rather than financial motives.

The final positive example is a project called SESAME, which will be the Middle East's first major international research centre as a cooperative venture by scientists and governments in the region. The acronym stands for 'Synchrotron-light for Experimental Science and Applications in the Middle East'. Synchrotron radiation is a form of high energy light that is emitted by electrically charged subatomic particles when they are accelerated in a magnetic field to near light speed. A number of synchrotron facilities have been built around the world and are used for a whole host of cutting-edge research work.

When in 1997 Germany decided to decommission its synchrotron research facility BESSY, it agreed to donate its components to the SESAME project, which was quickly developed under the auspices of Unesco. It is now being built in Jordan, which had to fight off strong competition from other countries in the region. The research to be carried out at SESAME will include material science, molecular biology, nano-technology, x-ray imaging, archaeological analysis and clinical medical applications. Its current membership, along with the hosts, includes Israel, the Palestinian Authority, Egypt, Turkey, Iran, Pakistan, Bahrain and Cyprus, and this group is likely to expand as several other countries join the collaboration. New science should start to be done in 2012.

So, is there a brighter future ahead for science in the Islamic world? Of course, scientific researchers require more than just the latest, shiniest equipment and political rhetoric. The whole infrastructure of the research environment needs to be addressed, from laboratory technicians who understand how to use and maintain the equipment to the exercise of real intellectual freedom and a healthy scepticism and the courage to question experimental results, something that we found in abundance in Baghdad's House of Wisdom and that was preached unambiguously by Ibn al-Haytham.

Just spending vast sums of money will not be enough to reignite and rebuild a scientific culture in the Muslim world. In addition to this, a clear separation of science from theology must be ensured. On a recent visit to Iran, I visited the Royan Institute in Tehran where research in genetics, infertility treatment, stem-cell research and ani-mal cloning is carried out in an atmosphere of openness that was quite dramatically at odds with my expectations. Much of the work at the Royan is therapeutic and centred on infertility treatment, but it was clear that their basic research in genetics was of a high standard.

What struck me in particular was the way the authorities overseeing the research seem to have dealt with the ethical minefields of parts of the work. I spoke to one of the imams who sits on the institute's 'ethics committee'. He explained that every research project proposed must be justified to his committee to ensure that it does not conflict with Islamic teaching. Thus, while issues such as abortion are still restricted (it is allowed only when the mother's life is in danger), research on human embryos is allowed.

According to Islamic teaching, the foetus becomes a full human being only when it is 'ensouled' between forty and a hundred and twenty days from the moment of conception, and so the research at Royan on human embryonic stem cells is not seen as playing God, as it takes place at a much earlier stage. It is of course quite understandable that areas of science that touch upon ethical issues must be considered carefully and sensitively, and, in an Islamic state like Iran, ethical values and moral issues are guided by religious teaching. Nevertheless, for those of us in the secular West, a process whereby the science that can or cannot be pursued is decided by religion is viewed with foreboding, for it is not religion that should be guiding science, and religion should certainly not be seen to hold a monopoly on ethics and morality. We saw how astronomical research in the Islamic world began to wane, Ibn al-Shātir notwithstanding, once it became a mere service industry for Islam rather than a scholarly pursuit for its own sake. This is not the way to go.

The Iranian philosopher Abdolkarim Soroush, who is one of the most influential intellectuals in the Muslim world today,[9] has stressed that censorship in today's Muslim world is stronger than at any other time in history. A cultural renaissance leading to a knowledge-based society is urgently required if wider Muslim society is to accept and embrace not only the bricks and mortar of modern research laboratories along with the shiny particle accelerators and electron microscopes that they house, but that spirit of curiosity that drives mankind to try to understand nature, whether it is to marvel at divine creation or just to know how and why things are the way they are.

The golden age of Arabic science did not last for just two hundred years. It began with Jābir ibn Hayyān in the eighth century and continued until al-Kāshi in the fifteenth – seven hundred years of rise and decline, with different centres across three continents taking their turn in the limelight to shine as bright as supernovas before dimming and bowing out. A scientific renaissance will not happen overnight and requires not only the political will but also and understanding of the meaning of both academic freedom and the scientific method itself. But if the Islamic world managed it before, it can do so again.

Notes

CHAPTER 1. A DREAM OF ARISTOTLE

1. Anthony Cutler, 'Gifts and Gift Exchange as Aspects of the Byzantine, Arab, and Related Economies', *Dumbarton Oaks Papers*, 55 (2001), p. 260.

2. Michael F. Hendy, *Studies in the Byzantine Monetary Economy c. 300–1450* (Cambridge University Press, 2008).

3. The silver dirham was an Islamic coin, and is a unit of currency still used in several Arab countries today, worth less than the gold dinar.

4. While there is no record of any census, a number of medieval Arab writers had attempted to make crude estimates of Baghdad's population. They would typically look at factors such as the consumption of foodstuffs, the numbers of people with specialized occupations or the number of houses and mosques. They would then choose what they subjectively felt were sensible multipliers to extrapolate these numbers. At the most ridiculous extreme is an estimate of 96 million, attributed to an eleventh-century Baghdadi writer by the name of Hilāl al-Sābi', who calculated Baghdad's peak population based on the number of bathhouses in the city. Conservative estimates, comparing Baghdad in size to Constantinople, which had a population of at least 150,000, means Baghdad would have been home to around half a million inhabitants (see Jacob Lassner, 'Massignon and Baghdad: The Complexities of Growth in an Imperial City', *Journal of the Economic and Social History of the Orient*, 9/1–2 (1966), pp. 1–27). However, many historians argue that Baghdad was the world's first city with a population of a million.

5. The most famous of the early Abbāsid structures still surviving is undoubtedly the great mosque of Sāmarra north of Baghdad. Built in 851, this 50-metre-high iconic structure with its distinctive spiralling cone minaret (*malwiyya*) was part of what was once the largest mosque in the world. The few surviving Abbāsid buildings in Baghdad itself are from later periods, such as the Nasiriyya Palace (known today simply as the Abbāsid Palace) built by the Caliph al-Nāsir (r. 1180–1225) and the Mustansiriyya school

built during the reign of al-Mustansir (r. 1226–42). Both these caliphs lived during a time when the Abbāsids, and Baghdad, briefly regained their early glories during the period between the occupations of the Seljuks and the Mongols.

6. Michael Cooperson, *Al-Ma'mūn* (OneWorld, 2005), p. 21.

7. Tayeb El-Hibri, 'Harūn al-Rashīd and the Mecca Protocol of 802: A Plan for Division or Succession?', *International Journal of Middle East Studies*, 24/3 (1992), pp. 461–80.

8. This may not be the real reason for the execution of Ja'far al-Barmaki. One account claims that Ja'far had slept with al-Rashīd's sister and, although the caliph had agreed that they could marry, it had been on the condition that the marriage was never consummated. Yet another reason may have been simply al-Rashīd's jealousy of the power and wealth that the Barmaki family had amassed.

9. Michael Cooperson, 'Baghdad in Rhetoric and Narrative', *Muqarnas*, 13 (1996), p. 99.

10. Sunni and Shi'a are the two major denominations of Islam. Sunnis make up the much larger fraction within the Islamic world whereas Shi'a form the majority of the population in Iran, Iraq, Lebanon, Bahrain and Azerbaijan. The historic background of the Sunni–Shi'a split can be traced back to the schism that took place after the Prophet Muhammad died in the year 632, leading to a dispute over succession, particularly surrounding the rights of Ali ibn abi Tālib, the fourth caliph and son-in-law of the Prophet. Over the years Sunni–Shi'a relations have been marked by both cooperation and conflict, with conflict predominating, most recently in Iraq following the overthrow of Saddam.

11. Dimitri Gutas, *Greek Thought, Arabic Culture* (Routledge, 1998), p. 98.

CHAPTER 2. THE RISE OF ISLAM

1. A good discussion can be found in Albert Hourani's excellent *A History of the Arab Peoples* (Faber and Faber, 2005), pp. 12–14.

2. Historians cannot agree on whether or not Mecca was actually called Macoraba in ancient times. The name is mentioned in the writings of the Alexandrian astronomer and geographer Ptolemy, in the second century CE. According to Islamic tradition, the Ka'ba (the holiest of all Muslim shrines) is supposed to have been built by the prophet Abraham around 2000 BCE. As for Yathrib (Medina), its first documented mention is in Assyrian texts dating back to the sixth century BCE. Ptolemy refers to it in his writings as *Lathrippa*.

3. Non-Arabs who converted to Islam, such as Egyptians, Persians and Turks, were known as *Mawāli*.

4. The Abbāsid dynasty is often mistakenly believed to be named after its first caliph, Abū al-Abbās. In fact, it refers to an uncle of the Prophet by the name of al-Abbās. The caliph with the similar name was the head of a branch of the Banū Hāshim tribe, who trace their lineage to the great-grandfather of the Prophet, via al-Abbās.

5. R. Coke, *Baghdad: The City of Peace* (Thornton Butterworth Ltd., London, 1927), p. 32.

6. Al-Tabari, *The Early Abbāsi Empire*, trans. J. A. William, 2 vols., vol. 1: *The Reign of Abū Ja'far al-Mansūr AD 754–775* (Cambridge University Press, 1998), p. 145.

7. Jacob Lassner, 'Massignon and Baghdad: The Complexities of Growth in an Imperial City', *Journal of the Economic and Social History of the Orient*, 9/1–2, (1966), p. 6.

CHAPTER 3. TRANSLATION

1. Dimitri Gutas, *Greek Thought, Arabic Culture* (Routledge, 1998), p. 2.

2. It is important to note that translations from Pahlavi into Arabic did in fact take place decades before the arrival of the Abbāsids, but these were few and far between and mostly dealt with administrative matters such as Sasanian financial and tax records for the Umayyads. (See, for instance, M. Sprengling, 'From Persian to Arabic', *American Journal of Semitic Languages and Literatures*, 56/2 (1939), pp. 175–224.)

3. Michael Cooperson, *Al-Ma'mūn* (OneWorld, 2005), p. 32.

4. David Pingree, 'Classical and Byzantine Astrology in Sasanian Persia', *Dumbarton Oaks Papers*, 43 (1989), pp. 227–39.

5. David Pingree, 'The Fragments of the Works of Al-Fazārī', *Journal of Near Eastern Studies*, 29/2 (April 1970), pp. 103–23.

6. The importance of geometry in engineering is best exemplified by the Arabic word *handasa*, which to this day means both 'geometry' and 'engineering'.

7. Martin Levey, 'Mediaeval Arabic Bookmaking and its Relation to Early Chemistry and Pharmacology', *Transactions of the American Philosophical Society*, new series, 52/4 (1962), pp. 1–79.

8. This is certainly what is claimed in De Lacy O'Leary's *How Greek Science Passed on to the Arabs* (Routledge & Kegan Paul, 1949), pp. 104–9, but is a view not by any means universally accepted today.

9. The astrolabe is an ancient astronomical device invented by the Greeks, typically made of brass and the size of small plate, although much larger and smaller

ones were made. It was used by astronomers, navigators and astrologers for solving problems relating to the position and motion of the heavenly bodies across the sky. By far the most popular type was the planispheric astrolabe, on which the celestial sphere is projected onto the plane of the equator. To use one, the moveable components are adjusted to a specific date and time. Once set, the entire sky, both visible and invisible, is represented on the face of the instrument.

A typical astrolabe has a circular plate, referred to as the mater, with a central peg on to which a set of smaller removable disks (the tympans) are placed. Each of these is made for a specific latitude and engraved with what is called a stereographic projection of a portion of the sky, which involves mapping points of a sphere on to a two-dimensional surface retaining their angular distribution. Angles are marked out around the rim of the mater. Next, sitting above the uppermost tympan is a rotating framework, called the rete, which is essentially a reference star chart that has engraved on it some of the most important constellations in the sky that are matched with the stars on the tympan below it. Above this is a pointer that also pivots around the central peg, which is marked with a scale showing angles of latitude in the sky.

On the other side of the astrolabe is a sighting arm, or alidade, which is used to make a reading of the angle of inclination of the object being viewed in the sky when the astrolabe is hung vertically.

10. Al-Mansūr's interest in Euclid's *Elements* is mentioned in the great work of the fourteenth-century historian Ibn Khaldūn (1332–1406), *Al-Muqaddima* (*An Introduction to History*), trans. Franz Rosenthal (Princeton University Press, 2005), p. 374.

CHAPTER 4. THE LONELY ALCHEMIST

1. Henceforth, since this is how I write my own name, I will depart from the more 'correct' way of writing an Arabic family name with a lower-case letter 'a' in the definite article.

2. Not to be confused with Euclid's mathematical text the *Elements*, an element in chemistry is defined as a substance that cannot be decomposed into a simpler one by chemical means. We now know that there are more than 100 elements that make up all matter, some of which are created artificially and are highly unstable.

3. W. R. Newman and L. M. Principe, 'Alchemy versus Chemistry: The Etymological Origins of a Historiographic Mistake', *Early Science and Medicine*, 3/1 (1998), pp. 32–65.

4. Quoted in S. E. Al-Djazairi, *The Golden Age and Decline of Islamic Civilisation* (Bayt Al-Hikma Press, Manchester, 2006), p. 320.

5. Quoted in E. J. Holmyard, *Makers of Chemistry* (Clarendon Press, 1931), p. 60.

6. Bayard Dodge (ed. and trans.), *The Fihrist of al-Nadīm* (Columbia University Press, 1970), vol. 2, p. 855.

7. Newman and Principe, 'Alchemy versus Chemistry', p. 38.

8. Ibid., p. 40.

9. See, for instance, the discussion about al-Kindi in Lynn Thorndike, *Arabic Occult Science of the Ninth Century*, (Kessinger Publishing, 2005), an extract from the same author's *History of Magic and Experimental Science*, vol. 1 (Columbia University Press, 1923).

10. This is a little unfair as some Greek scholars, such as Archimedes and Hipparchus, were certainly careful experimentalists.

11. In W. R. Newman, *The 'Summa Perfectionis' of Pseudo-Geber: A Critical Edition, Translation and Study*, Collection de Travaux de l'Académie Internationale d'Histoire des Sciences, 35 (Brill, annotated edn., 1997).

12. J. M. Stillman, 'Falsifications in the History of Early Chemistry', *Scientific Monthly*, 14/6 (1922), pp. 560–67.

13. E. J. Holmyard, 'A Critical Examination of Berthelot's Work upon Arabic Chemistry', *Isis*, 6/4 (1924), pp. 479–99.

14. S. N. Haq, *Names, Natures and Things: The Alchemist Jābir ibn Hayyān and his Book of Stones* (Kluwer Academic Publishers, 1994), p. 11.

15. P. Lory, *L'Élaboration de l'Élixir Suprême: Quatorze traités de Gābir ibn Hayyān sur le œuvre alchimique* (Bibliothèque Damas: Institut Français de Damas; Maisonneuve, Paris, 1988).

16. Haq, *Names, Natures and Things*, p. 25.

17. J. R. Partington, *A History of Greek Fire and Gunpowder* (Johns Hopkins University Press, 1998), p. 307.

18. V. Karpenko and J. A. Norris, 'Vitriol in the History of Chemistry', *Chemické Listy*, 96 (2002), pp. 997–1005.

19. E. J. Holmyard, *Alchemy* (Penguin, 1957; repr. Dover Publications, 1991), p. 81; C. Singer, *The Earliest Chemical Industry* (Folio Society, 1958), p. 61.

20. Holmyard, *Alchemy*, p. 139.

CHAPTER 5. THE HOUSE OF WISDOM

1. Michael Cooperson, *Al-Ma'mūn* (OneWorld, 2005), p. 81.

2. See, for instance, Dimitri Gutas, *Greek Thought, Arabic Culture* (Routledge, 1998), p. 53, or George Makdisi, *The Rise of Colleges: Institutions of Learning in Islam and the West* (Edinburgh University Press, 1981), p. 26.

3. Gutas, *Greek Thought, Arabic Culture*, p. 54.

4. S. E. Al-Djazairi, *The Golden Age and Decline of Islamic Civilisation*

(Bayt Al-Hikma Press, Manchester, 2006), p. 187; Y. Eche, *Les Bibliothèques arabes* (Institut Français de Damas, Damascus, 1967), p. 11.

5. There are two accounts of this man, one from the historian al-Nadīm (Bayard Dodge (ed. and trans.), *The Fihrist of al-Nadīm* (Columbia University Press, 1970), vol. 2, p. 639) and the other by the Baghdadi scholar al-Jahith, a contemporary of al-Ma'mūn (A. F. L. Beeston (trans.), 'On the Difference between Enmity and Envy, by al-Jāhiz', *Journal of Arabic Literature*, 18 (1987), p. 31).

6. Gutas, *Greek Thought, Arabic Culture*, p. 57, and George Sarton, *Introduction to the History of Science*, vol. 1 (Carnegie Institution of Washington, 1927), p. 531.

7. Dodge (ed. and trans.), *The Fihrist of al-Nadīm*, vol. 2, p. 584.

8. Ibid., p. 19.

9. It is worth mentioning that Ishāq is the Arabic version of the name Isaac and is pronounced with the 's' and 'h' separated (iss-*hāq*).

10. Sarton, *Introduction to the History of Science*, vol. 1. Worth noting also is that this 'Time of al-Khwārizmi' is sandwiched between those of the two great contributors to the discipline of chemistry: the previous half century (750–800 CE) is referred to as 'The Time of Jābir ibn Hayyān', and the second half of the ninth century as 'The Time of al-Rāzi'.

11. Obviously, Muhammad ibn Mūsa knew nothing of the gravitational force of attraction between bodies, let alone its mathematical proportionality to the inverse square of the distance between them. His brilliance was in providing an early glimpse at the universality of the laws of nature, applying as they do to both earthly and heavenly bodies.

12. Teun Koetsier, 'On the Prehistory of Programmable Machines: Musical Automata, Looms, Calculators', *Mechanism and Machine Theory*, 36 (2001), pp. 589–603.

13. M. Mayerhof, 'New Light on Hunayn ibn Ishāq and his Period', *Isis*, 8/4 (1926), pp. 685–724.

14. Peter E. Pormann and Emilie Savage-Smith, *Medieval Islamic Medicine* (Edinburgh University Press, 2007), p. 65.

15. Al-Jahiz, *Kitab al-Haywān*, vol. 4 (Al-Matba'ah al-Hamīdīyah al-Misrīyah, Cairo, 1909), p. 23 (in Arabic).

16. Ibid., p. 24.

17. Ibid., p. 25.

CHAPTER 6. BIG SCIENCE

1. Hugh Thurston, 'Greek Mathematical Astronomy Reconsidered', *Isis*, 93/1 (2002), pp. 58–69.

2. Sonja Brentjes, in Thomas Hockey (ed.), *The Biographical Encyclopedia of Astronomers* (Springer, 2007), p. 1011.

3. Benno van Dalen, in Hockey (ed.), *The Biographical Encyclopedia of Astronomers*, pp. 1249–50.

4. e.g., E. S. Kennedy, 'A Survey of Islamic Astronomical Tables', *Transactions of the American Philosophical Society*, new series, 46/2 (1956), pp. 123–77.

5. Gregg DeYoung, in Hockey (ed.), *The Biographical Encyclopedia of Astronomers*, p. 357. On the issue of the theory of astrolabe construction, two later astronomers, al-Battāni and al-Bīrūni, would develop the mathematics considerably further than al-Farghāni.

6. It is well established that the word *zīj*, like a number of other technical terms, came from the Persian and originally meant a thread. It came to stand for the set of parallel threads making up the warp of a fabric and later to mean a table of numbers because of the resemblance between the closely drawn vertical lines of a numerical table and the warp set up in a loom. It finally came to denote whole sets of astronomical tables, which is the meaning here.

7. Marvin Bolt, in Hockey (ed.), *The Biographical Encyclopedia of Astronomers*, p. 740.

8. T. F. Glick, S. Livesey, F. Wallis (eds.), *Medieval Science, Technology and Medicine: An Encyclopaedia*, Routledge Encyclopaedias of the Middle Ages (Routledge, 2005), p. 64. See also Aydin Sayili, *The Observatory in Islam and its Place in the General History of the Observatory*, Publications of the Turkish Historical Society, 7/38 (Ayer Co. Pub., Ankara, 1988).

9. Quoted in David Woodward, 'The Image of the Spherical Earth', *Perspecta*, 25 (1989), p. 3.

10. Thurston, 'Greek Mathematical Astronomy Reconsidered', p. 66.

11. Posidonius had carried out his own measurements following Eratosthenes' method and agreed with his value of 250,000 stadia to begin with but then revised it downwards to 180,000, which is the value Ptolemy quotes.

12. Sonja Brentjes, in Hockey (ed.), *The Biographical Encyclopedia of Astronomers*, p. 1011.

13. *Mas'ūdi*, from *The Meadows of Gold*, trans. P. Lunde and C. Stone (Penguin, 2007), p. 48.

14. Michael Cooperson, *Al-Ma'mūn* (OneWorld, 2005), pp. 2–3.

CHAPTER 7. NUMBERS

1. R. L. Goodstein, 'The Arabic Numerals, Numbers and the Definition of Counting', *Mathematical Gazette*, 40/332 (1956), pp. 114–29.

2. It was also independently known to the Chinese, as the *Gou Gu* theorem, and to the Indians as the *Bakhshali* theorem.

3. It is most likely that the Indian iterative algorithm for computing square roots is based on an earlier Babylonian one, however.

4. Otto Neugebauer, *The Exact Sciences in Antiquity* (Brown University Press, 1957; Dover, 1969), p. 46.

5. J. D. Buddhue, 'The Origin of our Numerals', *Scientific Monthly*, 52/3 (1941), pp. 265–7.

6. D. E. Smith and L. C. Karpinski, *The Hindu-Arabic Numerals* (Ginn and Co., 1911).

7. G. Ifrah, *The Universal History of Numbers: From Prehistory to the Invention of the Computer* (Wiley, 2000).

8. G. Sarton, *Introduction to the History of Science* (Carnegie Institution of Washington, 1927), vol. 1, p. 585.

9. G. Sarton, 'Decimal Systems Early and Late', *Osiris*, 9 (1950), pp. 581–601.

10. Here is the technique the Romans used (which actually goes back to much earlier times and is similar to the method used by the ancient Egyptians). They would put the two numbers to be multiplied alongside each other and then underneath they would halve one number and double the other. This they learnt to do very well. They would keep doing this, ignoring the remainder when halving an odd number, until the number being halved got down to 1. Then they would cross out all those numbers on the doubling column that corresponded to an even number on the halving column and added up what was left on the doubled column. They could add their Roman numerals quite quickly.

To try this with our example I have written the Roman numerals with Hindu-Arabic numerals in brackets for you to follow:

Step 1 (double and halve):

XI (11)   CXXIII (123)
V (5)   CCXLVI (246)
II (2)   CDXCII (492)
I (1)   CMLXXXIV (984)

Step 2 (remove number adjacent to only even number on left):

XI (11)   CXXIII (123)
V (5)   CCXLVI (246)
II (2)
I (1)   CMLXXXIV (984)

Step 3 (add):

         MCCCLIII (1,353)

11. Roshdi Rashed, *The Development of Arabic Mathematics: Between Arithmetic and Algebra* (Kluwer Academic Publishers, 1994), p. 55.

12. Heinrich Hermelink, 'A Commentary upon Bīrūni's Kitab *Taḥdīd al-Amākin*, an 11th Century Treatise on Mathematical Geography by E. S. Kennedy', *Isis*, 67/4 (1976), pp. 634–6.

13. A good discussion on the Babylonian use of zero can be found in Neugebauer, *The Exact Sciences in Antiquity*, pp. 14–20.

14. C. B. Boyer, 'An Early Reference to Division by Zero', *American Mathematical Monthly*, 50/8 (1943), pp. 487–91.

15. Bibhutibhusan Datta, 'Early Literary Evidence of the Use of the Zero in India', *American Mathematical Monthly*, 38 (1931), pp. 566–72.

16. C. B. Boyer, 'Zero: The Symbol, the Concept, the Number', *National Mathematics Magazine*, 18/8 (1944), pp. 323–30.

17. A. S. Sa'īdān, 'The Earliest Extant Arabic Arithmetic: *Kitab al-Fusūl fī al-Hisāb al-Hindī* of Abū al-Hasan Ahmed ibn Ibrāhīm al-Uqlīdisī', *Isis*, 57/4 (1966), pp. 475–90.

18. J. L. Berggren, *Episodes in the Mathematics of Medieval Islam* (Springer-Verlag, 2000), p. 36.

19. The three examples of al-Uqlīdisi's use of decimals in specific problems are (a) halving an odd number a certain number of times, (b) increasing or decreasing a number by a tenth of its value a certain number of times, and (c) the extraction of square and cube roots of numbers.

20. Rashed, *The Development of Arabic Mathematics*, p. 124.

21. There is still some debate over the title of this great book. The problem is in the second word *hussāb*, which means 'calculators' (those who calculate). But because of the absence of the first, shorter, vowel in the Arabic word it could also be read as *hisāb*, meaning 'arithmetic'. This is why two highly acclaimed historians of mathematics, Berggren and Rashed, refer to the book as *The Calculators' Key* and *The Key to Arithmetic*, respectively.

22. The only other mathematician who seems to have picked up on the subject properly was Abū Mansūr al-Baghdādī (d. 1037) in his book *Al-Takmila fī 'Ilm al-Hisāb* (MS 2708, Lala-Li Library, Istanbul).

23. J. Needham, *Science and Civilisation in China* (Cambridge University Press, 1959), vol. 3, pp. 33–91.

24. Of course, while in English we use a decimal 'point' (e.g. 1.5 to mean one and a half), in French, as well as in Arabic, a comma is used to separate the units from the fractions (e.g. 1,5).

25. A. S. Sa'īdān, 'The Earliest Extant Arabic Arithmetic', p. 487.

CHAPTER 8. ALGEBRA

1. Muhammad b. Mūsa al-Khwārizmi (trans. F. Rosen), *The Algebra of Muhammad ibn Mūsa* (Oriental Translation Fund, London, 1831).

2. Fermat's copy of *Arithmetica* was the version published in 1621 and translated from Greek into Latin by Claude Gaspard Bachet de Méziriac.

3. e.g. Roshdi Rashed, *The Development of Arabic Mathematics: Between Arithmetic and Algebra* (Kluwer Academic Publishers, 1994), p. 13.

4. S. Gandz, 'The Sources of al-Khwārizmi Algebra', *Osiris*, 1 (1936), pp. 263–77.

5. G. Sarfatti, *Mathematical Terminology in Hebrew Scientific Literature of the Middle Ages* (Magnus Press, Jerusalem, 1969).

6. Al-Khwārizmi, *The Algebra of Muhammad ibn Mūsa*, p. 3.

7. A calendar is any table or register that marks the passage of time by organizing days into constant time units of weeks, months and years following the naturally repeating cycles of the seasons and the motion of the sun and moon across the sky.

8. A. Youschkevitch and B. A. Rosenfeld, 'Al-Khayyāmī', in Charles Coulston Gillispie (ed.), *Dictionary of Scientific Biography* (Charles Scribner's Sons, 1973), vol. 7, pp. 323–34.

CHAPTER 9. THE PHILOSOPHER

1. John A. Nawas, 'A Reexamination of Three Current Explanations for Al-Ma'mun's Introduction of the *Miḥna*', *International Journal of Middle East Studies*, 26/4 (1994), pp. 615–29.

2. Peter Adamson, *Al-Kindi*, Great Medieval Thinkers (Oxford University Press, 2006), p. 4.

3. Socrates did not himself leave any philosophical writings. His ideas reach us only through the writings of his contemporaries and students, most notably Plato.

4. Quoted in Richard Walzer, 'The Rise of Islamic Philosophy', *Oriens*, 3/1 (1950), p. 9.

5. Simon Singh, *The Code Book* (Fourth Estate, 2000), pp. 14–20.

6. Lynn Thorndike, *Arabic Occult Science of the Ninth Century* (Kessinger Publishing, 2005), p. 649.

7. Alfred L. Ivry, 'Al-Kindi and the Mu'tazila: A Philosophical and Political Reevaluation', *Oriens*, 25 (1976), p. 82.

8. Adamson, *Al-Kindi*, p. 5.

9. Seyyed Hossein Nasr and Oliver Leaman (eds.), *History of Islamic Philosophy* (Routledge, 1996), p. 166.

CHAPTER 10. THE MEDIC

1. The author of this treatise should not be confused with the philosopher Ya'qūb ibn Ishāq al-Kindi; he is an Egyptian-Jewish physician who wrote these words following a visit to Damascus in 1202.

2. I do not mention Chinese medicine here only because it had less of an influence on the Muslim world than Indian and Greek medicine and so is not a part of my story, which is not of course to downplay its importance or impact on the world to this day.

3. Bayard Dodge (ed. and trans.), *The Fihrist of al-Nadīm* (Columbia University Press, 1970), vol. 2, p. 702.

4. P. E. Pormann and E. Savage-Smith, *Medieval Islamic Medicine* (American University in Cairo Press, 2007), p. 96.

5. Later, much larger hospitals would be built, such as the Adudi hospital in 982, the Nūri hospital in Damascus in the mid-twelfth century and the massive Mansūri hospital in Cairo in 1284.

6. Ibn Jubayr, *Travels of Ibn Jubayr*, trans. J. C. Broadhurst (Goodword Books, New Delhi, 2004), p. 234.

7. Pormann and Savage-Smith, *Medieval Islamic Medicine*, p. 117.

8. Described in detail by Albert Zaki Iskandar, 'Al-Rāzi, the Clinical Physician', in P. E. Pormann (ed.), *Islamic Medical and Scientific Tradition* (Routledge, 2010).

9. P. E. Pormann, 'Medical Methodology and Hospital Practice: The Case of Tenth-Century Baghdad', in P. Adamson (ed.), *In the Age of al-Farabi: Arabic Philosophy in the 4th/10th Century*, Warburg Institute Colloquia, 12 (Warburg Institute, 2008), pp. 95–118.

10. M. Dunlop, *Arab Civilisation, to AD 1500* (Longman/Librairie du Liban, 1971), p. 235, an extract from the *Treatise on Smallpox and Measles*.

11. G. Wiet, V. Elisseeff, P. Wolff and J. Naudu, *History of Mankind*, vol. 3: *The Great Medieval Civilizations*, trans. from the French (George Allen & Unwin/Unesco, 1975), p. 654.

12. Quoted in Jennifer Michael Hecht, *Doubt: A History. The Great Doubters and their Legacy of Innovation from Socrates and Jesus to Thomas Jefferson and Emily Dickinson* (HarperOne, 2006), p. 227.

13. L. E. Goodman, 'Al-Razi', in C. E. Bosworth *et al.* (eds.), *The Encyclopedia of Islam* (Brill, 1995), pp. 474–7.

14. Quoted in Hecht, *Doubt*, p. 31.

15. It is interesting that 'zenith' actually derives from the Arabic word *samt*

(meaning 'path' and coming from *samt al-ra's*, or 'path over the head'), but the word was transcribed incorrectly into medieval Latin as *senit*. Likewise, the word 'nadir', the opposite of 'zenith', comes from the Arabic *nadir al-samt*.

CHAPTER 11. THE PHYSICIST

1. I do not make this claim lightly, for Newton followed some truly great scientists, such as Descartes, Galileo and Kepler.

2. Like some of the other best-known Islamic scholars in the West, such as al-Rāzi (Rhazes), Ibn Sīna (Avicenna) and Ibn Rushd (Averroës), Ibn al-Haytham is probably still far better known as Alhazen, as I found when researching for this book and having to look his work up in library catalogues under 'A' rather than 'I' or 'H'.

3. Some have argued that *Dar al-Hikma* translates as 'Hall of Wisdom' – as in 'Hall of Fame'.

4. Roshdi Rashed, 'A Pioneer of Anaclastics: Ibn Sahl on Burning Mirrors and Lenses', *Isis*, 81/3 (September 1990), p. 465.

5. Kurt Bernardo Wolf and Guillermo Krötzsch, 'Geometry and Dynamics in Refracting Systems', *European Journal of Physics*, 16 (1995), pp. 14–20.

6. D. C. Lindberg, *Theories of Vision from al-Kindi to Kepler* (University of Chicago Press, 1976), p. 209.

7. David Lindberg, 'Alhazen's Theory of Vision and its Reception in the West', *Isis*, 58/3 (1967), p. 331.

8. Nader El-Bizri, 'A Philosophical Perspective on Alhazen's Optics', *Arabic Sciences and Philosophy*, 15/2 (2005), pp. 189–218.

9. G. J. Holton and S. G. Brush, *Physics, the Human Adventure: From Copernicus to Einstein and Beyond* (Rutgers University Press, 2001), p. 32.

10. *Opticae Thesaurus*, vol. 1, sect. 1, p. 1, quoted in Lindberg, 'Alhazen's Theory of Vision and its Reception in the West', p. 322.

11. Ibid.

12. Contrary to popular myth, Ibn al-Haytham did not invent the camera obscura, nor is his writing the first mention of it, for its actions were crudely understood by the ancient Chinese before 300 BCE (found in a passage of the *Mo Ching*). But Ibn al-Haytham was the first to describe mathematically how it worked.

13. W. H. Lehn and S. van der Werf, 'Atmospheric Refraction: A History', *Applied Optics*, 44 (2005), pp. 5624–36.

14. H. J. J. Winter, 'The Optical Researches of Ibn al-Haitham', *Centaurus*, 3 (1954), p. 196.

15. Nader El-Bizri, 'In Defence of the Sovereignty of Philosophy: Al-Baghdādī's

Critique of Ibn al-Haytham's Geometrisation of Place', *Arabic Sciences and Philosophy*, 17/1 (2007), pp. 57–80.

16. A. I. Sabri, 'The authorship of *Liber de crepusculis*, an Eleventh-century Work on Atmospheric Refraction', *Isis*, 58 (1967), pp. 77–85.

17. Books I–IV survive in the original Greek while Books V–VII reach us only from their Arabic translation made in the ninth century by the Banū Mūsa brothers.

18. Peter M. Neumann, 'Reflections on Reflection in a Spherical Mirror', *American Mathematical Monthly*, 105 (1998), pp. 523–8.

19. Roshdi Rashed, 'The Celestial Kinematics of Ibn al-Haytham', *Arabic Sciences and Philosophy*, 17 (2007), p. 8.

20. Quoted in ibid., p. 11.

21. Gerhard Endress, in J. P. Hogendijk and A. I. Sabra (eds.), *The Enterprise of Science in Islam* (MIT Press, 2003), p. 148.

22. Bradley Steffens, *Ibn al-Haytham: First Scientist* (Morgan Reynolds Publishing, 2005), p. 62.

23. Robert Briffault, *The Making of Humanity* (The Macmillan Co., 1930), p. 141, quoted in Mohaini Mohamed, *Great Muslim Mathematicians* (Penerbit UTM, 2000), p. 52.

CHAPTER 12. THE PRINCE AND THE PAUPER

1. The Greek Leucippus, who flourished in the fifth century BCE, is regarded as the father of atomic theory. His ideas were extended and developed by his student and disciple Democritus (c. 460–370 BCE). According to them, all matter – indeed the whole universe – consists of fundamental building blocks (atoms) and the void. Aristotle criticized this view.

2. H. M. Said and A. Z. Khan, *Al-Bīrūni: His Times, Life and Works* (Renaissance Publishing House, Delhi, 1990), p. 105.

3. The full correspondence, known as *Al-As'ila wal-Ajwiba* (*The Questions and Answers*) is reproduced in a series of eight journal articles by Rafik Berjak and Muzaffar Iqbal in *Islam & Science*, 1/1 (2003), p. 91; 1/2 (2003), p. 253; 2/1 (2004), p. 57; 2/2 (2004), p. 181; 3/1 (2005), p. 57; 3/2 (2005), p. 166; 4/2 (2006), p. 165; 5/1 (2007), p. 53.

4. This is known today as the Amu Darya river and flows down from the Pamir Mountains to the west of the Himalayas, winding its way west and north through the region of Khwārizm until it finally spills into the southern tip of the Aral Sea.

5. Aisha Khan, *Avicenna* (The Rosen Publishing Group, New York, 2006), p. 39.

6. Because of the different spelling of the two cities Gorgan (Jurjān) and

Gurgānj (Old Urganch, Kunya Urgench or Jurjāniah), the two are often confused with each other. The former is today a thriving city in northern Iran; the latter, in its heyday one of the greatest cities in Central Asia, was razed to the ground by Genghis Khan in 1221.

7. i.e. those who study the languages, literature, history and cultures of the Indian subcontinent.

8. Lenn E. Goodman, *Avicenna* (Cornell University Press, 2006), p. 155.

9. Not forgetting of course Tycho Brahe's careful observations and Johannes Kepler's brilliant deductions.

10. Jamil Ali, *The Determination of the Coordinates of the Cities: Al-Bīrūni's Tahdīd al-Amākin* (Centennial Publications, The American University of Beirut, 1967), p. 188.

11. Ibid., p. 183.

12. I should point out though that the ancient Greeks also had some understanding of how land is recovered from the sea from their discovery of marine fossils high above ground (see the beginning of Plato's *Timaeus*).

13. Abdus Salam, 'Islam and Science', in C. H. Lai and Azim Kidwai (eds.), *Ideals and Realities: Selected Essays of Abdus Salam* (World Scientific, Singapore, 1987), pp. 179–213.

14. Ali, *The Determination of the Coordinates of the Cities*, p. 2.

CHAPTER 13. ANDALUSIA

1. Ivan Van Sertima, *Golden Age of the Moor* (Transaction Publishers, 1991), p. 17.

2. It is a coincidence that the three most famous Andalusian rulers are all called Abd al-Rahmān, for there were others who ruled in between, and there would be five caliphs in total with this name.

3. George F. Hourani, 'The Early Growth of the Secular Sciences in Andalusia', *Studia Islamica*, 32 (1970), p. 149.

4. However, it is most likely that the present name originates from the pre-Islamic toponym, *Sumrā* in Syriac, and that the popular name of *Surra man Ra'a* itself derived from Sāmarra.

5. Hugh Kennedy, in D. Luscombe and J. Riley-Smith (eds.), *The New Cambridge Medieval History* (Cambridge University Press, 2004), vol. 4, p. 601.

6. M. S. Spink and G. L. Lewis, *Albucasis on Surgery and Instruments* (Wellcome Institute of the History of Medicine, 1973), p. 8.

7. Ibid., p. 406.

8. G. Sarton, *Introduction to the History of Science* (Carnegie Institution of Washington, 1927), vol. 1, p. 694.

9. Alexander Broadie, in Seyyed Hossein Nasr and Oliver Leaman (eds.), *History of Islamic Philosophy* (Routledge, 1996), p. 725.

10. Hourani, 'The Early Growth of the Secular Sciences in Andalusia', p. 153.

11. R. W. Southern, *The Making of the Middle Ages* (Yale University Press, 1953), p. 121.

12. David C. Lindberg (ed), *Science in the Middle Ages* (University of Chicago Press, 1976), p. 60.

13. He is also known by the misspelt 'Albucasis'.

14. S. P. Scott, *History of the Moorish Empire in Europe* (Lippincott, 1904), vol. 3, pp. 461–2.

CHAPTER 14. THE MARĀGHA REVOLUTION

1. F. Jamil Ragep, 'Freeing Astronomy from Philosophy: An Aspect of Islamic Influence on Science', *Osiris*, 16 (2001), p. 51.

2. Ibid., p. 50.

3. In the Ptolemaic model, the sun revolves around in a circular orbit that is not centred on the earth. So there is a point in its orbit when it is at its furthest point from the earth: the apogee. Imagine two almost completely overlapping circles of the same size, with the earth at the centre of one and the sun revolving around the other. The measurement made by the Greeks and corrected by Islamic astronomers is that of the longitudinal angle of the sun in the sky at this point in its cycle.

4. Rudolf von Erhardt and Erika von Erhardt-Siebold, 'Archimedes' Sand-Reckoner: Aristarchos and Copernicus', *Isis*, 33/5 (1942), pp. 578–602; O. Neugebauer, 'Archimedes and Aristarchus', *Isis*, 34/1 (1942), pp. 4–6.

5. William Harris Stahl, 'The Greek Heliocentric Theory and Its Abandonment', *Transactions and Proceedings of the American Philological Association*, 76 (1945), pp. 321–32.

6. Noel Swerdlow, 'A Lost Monument of Indian Astronomy', *Isis*, 64/2 (1973), pp. 239–43.

7. Jose Wudka, *Space-Time, Relativity and Cosmology* (Cambridge University Press, 2006), p. 46.

8. Hugh Thurston, *Early Astronomy* (Springer, 1994), p. 178.

9. Aydin Sayili, *The Observatory in Islam and its Place in the General History of the Observatory*, Publications of the Turkish Historical Society, 7/38 (Ayer Co. Pub., Ankara, 1988).

10. The term was coined by historian Edward Kennedy in his paper 'Late Medieval Planetary Theory', *Isis*, 57 (1966), pp. 365–78.

11. Noel Swerdlow, 'The Derivation and First Draft of Copernicus' Planetary

Theory: A Translation of the *Commentariolus* with Commentary', *Proceedings of the American Philosophical Society*, 117 (1973), p. 426.

12. Willy Hartner, 'Copernicus, the Man, the Work, and its History', *Proceedings of the American Philosophical Society*, 117 (1973), pp. 413–22.

13. Swerdlow, 'The Derivation and First Draft of Copernicus' Planetary Theory', p. 423.

14. Stahl, 'The Greek Heliocentric Theory and its Abandonment', p. 322.

15. George Saliba, *A History of Arabic Astronomy* (New York University Press, 1994), p. 26.

CHAPTER 15. DECLINE AND RENAISSANCE

1. Dorothee Metlitzki, *The Matter of Araby in Medieval England* (Yale University Press, 1977), p. 35.

2. George Sarton, *Introduction to the History of Science* (Carnegie Institution of Washington, 1927), vol. 2, p. 126.

3. A. Gonzalez Palencia, 'Islam and the Occident', *Hispania*, 18 (1935), pp. 245–76.

4. George Saliba, *Islamic Science and the Making of the European Renaissance* (MIT Press, 2007), p. 234.

5. While this book is not usually named as the first book to be printed in England (one or two others may have beaten it by a year), it is certainly the first that can be reliably confirmed, since it contains not only the date, but a printer's colophon showing for the first time in England the name of the printer, William Caxton (*c.* 1422–92), and the place of publication, Westminster. Caxton had set up the first printing press in England in 1476. Among the many books he printed was Chaucer's *Canterbury Tales*.

6. The book was written by a little-known scholar from Egypt called Mubāshir ibn Fātik. See Bernard Lewis, 'Translation from Arabic', *Proceedings of the American Philosophical Society*, 124 (1980), pp. 41–7.

7. See Angela Nuovo, 'A Lost Arabic Koran Rediscovered', *The Library*, 6th series, 12 (1990), p. 17.

8. Peter E. Pormann and Emilie Savage-Smith, *Medieval Islamic Medicine* (Edinburgh University Press, 2007), p. 47.

9. Ibrahim M. Oweiss, *Arab Civilization: Challenges and Responses* (SUNY Press, 1988), p. 123.

10. Jean David C. Boulakia, 'Ibn Khaldūn: A Fourteenth-Century Economist', *Journal of Political Economy*, 79 (1971), pp. 1105–18.

11. Arnold J. Toynbee, *A Study of History* (London, 1935), vol. 3, p. 322.

12. J. L. Berggren, *Episodes in the Mathematics of the Medieval World* (Springer, 1986), p. 21.

CHAPTER 16. SCIENCE AND ISLAM TODAY

1. M. A. Anwar and A. B. Abū Bakar, 'Current State of Science and Technology in the Muslim World', *Scientometrics*, 40 (1997), pp. 23–44.

2. The Atlas of Islamic-World Science and Innovation project, Royal Society Science Policy Centre: http://royalsociety.org/aiwsi/.

3. Pervez Amirali Hoodbhoy, 'Science and the Islamic World – The Quest for Rapprochement', *Physics Today,* 49 (2007), pp. 49–55.

4. See also Statistical, Economic and Social Research and Training Centre for Islamic Countries, Academic Rankings of Universities in the OIC Countries (April 2007): http://www.sesrtcic.org/files/article/232.pdf/.

5. Paper by Abdus Salam entitled 'The Future of Science in Islam', delivered to the Islamic Summit Conference held in Kuwait in January 1987.

6. See, for example, Osman Bakar, 'The History and Philosophy of Islamic Science', *Islamic Texts Society* (1999), p. 232.

7. Nader Fergany, 'Steps Towards Reform', *Nature*, 444 (2006), pp. 33–4.

8. Professor Choon Fong Shih and KAUST President: Opening Remarks at the Discover KAUST Global Gathering, 5 January 2009, Jeddah, Saudi Arabia.

9. He was voted the seventh most influential popular intellectual in the world, according to a poll carried out by *Prospect Magazine* in 2008. One needs to be careful, however, with such statistics, for all top ten on the list were from Muslim countries or Muslim backgrounds, pushing Noam Chomsky (who was ranked at number 1 in the previous poll in 2005) into eleventh place. This result clearly has more to do with the connectivity of the Muslim world through the Internet and the power of organized campaigns by followers of particular personalities, particularly in countries such as Turkey, Egypt and Iran, than with true global influence.

Glossary of Scientists

This list of scholars of the Islamic Empire is by no means exhaustive and includes, in addition to those who appear in the main text, several not mentioned but important enough to be listed. The only Christian Europeans included are those prominent in the translation movement from Arabic to Latin.

Note on alphabetical arrangement: If a scholar has a *laqab* (nickname or family name) then that is used to place him. If not – if he is just *X* son of *Y* – then it is his first name that is used, unless he is better known by his father's name. Sometimes, it is simply a case of tradition; thus, both Ibn al-Haytham and al-Hajjāj ibn Yūsuf are found under 'H'.

Adelard of Bath English philosopher, mathematician and scientist (1080–1152) known both for his original works and for translating many important Arabic works on astrology, astronomy, philosophy and mathematics into Latin, as well as an Arabic version of Euclid's *Elements*, which for centuries served as the chief geometry textbook in the West. He studied and taught in France and travelled widely before returning to England, and becoming a teacher of the future King Henry II. His writings on human nature, meteorology, astronomy, botany and zoology are based on Arabic science. He also wrote on the abacus and the astrolabe. He was the greatest English scholar before Roger Bacon.

Ali ibn Īsa Flourished in Baghdad in first half of eleventh century; Christian scholar and the most famous Arab oculist. His *Tathkirat* *al-Kahhālīn* is the oldest Arabic work on ophthalmology and deals with the anatomy, physiology and diseases of the eye, and characterizes more than a hundred different drugs.

Ali ibn Sahl (*c.* 838–70) Son of Sahl al-Tabari; physician and Jewish convert to Islam who flourished in Baghdad under the caliphate of al-Mutawakkil (847–61); tutor to the great al-Rāzi. His most famous work, completed in 850, is *The Paradise of Wisdom* (*Firdaws al-Hikma*), which was primarily on medicine but also covered philosophy, astronomy, meteorology, zoology and psychology. It was predominantly based on Greek and Hindu sources rather than an original work.

al-Ash'ari Abū al-Hassan Ali ibn Isma'īl al-Ash'ari (873–935); Arab theologian who flourished in Baghdad. He is included here, not because of any achievements in science, but because of the widely perceived negative influence of his theological teachings (he was a Mu'tazilite who converted to Sunni orthodoxy) on the spirit of free scientific enquiry. He is regarded as the founder of Muslim scholasticism and the greatest theologian of Islam before al-Ghazāli.

Ibn Bājja Abū Bakr Muhammad ibn Yahya, generally known as Ibn Bājja, Latin, Avempace; Andalusian Muslim philosopher, scientist and physician; born in Saragossa before 1106, lived in Granada and died in Fez in 1139 (possibly poisoned). He was critical of the Ptolemaic model and yet attacked Ibn al-Haytham's criticism of Ptolemy for being too simplistic. He was widely criticized himself because of his 'atheism'. He was a big influence on the work of other Andalusian scholars such as Ibn Tufayl, al-Bitrūji and Ibn Rushd.

Abū Ma'shar al-Balkhi Abū Ma'shar Ja'far ibn Muhammad ibn Umar al-Balkhi (*c.* 787–886), Latin, Albumasar; Persian astrologer who had great influence on twelfth-century Europeans. He studied the texts of Ptolemy and Aristotle. Many of his works were translated into Latin in the first half of the twelfth century and so he was many European scholars' first encounter with Aristotle's philosophy.

Ibn Sahl al-Balkhi Abū Zaid Ahmed ibn Sahl al-Balkhi (850–934), born in the Persian city of Balkh, now in northern Afghanistan;

geographer and mathematician. His *Figures of the Climates* (*Suwar al-Aqālīm*) consisted chiefly of maps and led to him founding the 'Balkhi school' of terrestrial mapping style. He also wrote on medicine and psychology.

Banū Mūsa The three sons of Mūsa ibn Shākir: Muhammad, Ahmed and Hassan, all born in the first decade of the ninth century; mathematicians, engineers, astronomers and wealthy patrons of the translation movement. Among the famous translators they employed were Hunayn ibn Ishāq and Thābit ibn Qurra. It is difficult to disentangle the many contributions each brother made to science, but Muhammad (d. 872/3) seems to have been the most important.

al-Battāni Abū Abdallah Muhammad ibn Jābir ibn Sinān al-Battāni (*c.* 858–929), Latin, Albatenius or Albategnius. The origin of his name, al-Battāni, is not known. He was a Sabian who converted to Islam; born in Harrān and flourished in Raqqah in Syria; died in Sāmarra. He was one of the world's greatest medieval astronomers, who made astronomical observations and measurements of remarkable range and accuracy. He improved on many of the measurements of the Greeks and was quoted extensively by Europeans, including Copernicus. He also made many original advances in trigonometry.

al-Bīrūni Abū Rayhān Muhammad ibn Ahmed al-Bīrūni, born in Khwārizm (Khiva) in 973, died in 1048, probably in Ghazna, Sijistān (Afghanistan); Persian Muslim (but probably agnostic) and one of the greatest scientists and polymaths in history; philosopher, mathematician, astronomer, geographer, anthropologist and encyclopedist. He travelled widely throughout Central Asia; he wrote in Arabic and Persian but was strongly anti-Arab in his sentiments. His most important works were *The Chronology of Ancient Nations*, *The Mas'ūdi Canon* and *The History of India*. He made many original contributions in astronomy and mathematics and was famous for measuring the size of the earth to greater accuracy than anyone had done before.

al-Bitrūji Abū Ishāq Nūr al-Dīn al-Bitrūji (died *c.* 1204), Latin, Alpetragius; Arab astronomer and philosopher, from the town of Pedroche, north of Córdoba; flourished in Seville; disciple of Ibn

Tufayl and contemporary of Ibn Rushd. He advanced a theory on planetary motion that avoided both epicycles and eccentrics by compounding rotations of homocentric spheres. Although still a geocentric model, it was regarded at the time as having revolution-ized Ptolemaic cosmology.

al-Fadl ibn Nawbakht Abū Sahl al-Fadl ibn Nawbakht (died c. 815); Persian Muslim astronomer/astrologer and Harūn al-Rashīd's chief librarian; son of al-Mansūr's astrologer Nawbakht. He made a number of translations of astrological texts from Persian into Arabic.

al-Farābi Abū Nasr Muhammad ibn Muhammad ibn Tarkhān ibn Uzlagh al-Farābi, Latin, Alpharabius; born near Fārāb, Turkestan, of a Turkish family; studied in Baghdad, flourished in Aleppo; died in Damascus in 950 aged about 80; Muslim encyclopedist and one of the great philosophers of medieval times. He continued the work of al-Kindi, developed further by later scholars such as Ibn Sīna and Ibn Rushd, in reconciling and harmonizing Greek philo-sophy with Islamic theology. He was known as 'the Second Teacher', Aristotle being the first.

al-Farghāni Abū al-Abbās Ahmed ibn Muhammad ibn Kathīr al-Farghāni, Latin, Alfraganus, born in Farghānā in Transoxiana; died after 861; Muslim astronomer who flourished under al-Ma'mūn. His most famous text was *Kitab fi Harakāt Samāwiyya wa Jawwāmi' 'ilm al-Nujūm* (*Book of Motion of Heavenly Bodies and Elements of Astronomy*), which was translated into Latin in the twelfth century and was very influential in Europe. In 861 he oversaw the building of the Nilometer in Cairo.

al-Fārisi Kamal al-Dīn al-Hassan ibn Ali ibn al-Hassan al-Fārisi (1267–1318); Persian Muslim physicist and mathematician, born in Tabriz; pupil of al-Shirāzi. He revised and extended Ibn al-Haytham's *Optics* in his *Kitab Tanqīh al-Manāthir* (*The Revi-sion of the Optics*). He gave the first mathematically satisfactory explanation of the rainbow by experimenting with a glass sphere filled with water to model a raindrop, and made a number of important contributions to number theory.

al-Fazāri Muhammad ibn Ibrahīm al-Fazāri; Arab (some sources say Persian) astronomer/astrologer and mathematician and one of the earliest in Islam; flourished in Baghdad in the second half of the eighth century; not to be confused with his father, Ibrahīm al-Fazārī, who was also an astronomer/astrologer and translator. He helped al-Mansūr with the foundation of the Round City of Baghdad in 762 and was the first Muslim to build an astrolabe. He translated a number of texts into Arabic, including Brahmagupta's *Siddhanta* (*Sindhind*), possibly in collaboration with his father.

Abbās ibn Firnās Abū al-Qāsim Abbās Ibn Firnas; Berber polymath, born in Ronda, Spain, flourished in Córdoba in the second half of the ninth century; inventor, engineer, physician, poet and musician. He was famous for a supposedly early attempt at aviation with a set of wings he built and strapped to his back, and he devised a means of manufacturing colourless glass, and made corrective lenses ('reading stones').

Gerard of Cremona Italian scholar (1114–87) and the greatest of all the Arabic–Latin translators. Motivated by a desire to read the *Almagest*, which did not yet exist in Latin, he studied Arabic in Toledo, then stayed on there to translate the work of most of the great Muslim scholars as well as the Arabic versions of many Greek texts. While some translators are known for one or two books, Gerard's list runs to almost a hundred, making him possibly the most prolific translator of all time.

Gerbert d'Aurillac Born *c.* 945 near Aurillac, Auvergne; died in Rome in 1003; the first French pope, under the name of Sylvester II; spent several years in Barcelona, where he studied and translated texts from Arabic. He wrote on the abacus and astrolabe and was one of the very first to introduce Christian Europe to Hindu-Arabic numerals (but not the zero).

al-Ghazāli Abū Hāmid Muhammad ibn Muhammad al-Tūsi al-Shāfi'i al-Ghazāli, Latin, Algazel; born in Tūs in 1058, flourished in Nishapūr and Baghdad, travelled to Alexandria before returning to Tūs, where he died in 1111. He was the greatest and most famous theologian in Islamic history; an original thinker who made contributions to science, but is best known for his attack on Aristotelian philosophy and its proponents, such as Ibn Sīna, in his book *Tahāfut al-Falāsifa* (*The Incoherence of the Philosophers*). He was blamed (unfairly) for the decline of the golden age of Arabic science.

al-Hajjāj ibn Yūsuf Al-Hajjāj ibn Yūsuf ibn Matar, flourished between 786 and 833, probably in Baghdad; early Muslim translator. He was important because he was the first translator of both Euclid's *Elements* and Ptolemy's *Almagest* into Arabic. He translated the *Elements* twice, once for al-Rashīd and then again for al-Ma'mūn. His *Almagest* translation, from a Syriac version, was completed around 830.

Ibn al-Haytham Abū Ali al-Hassan ibn al-Hassan (or al-Hussein) ibn al-Haytham, Latin, Alhazen; born *c.* 965 in Basra, flourished in Egypt under al-Hākim and died (probably) in Cairo in 1039; the greatest physicist of medieval times and probably the greatest during the two-thousand-year span between Archimedes and Newton. He made many contributions in optics and astronomy. His *Kitab al-Manāthir* (*Book of Optics*) had a huge influence on the development of Western science. He is regarded as one of the earliest advocates of the scientific method and as such is often referred to as the 'first true scientist'. He was the first to explain correctly how vision works in terms of geometric optics. He made advances in 'mathematizing' astronomy and wrote on celestial mechanics. He was one of the three greatest scientists of Islam (along with his contemporaries, al-Bīrūni and Ibn Sīna).

Ibn Hazm Abū Muhammad Ali ibn Ahmed ibn Hazm (994–1064); Muslim philosopher, theologian, historian and statesman; born in Córdoba; one of the most important and original scholars in Muslim Spain. He wrote an accurate account of the different sects in Islam, in which he also discussed Christianity, Judaism and Zoroastrianism, called the *Book of Religions and Sects*.

Hunayn ibn Ishāq Abū Zaid Hunayn ibn Ishāq al-Ībādi (809–77), Latin, Joannitius, born in Hīra, flourished in Gondēshāpūr then Baghdad; Nestorian Christian physician and the greatest of the Baghdad translators. He was employed by the Banū Mūsa brothers to translate Greek works into Arabic, in particular the medical texts of Galen. It is unclear if he was employed in the House of Wisdom itself but it is recorded that the Caliph al-Mutawakkil endowed a translation school under his supervision. He translated a prodigious number of books over a period of half a century.

al-Idrīsi Abū Abdallah Muhammad ibn Muhammad al-Idrīsi; Muslim geographer and one of the greatest cartographers of the Middle Ages; born in Ceuta *c.* 1100, studied in Córdoba and later flourished in Palermo; died in 1166. He described the then known world in his *al-Kitab al-Rujāri* (*The Book of Roger*).

Ishāq ibn Hunayn Abū Ya'qūb Ishāq ibn Hunayn ibn Ishāq al-Ibādi, died in Baghdad in 910; Christian translator and son of the more famous Hunayn ibn Ishāq. He was a physician and mathematician who is credited with the translation (into Arabic and Syriac) of the texts of some of the greatest of the Greeks, such as Aristotle, Euclid, Archimedes and Ptolemy.

Jābir ibn Hayyān Abū Mūsa Jābir ibn Hayyān al-Azdī (*c.* 721–*c.* 815); Arab chemist and one of the first great scientists of Islam; flourished mostly in Kūfa *c.* 776. He was known as Geber the Alchemist in Europe (although he had remarkably sound views on the methods of chemical research and processes). He was an advocate of the so-called sulphur-mercury theory of metals (that all metals are composed of differing proportions of sulphur and mercury).

al-Jāhith Abū Uthmān Amr ibn Bahr al-Jāhith ('the Goggle-Eyed') (*c.* 776–*c.* 869), flourished in Basra and Baghdad; man of letters with an interest in the biological sciences and one of the leaders of the Mu'tazilite movement. His most famous scientific work is his *Kitab al-Haywān* (*Book of Animals*), which was more theological and folkloric than scientific, although based on the work of Aristotle. However, it contained the germs of important ideas such as evolution, adaptation and animal psychology.

al-Jawhari Al-Abbās ibn Sa'īd al-Jawhari; astronomer who flourished under al-Ma'mūn. He was one of the group of astronomers known as the *Asshāb al-Mumtahan* ('Companions of the Verified Tables') who carried out important astronomical measurements at the observatories in Baghdad (829–30) and Damascus (832–3).

Ibn Isma'il al-Jazari Abū al-'Iz ibn Ismā'īl ibn al-Razāz al-Jazari (1136–1206); prominent Arab engineer, craftsman, artist and inventor from Al-Jazīra, a region in northern Mesopotamia between the Tigris and the Euphrates. He is best known for writing the *Kitab fi Ma'rifat al-Hiyāl al-Handasiyya* (*Book of Knowledge of Ingenious Mechanical Devices*), which described fifty mechanical devices and gave instructions on how to construct them, in the style of a modern 'do-it-yourself' manual.

Ibn Jubayr Ibn Jubayr (1145–1217); Arab geographer, traveller and poet from Andalusia; born in Valencia, descendant of a tribe of Andalusian (Visigoth) origins; studied at Granada. He travelled widely around the Muslim world and wrote extensively about the people and customs in his *Rihlat Ibn Jubayr* (*Ibn Jubayr's Journey*).

Abū Kāmil Abū Kāmil Shujā al-Hāsib al-Masri ('the Egyptian Calculator'); Egyptian mathematician who flourished in the late ninth and early tenth century. He developed al-Khwārizmi's work on algebra and studied geometric shapes algebraically. His work in turn influenced al-Karkhi and Leonardo of Pisa (Fibonacci).

al-Karkhi Abū Bakr Muhammad ibn Hassan al-Hāsib ('the Calculator') al-Karkhi (from the Baghdad suburb of Karkh); also known as al-Karaji (since his family originated from the Persian city of Karaj); flourished in Baghdad during first decades of the eleventh century; died *c.* 1029; Muslim mathematician who made important advances in arithmetic and algebra. Little is known about his life, as his original Arabic manuscripts are lost. His most significant contribution is his table of binomial coefficients (the numbers that multiply powers of x in polynomial expansions). He also advanced algebra beyond the work of al-Khwārizmi by distancing it further from the shackles of Greek geometric solutions.

al-Kāshi Ghiyāth al-Dīn Jamshīd ibn Mas'ūd al-Kāshi, born in Kāshān, central Iran, *c.* 1380; died in Samarkand in 1429; Persian astronomer and mathematician and one of the last of the great scholars of Arabic science. He worked at Ulugh Beg's scientific institute in Samarkand, produced a *zīj* entitled the *Khaqani Zīj* and wrote on the determination of distances and sizes of heavenly bodies. He wrote a treatise on astronomical observational instruments and invented several new devices himself to solve a range of planetary problems. He is best known for providing the first explicit statement of the cosine rule (still known in French as the *théorème d'al-Kashi*).

Ibn Khaldūn Abū Zayd 'Abd al-Rahmān ibn Muhammad ibn Khaldūn al-Hathrami (1332–1406); Arab polymath: economist, historian, jurist, theologian, mathematician, astronomer, philosopher, social scientist and statesman; born in Tunis into an upper-class Andalusian family, the Banū Khaldūn, which had emigrated to Tunisia after the fall of Seville to the Christians. He was the founder of several social scientific disciplines: demography, cultural history, historiography and sociology, and is widely regarded as the father of economics. Best known for his *Muqaddima* (*The Prolegomenon*).

Ibn al-Khatīb Lisan al-Dīn ibn al-Khatīb, born 1313 near Granada; died 1374; Andalusian poet, writer, historian, philosopher, physician and politician. He spent most of his life as vizier to Muhammad V, the Nasrid sultan of Granada, but was exiled to Morocco.

Omar Khayyām Abū al-Fatah Umar ibn Ibrahīm al-Khayyāmi, born and died in Nishapūr (1048–1131); his *laqab, al-Khayyāmi*, means 'tentmaker'; Persian mathematician, astronomer and poet; one of the greatest mathematicians of the medieval world. He made contributions to the geometric solution of cubic equations and played a major role in devising the Persian Jalali calendar, based on his highly accurate measurement of the length of the year.

al-Khwārizmi Abū Abdullah Muhammad ibn Mūsa al-Khwārizmi, Latin, Algorithmus; Muslim mathematician, astronomer and geographer and one of the greatest scientists of the medieval world; born *c.* 780 in Khwārizm, south of the Aral Sea, and flourished in Baghdad under al-Ma'mūn; died *c.* 850. He brought together Greek geometry and Hindu arithmetic and wrote most famously the first book on algebra, *Kitab al-Jebr*. He was influential in promoting the Hindu decimal system, to both the Islamic world and Europe; he produced a famous star chart and associated trigonometric tables as well as a geographical text that improved on the work of Ptolemy.

al-Kindi Abū Yūsuf Ya'qūb ibn Ishāq ibn al-Sabbāh al-Kindi, Latin, Alkindus; born in Basra at the beginning of the ninth century, flourished in Baghdad under al-Ma'mūn and al-Mu'tasim (813–42); died *c.* 873; known as 'the Philosopher of the Arabs'. His numerous works covered mathematics, physics, astronomy, music, medicine, pharmacy and geography. He wrote several books on Hindu numerals (introducing them to the Muslim world, along with al-Khwārizmi). Many translations from Greek to Arabic were made by him or under his direction.

Kūshyār ibn Labbān Abū al-Hassan Kūshyār ibn Labbān ibn Bāshahri al-Jīli (from Jīlān, south of the Caspian Sea); flourished *c.* 971–1029. A Persian mathematician and astronomer who made contributions in trigonometry and compiled astronomical tables, *al-Zīj al-Jāmi' wal-Bāligh* (*The Comprehensive and Mature Tables*).

Maimonides (Mūsa ibn Maymūn) Arabic: Abū 'Imrān Mūsa ibn Maymūn ibn Abdallah al-Qurtubi al-Isra'īli; Hebrew: Moses ben Maimon; Hispano-Jewish philosopher, theologian, astronomer; born in Córdoba 1135; died in Cairo 1204. A contemporary of Ibn Rushd and just as great a scholar, though he worked independently; almost all his works were in Arabic, but were promptly translated into Hebrew, in which form they were far more influential. His most famous text was his *Dalālat al-Hā'irūn* (*The Guide for the Perplexed*). He was influenced by Ibn Sīna and his Aristotelianism and attempted to reconcile it with Jewish theology, just as others had done for Islamic theology (combining faith with reason).

al-Marwarrūdhi Khālid ibn abd al-Malik al-Marwarrūdhi; Muslim astronomer who flourished under al-Ma'mūn. He took part in the solar observations in Damascus in 832–3.

Mashā'allah The name means (in Arabic) 'What God has willed', but his real name was probably Manasseh; an Egyptian Jew who flourished in Baghdad under al-Mansūr in the second half of the eighth century. He was one of the earliest astronomers/astrologers in Islam and took part in the preliminary surveys of the site of the foundation of Baghdad. Only one of his writings is extant in Arabic, though many translations in Hebrew and Latin survive. His most popular work in the Middle Ages was the *De scientia motus orbis*, translated by Gerard of Cremona.

Ibn al-Nadīm Abū al-Faraj Muhammad ibn Ishāq ibn abī Ya'qūb al-Nadīm al-Warrāq al-Baghdādi ('the Stationer of Baghdad'); died 995; historian and biographer, who wrote the famous *Fihrist al-Ulūm* (*Index of the Sciences*) or, simply, *al-Fihrist*. This invaluable reference book (completed in 988 in Constantinople) was, in al-Nadīm's own words, 'an index of all the books of all peoples of the Arabs and non-Arabs whereof somewhat exists in the language and script of the Arabs on all branches of knowledge'. It also included useful biographies of all the authors. Only a tiny fraction of the books mentioned in the *Fihrist* survived the sacking of Baghdad in 1258.

Ibn al-Nafīs Ala' al-Dīn Abū al-Hassan Ali ibn Abi al-Hazm al-Nafīs al-Qurāshi al-Dimashqi; born Damascus 1213, died Cairo 1288; Arab Muslim polymath: physician, anatomist, physiologist, surgeon, ophthalmologist, lawyer, Sunni theologian, philosopher, logician and astronomer. His most famous work, *Sharh Tashrīh al-Qānūn* (*Commentary on Anatomy in Ibn Sīna's Canon*), contained many new anatomical discoveries, most importantly his discovery of pulmonary and coronary circulations. His huge *Comprehensive Book on Medicine* remains one of the largest medical encyclopedias of all time. He was a proponent of post-mortem autopsies and human dissection.

Nawbakht Persian astronomer/astrologer and engineer; flourished in Baghdad under al-Mansūr; died *c.* 777. Together with Mashā'allah, he made preliminary surveys of the site for the construction of the Round City of Baghdad.

al-Qalasādi Abū al-Hassan ibn 'Ali al-Qalasādi; born Baza, Spain, 1412, flourished in Granada, died in Tunisia 1486; Arab Muslim mathematician who wrote numerous books on arithmetic and algebra, including *al-Tafsīr fi 'Ilm al-Hisāb* (*Clarification of the Science of Arithmetic*). He developed symbolic algebra beyond the early notations of Diophantus and Brahmagupta by using, for the first time, symbols for mathematical operations as well as numbers.

Qusta ibn Luqqa Qusta ibn Luqqa al-Ba'labakki (that is, from Baalbek, or Heliopolis); died *c.* 912; Christian of Greek origin who flourished in Baghdad as a physician, philosopher, mathematician and astronomer. He translated a number of Greek texts into Arabic and wrote many original works on medicine and geometry, including a treatise on the astrolabe.

Fakhr al-Dīn al-Rāzi Abū Abdallah Muhammad ibn Umar Fakhr al-Dīn al-Rāzi (1149–1210), often called Imām al-Rāzi; born in

Rayy; Persian philosopher, historian, mathematician, astronomer, physician, theologian. He wrote prodigiously in both Arabic and Persian. He dealt with the physical sciences and cosmology from an Islamic perspective and, like his predecessor al-Ghazāli, was critical of Ibn Sīna and Aristotle.

Ibn Zakariyya al-Rāzi Abū Bakr Muhammad ibn Zakariyya al-Rāzi, Latin, Rhazes (c. 854–c. 925); born in Rayy; physician, philosopher, chemist, and the greatest clinician of Islam and the Middle Ages. He flourished in Rayy and Baghdad, where he oversaw the running of several hospitals. In medicine, he combined Galenic theory with Hippocratic wisdom. His *Kitab al-Hāwi* (*Liber continens*) and his monograph on smallpox and measles, *Kitab al-Judari wal-Hasba*, were two of the most important medical books in Europe for many centuries. He made one of the earliest serious attempts to classify the chemical elements, was an early proponent of the scientific method and even carried out one of the first clinical trials.

Robert of Chester English mathematician, astronomer, alchemist and translator from Arabic into Latin; flourished in Spain in the first half of the twelfth century before returning to London. He completed the first Latin translation of the Qur'an in 1143 as well as the first Latin translation of al-Khwārizmi's *Kitab al-Jebr*. He is therefore regarded as the first person to introduce algebra into Europe.

Ibn Rushd Abū al-Walīd Muhammad ibn Ahmed ibn Muhammad ibn Rushd, Latin, Averroës (1126–98); one of the greatest and certainly best-known philosophers of medieval times. He was responsible more than any other for introducing Aristotelian philosophy to Europe. Born in Córdoba, he studied law and medicine and even worked as the Almohad caliph's personal physician in Marrakesh. He was the last of the great Muslim philosophers, and deeply influenced both Christian and Jewish thought.

Ibn Sahl Abu Sa'ad al-'Alā' ibn Sahl (c. 940–1000); Muslim mathematician and physicist, who flourished in Baghdad. His treatise *On the Burning Instruments* set out his understanding of the refraction of light that was to influence Ibn al-Haytham shortly after. Famous for his discovery of the law of refraction, today known as Snell's law, over six centuries before Snell himself.

Sahl al-Tabari Jewish astronomer and physician (*c.* 786–845), also known as Rabbān al-Tabari ('The Rabbi of Tarabistan'). He flourished in Baghdad and is said to have made one of the first translations into Arabic of Ptolemy's *Almagest.*

al-Samaw'al Al-Samaw'al Ibn Yahyā al-Maghribī; born in Baghdad *c.* 1130, died in Marāgha *c.* 1180; Arab mathematician and astronomer; Muslim convert and son of a Jewish rabbi from Morocco. He wrote the treatise *al-Bahir fi al-Jebr* (*The Brilliant in Algebra*) at the age of 19; later he developed the concept of proof by mathematical induction, which he used to extend the work of al-Karkhi on the binomial theorem.

Sanad ibn Ali Abū al-Tayyib Sanad ibn Ali al-Yahūdi; Muslim astronomer, the son of a Jewish astrologer; flourished under al-Ma'mūn; died after 864. He constructed the Shammāsiyya observatory in Baghdad to carry out al-Ma'mūn's mission of checking and improving many of the astronomical observations of the Greeks.

Ibn al-Shātir Ala' al-Dīn Abu'l-Hassan Ali ibn Ibrahīm ibn al-Shātir (1304–75); one of the greatest Arab astronomers; worked as a *muwaqqit* (timekeeper) at the Umayyad mosque in Damascus. He reformed and improved the Ptolemaic system by eliminating the cumbersome eccentrics and equants in the lunar and planetary models. His mathematical models were in better agreement with observations than Ptolemy's and were used by Copernicus a hundred and fifty years later. He constructed a magnificent sundial for one of the minarets of the Umayyad mosque, the fragments of which are in a Damascus museum, making it the oldest polar-axis sundial still in existence.

al-Shirāzi Qutb al-Dīn Shirāzi (1236–1311); Persian Muslim polymath who made contributions in astronomy, mathematics, medicine, physics, music theory and philosophy. Born in Shiraz in 1236, he studied medicine under his father and uncle, both physicians, and astronomy under al-Tūsi at Marāgha; then spent time in Khurasan, Qazwīn, Isfahan and Baghdad. He wrote important treatises on astronomy and optics and began the work that would lead to his student al-Fārisi's explanation of the rainbow.

al-Sijzi Abū Sa'īd Ahmed ibn Muhammad al-Sijzi (al-Sijistāni) (*c.* 950–*c.* 1020); astronomer and mathematician who developed geometrical solutions of algebraic equations. He was a contemporary of al-Bīrūni; little is known about him but he is said (by al-Bīrūni) to have built a heliocentric astrolabe.

Ibn Sīna Abū Ali al-Hussein ibn Abdullah ibn Sīna, Latin, Avicenna; born 980 at Afshāna near Bukhara, died in Hamadan 1037; by far the most famous and influential scholar in Islam and one of the most important thinkers in history. He is best known as a philosopher and a physician and was hugely influential in Europe in both disciplines for many centuries. His two greatest works were his *Qānūn fi al-Tibb* (*Canon of Medicine*), a codification of all medical knowledge, and the philosophical encyclopedia *Kitab al-Shifā'* (*Book of Healing*). He is regarded as almost as influential on Western philosophy as Aristotle. His ideas in mathematics and physics were more philosophical than technical (as distinct from his two contemporaries al-Bīrūni and Ibn al-Haytham). Nevertheless, he made a profound study of such concepts as light, heat, force, motion, vacuum and infinity, and was strongly influenced by the work of Aristotle. In a sense, his contribution to science was so complete that it discouraged further original investigations and sterilized intellectual life in the Muslim world.

Sinān ibn Thābit Abū Sa'īd Sinān ibn Thābit ibn Qurra; Muslim physician, mathematician and astronomer; flourished in Baghdad; died 943; son of the more famous Thābit ibn Qurra. A brilliant administrator of a number of Baghdad hospitals, he worked tirelessly to raise the scientific standards of the medical profession.

al-Tabari Abū Ja'far Muhammad ibn Jarīr al-Tabari; born in Tabaristan *c.* 839; flourished in Baghdad where he died 923; Persian historian and theologian and one of the most important historians in Islam. His most famous work is a history of the world, written in Arabic, from creation to the year 915, his *Akhbār al-Rusūl wal-Mulūk* (*Annals of the Prophets and Kings*).

Ibn Tāhir al-Baghdādi Abū Mansūr 'Abd al-Qāhir ibn Tāhir ibn Muhammad al-Baghdādi; historian, philosopher, theologian and mathematician; born and grew up in Baghdad but flourished at Nishapūr (d. 1037). He wrote on philosophy and theology, but his most famous work was on algebra, called *Kitab al-Takmīl* (*The Completion*).

Thābit ibn Qurra Abū al-Hassan Thābit ibn Qurra ibn Marwān al-Harrāni (c. 836–901); pagan Arab from Harrān in north-west Mesopotamia who flourished in Baghdad; mathematician, astronomer, physician and one of the greatest translators from Greek and Syriac into Arabic. He made a number of impressive advances in number theory.

Ibn Tufayl Abū Bakr Muhammad ibn abd al-Malik ibn Muhammad ibn Muhammad ibn Tufayl, Latin, Abubacer; Andalusian Muslim philosopher and physician; born in the first decade of the twelfth century near Granada; died 1185. He wrote one of the most original and best-known books of the Middle Ages, *Asrār al-Hikma al-Ishrāqiyya* (*Secrets of Illuminative Philosophy*), which was a theological romance, often described as a metaphysical *Robinson Crusoe*.

Nasr al-Dīn al-Tūsi Muhammad ibn Muhammad ibn Hasan al-Tūsi, better known as Nasr al-Dīn al-Tūsi; born 1201 in Tūs, Khurasan, died Baghdad 1274; Persian polymath and one of the great scholars of medieval times. He was an astronomer, biologist, chemist, mathematician, philosopher, physician, physicist and theologian. He fled the Mongols to join the Hashashīn, an offshoot of the Isma'īlis, in their fort at Alamūt, where he made his most important contributions in science, but later joined Hūlāgū Khān's ranks and persuaded the Mongol leader to build him a new observatory in Marāgha, which became the most important centre for astronomy in the world for several centuries. He invented a geometrical technique called a Tūsi-couple, which improved on Ptolemy's problematic equant. He was the first to present observational evidence of the earth's rotation. He also wrote extensively on biology and was the first to treat trigonometry as a separate mathematical discipline, distinct from astronomy.

al-Uqlīdisi Abū al-Hassan Ahmad ibn Ibrahīm al-Uqlīdisi; Arab mathematician who flourished in Damascus and Baghdad; his name derives from *Uqlīdis* (Arabic for 'Euclid'), suggesting his main occupation was as a translator or copier of Euclid's texts. He is famous for writing the earliest known text on decimal fractions around the mid-tenth century, five hundred years before the work of al-Kāshi in Samarkand, who was commonly believed to have been the first to use decimal fractions.

al-'Urdi Mu'ayyad al-Dīn al-'Urdi (died 1266); Arab astronomer, mathematician, architect and engineer; born in Aleppo and flourished at the Marāgha observatory under the guidance of al-Tūsi. He was the first of the Marāgha School to develop a non-Ptolemaic model of planetary motion. The methods he developed were later used by Ibn al-Shātir in the fourteenth century and in the heliocentric model of Copernicus in the sixteenth.

Abū al-Wafā' Abū al-Wafā' Muhammad ibn Muhammad al-Būzjāni (940–98); astronomer and mathematician; born Būzjān, Qūhistān. One of the last Arabic translators and commentators on Greek works, he wrote an astronomical text (probably based on the *Almagest*) called *al-Kitab al-Kāmil (The Complete Book)*; he contributed to trigonometry and was probably the first to show how the sine rule generalizes to spherical angles.

Ibn Wahshiyya Abū Bakr Ahmed ibn Ali ibn Wahshiyya al-Kaldāni; born Iraq of Chaldaean/Nabataean (descendants of the Babylonians) family; alchemist who flourished at end of the ninth and beginning of the tenth century. He partially deciphered Egyptian hieroglyphics and Babylonian cuneiform texts.

Yahya ibn abi Mansūr Abū Ali Yahya ibn abi Mansūr; Persian Muslim astronomer who flourished in Baghdad under the patronage of al-Ma'mūn; died *c.* 831. He was one of the *Asshāb al-Mumtahan* ('Companions of the Verified Tables'), the group of astronomers in Baghdad (with al-Khwārizmi and Sanad) who carried out the famous observations in 829–30.

Yuhanna ibn Māsawayh Abū Zakariyya Yuhanna ibn Māswayh, Latin, Mesuë (or Mesuë the Elder); Persian Christian physician, born in Gondēshāpūr; flourished in Baghdad; died 857. He wrote in Arabic but also translated medical works from Greek into Syriac. He was tutor to Hunayn ibn Ishāq. Famously, he carried out dissection of apes to study anatomy during the reign of al-Mu'tasim, *c.* 836.

Ibn Yūnus Abū al-Hassan Ali ibn Sa'īd ibn Ahmed ibn Yūnus (*c.* 950–1009); considered by many as the greatest Muslim astronomer; worked in Cairo in a well-equipped laboratory where he compiled astronomical tables called the Hakimite Tables (dedicated to the Fātimid Caliph al-Hākim). He made several contributions to trigonometry, though not as great as those made by Abū al-Wafā' and al-Bīrūni.

Abū al-Qāsim al-Zahrāwi Abū al-Qāsim Khalaf ibn Abbās al-Zahrāwi, Latin, Abulcasis (or Albucasis) (*c.* 936–*c.* 1013); flourished in Medīnat al-Zahrā', near Córdoba; greatest surgeon of Islam and the medieval world. He wrote a medical encyclopedia of which the most important sections were on surgery and described many new surgical instruments. It was translated into Latin by Gerard of Cremona, making al-Zahrāwi famous across Europe. He was influenced strongly by the physician Paulos Aegineta, a Greek from Alexandria, who flourished *c.* 640.

al-Zarqāli Abū Ishāq Ibrahīm ibn Yahya al-Naqqāsh al-Zarqāli, Latin, Arzachel (*c.* 1029–87); observational astronomer who flourished in Córdoba. He made important astronomical measurements and edited the Toledan Tables of planetary motion, which were very popular in Europe. He also invented an improved astrolabe, called a *safiha* (the *saphaea Arzachelis*).

Ziryāb Abu al-Hassan Ali ibn Nāfi' (*c.* 789–857), nicknamed Ziryāb (Blackbird); Iraqi (possibly Kurdish) poet, musician, singer, fashion designer, celebrity, trendsetter, as well as astronomer, botanist and geographer. He first achieved notoriety in his city of birth, Baghdad, as a performer and a student of the great musician and composer al-Mawsili. He flourished in Córdoba where he became a prominent cultural figure, creating a unique and influential style of musical performance, and writing songs that were performed in Andalusia for generations. He introduced the Persian lute, which became the Spanish guitar.

Ibn Zuhr Abū Marwān Abd al-Malik ibn abi-l-'Ala' Zuhr, Latin, Avenzoar; born in Seville *c.* 1091; died 1161; most illustrious member of the greatest medical family of Muslim Spain and the world's most famous physician of his time. Like al-Rāzi, he was mainly a clinician, with strong empirical tendencies, but did not quite have the Persian's originality.

Timeline: The Islamic World from Antiquity to the Beginning of the Modern Period

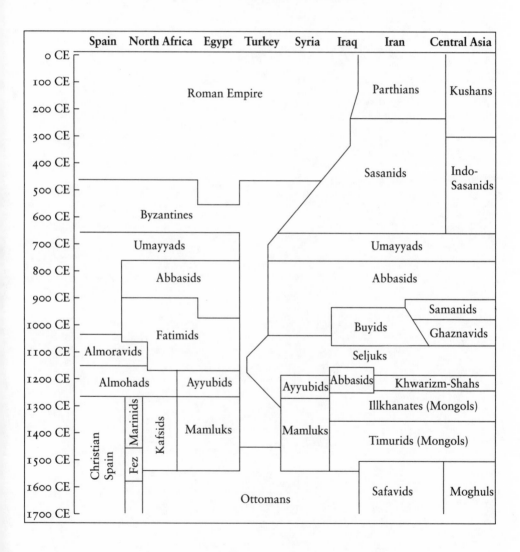

	Spain	North Africa	Egypt	Turkey	Syria	Iraq	Iran	Central Asia
0 CE								
100 CE		Roman Empire					Parthians	Kushans
200 CE								
300 CE							Sasanids	Indo-Sasanids
400 CE								
500 CE								
600 CE		Byzantines						
700 CE		Umayyads					Umayyads	
800 CE		Abbasids					Abbasids	
900 CE								Samanids
1000 CE		Fatimids				Buyids		Ghaznavids
1100 CE	Almoravids					Seljuks		
1200 CE	Almohads		Ayyubids		Ayyubids	Abbasids	Khwarizm-Shahs	
1300 CE	Christian Spain	Fez / Marinids / Kafsids	Mamluks		Mamluks		Illkhanates (Mongols)	
1400 CE							Timurids (Mongols)	
1500 CE								
1600 CE				Ottomans			Safavids	Moghuls
1700 CE								

Index